MARS ON EARTH

WANDERINGS
IN THE WORLD'S
DRIEST DESERT

BY MARK JOHANSON

RMB

T0370190

For information on purchasing bulk quantities of this book, or to obtain media excerpts or invite the author to speak at an event, please visit rmbooks.com and select the "Contact" tab.

RMB | Rocky Mountain Books Ltd.
rmbooks.com
@rmbooks
facebook.com/rmbooks

Cataloguing data available from Library and Archives Canada
ISBN 9781771606769 (hardcover)
ISBN 9781771606776 (electronic)

All photographs are by Mark Johanson unless otherwise noted.
Copy editor: Peter Norman
Proofreader: Peter Enman
Cover photo: iStock.com/MarcioDufranc

Printed and bound in Canada

We acknowledge the financial support of the Government of Canada through the Canada Book Fund and the Canada Council for the Arts, and of the province of British Columbia through the British Columbia Arts Council and the Book Publishing Tax Credit.

Disclaimer
The views expressed in this book are those of the author and do not necessarily reflect those of the publishing company, its staff, or its affiliates.

CONTENTS

NORTHERN CHILE

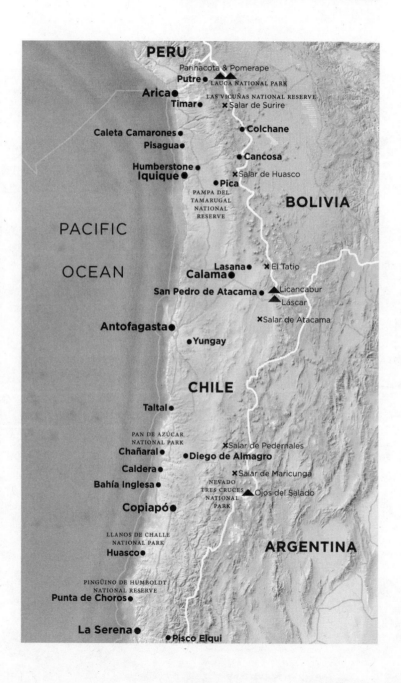

PERU

Parinacota & Pomerape
Putre ● ✕ LAUCA NATIONAL PARK
Arica ● LAS VICUÑAS NATIONAL RESERVE
Timar ● ✕ Salar de Surire

Caleta Camarones ● ● **Colchane**
Pisagua ●
● **Cancosa**
Humberstone ● ✕ Salar de Huasco
Iquique ● ● **Pica**
PAMPA DEL
TAMARUGAL
NATIONAL
RESERVE **BOLIVIA**

PACIFIC

OCEAN
Lasana ● ✕ El Tatio
Calama ●
San Pedro de Atacama ● ▲ Licancabur
▲ Láscar

Antofagasta ● ✕ Salar de Atacama

● **Yungay**

CHILE

Taltal ●

PAN DE AZÚCAR
NATIONAL PARK
Chañaral ● ✕ Salar de Pedernales
● **Diego de Almagro**
Caldera ● ✕ Salar de Maricunga
Bahía Inglesa ● NEVADO
TRES CRUCES ▲ Ojos del Salado
Copiapó ● NATIONAL
PARK

LLANOS DE CHALLE
NATIONAL PARK **ARGENTINA**
Huasco ●

PINGÜINO DE HUMBOLDT
NATIONAL RESERVE
Punta de Choros ●

La Serena ●
● **Pisco Elqui**

The Yungay sector of the Atacama Desert is both stunning and repulsive, an elegant bone-dry taunt. It's earthly and yet otherworldly, so aggressively uncomfortable I can't figure out why I love it. But there it is: the world's driest place. It gives me an awful kind of euphoria (highly recommended, yet highly confusing). It's as if Mars is right here on Earth.

Technically, scientists call the Atacama of northern Chile the driest *non-polar* desert on Earth. When they do it's places like this, Yungay, they're talking about. This remote flatland far from civilization has absolutely zero vegetation. It's desiccated. It's all salt-crumpled earth backed by an amphitheater of camel-colored hills. The ground has the texture of burnt pizza crust and cracks under the pressure of my feet. The air feels as if it's been whooshed into the valley from some giant unseen hair dryer.

If the Atacama is a collection of lonely landscapes – and it is – then Yungay is the loneliest of all. What it has in abundance is sweet, sweaty, soul-searching emptiness. As in any respectable desert, you get the looming sense of desertion. The sole presence of life I see is the odd minibus carrying mining men off to distant holes – hulking chasms filled with copper, iron or gold. It's the cursed and forsaken Atacama that Charles Darwin once referred to as "a barrier far worse than the most turbulent ocean." Yungay is one of the forgotten places; it transmits a stillness that's terrifying.

Geographers consider any place on Earth a desert if its average annual rainfall is less than ten inches (25 cm). In essence, precipitation – be it rain or fog or dew – shouldn't exceed the potential for evaporation (or transpiration from the surface to the atmosphere). By that measure, one-fifth of Earth's total land surface is considered desert, and deserts are found on every continent. Yet none (other than the McMurdo Dry Valleys of Antarctica) is quite so dry or forbidding as this.

A team of global researchers descended on Yungay in 2003 for an experiment that would forever alter its trajectory. Chris McKay, a square-jawed astrobiologist with NASA's Ames Research Center, wanted to repeat a series of studies conducted by the Viking landers, which touched down on Mars in the late 1970s. This time, he'd take samples from Yungay. What he discovered was that the results were nearly the same as those attained on Mars.

"In the driest part of the Atacama, we found that, if Viking had landed there instead of on Mars and done exactly the same experiments, we would also have been shut out [in the search for life]," McKay said in his report. "The Atacama appears to be the only place on Earth [that the] Viking would have found nothing."

Mars may be at least 34 million miles (54.7 million km) away from Earth at any given time, but the similarities between it and the Atacama have tantalized scientists ever since the first studies on the topic back in the 1960s. McKay's definitive paper on "Mars-like soils in the Atacama Desert," published in a November 2003 issue of *Science* magazine, set off a firestorm of new interest in the secluded Yungay region, cementing its reputation as an analogue for Mars on Earth.

Several factors make it a good fit. For one, it has a fantastic track record of being extremely arid for the past ten million years. And despite being considerably warmer than the Red Planet, it has remarkably similar soil chemistry, as well as extreme levels of ultraviolet radiation (30 percent higher, on average, than in the Mojave Desert of California). All of this has pushed life here to the limit.

Since you can't exactly test drills and other rover gadgets on Mars – these costly parts need to be perfect before they ever leave orbit – NASA sensed an opportunity to use the Atacama as a laboratory to perfect technologies for things like drilling and life-detection.

McKay's initial experiments showed that Yungay's soil was as disappointingly lifeless and depleted in organic material as that of Mars, but scientists have since discovered that the Atacama's hyper-arid core is not quite as comatose as it initially appeared. If the Atacama can hide signs of life, the theory goes, then perhaps Mars can, too?

Below the surface here, several feet beneath my own feet, are some remarkably hardy strains of fungi, bacteria and other microbes that have adapted to the region's dryness, saltiness and extreme ultraviolet radiation. Usually inactive, they awaken from their slumber when water makes its infrequent appearance. Though the Martian surface today is hard, dry and cold, ancient Mars may have been habitable for microbial life, too, because we know that it was once a warmer and wetter place. That's why NASA scientists have carried out numerous experiments in the Atacama, searching for microbial life to prep for future missions to Mars.

They believe that, due to the extreme radiation, clues about Martian life might only be found hidden deep beneath the desert's surface. The idea is that, if life exists on Mars – or if it existed at any time in the past – it most likely retreated underground as the planet's atmosphere made living on the surface more untenable. So, to find traces today, rovers will have to dig. To dig better, they'll need to be perfectly designed. To be

perfectly designed, they'll need to practice in the field. To practice in the field, they'll need a Martian analogue. And to find that
analogue, they'll have to keep coming back to Yungay.

It's funny: the closest landmark to Yungay is actually a colossal 36-foot (11 m) human hand reaching out from the depths
of the desert as if it belongs to some hidden sand monster. It
has the same peanut color as the earth itself and arrived here
back in 1992, before there was any geeky gossip of a Mars on
Earth. While this sculpture by Chilean artist Mario Irarrázabal
may protrude out of the ground, it seems to me as if it's waving toward the sky; it's almost like it's sending its greetings to
Mars, acknowledging the hidden life forms that may be waiting
in some twinland up above.

Or maybe my imagination is getting the best of me? Maybe I'm
already half-baked? It's becoming clearer to me now how deserts
distort reality. I feel it creeping up on me. I catch myself filling
empty spaces with memories. I'm stuffing voids with thoughts. A
forest might soothe my mind; this desert lights it on fire.

Of course, that's exactly what I came for. When I set off into
the Atacama, I felt like I was losing my sense of self, unsure how
life had deposited me in my current geography. I needed to get
out, at least for a while, and I wanted one of those lawless spots –
a place in the in-between – where the sureties of a predictable
city life disappear alongside its burdens. I wanted overpowering
landscapes, visual provocations, a Mars on Earth. And here I am,
in the driest of dry dwelling places, alone, on a journey more
consequential than I could have imagined at the start.

Back then, the Atacama was a means to an end. It was about
this high I need sometimes, or maybe more often than I'd like
to admit, of being completely out of my element. Out in some
unfamiliar place with rules I don't understand and people whose

internal clocks don't always tick the way mine tocks. I've been chasing that high ever since I can remember. First, I was a gay boy from the suburbs of America navigating the unfamiliar maps of a straight man's world. Then, I matured into a kind of itinerant stranger, piecing together the puzzles of foreign peoples' lands. That's been the cycle: start different by birth, tend toward the different by choice. Keep myself the other, in part, to hide my otherwise ordinariness.

I suppose that explains how I could end up in this desert. Maybe it's how I ended up in this country. Maybe that's how my life led me here. But it's not what this trip is about. It's not what this book is about, either. Not really. You might call it a strange love story. You might call it search for belonging. Or meaning. Or perspective. You might find it to be a meditation on deserts. Or dreams. Or democracy.

You decide.

For that, I suppose we should go back to a rooftop in Santiago, back to the fires, the fog and the fury that followed.

1 IT BEGAN WITH A SPARK

(CHI, CHI, CHI, LE, LE, LE...VIVA CHILE)

When it happens, when my neatly curated life abroad explodes for the first time, I'm on a rooftop, guzzling champagne.

My table at The Singular edges up against a thin sliver of a pool whose turquoise waters spill, "infinity" style, over the haphazard skyline of Chile's exuberant capital. It's a temperate October day. Young Brazilian lovers – honeymooners, I suppose – make pretzels out of their legs at the pool's edge. A leathery German on a lounger passes a cigarette to a fellow passenger in his group tour. She's wearing one of those floppy sun hats typically reserved for breezy beach vacations – the kind this trip was not destined to be. An Englishman in a baby-blue polo shirt – the one who held me captive on the nine-floor elevator ride up to this rooftop hotel bar, boasting of his adventures in Patagonia – is now recounting the same tale, word for word, to my waiter. All the while, a 73-foot-tall (22 m) statue of the Virgin Mary stares down on us from her perch atop Cerro San Cristóbal. Arms outstretched, eyes weary, she can already see the sparks flying around the corner.

"*Salud,*" I say, clinking my champagne flute against another one held by the Chilean artist JJ.

An American magazine has just assigned me a ten-page cover story on Santiago, which is the latest in a string of far-flung places I've called home in a decade of writing about travel. The idea is to follow five local personalities around the Chilean capital, extracting its often-elusive appeal on visits to their favorite spots. That's where JJ comes in. He's my first subject and (though my editors don't know it) a loyal friend.

JJ is a purveyor of the surreal. His magazine spreads take fashion photography out of its pretty little box, thrusting subjects into a more primal realm. Outside of the studio he comes off as boyish, despite a balding head. Yet he's confident in a way most Chileans aren't, always storming around Santiago like a peacock in winter, daring its drably dressed citizens to try just a little bit harder. Naturally, our day together has been as colorful as planned. We began in the early afternoon at a street market, where I learned of his not-so-flashy childhood as the son of an avocado farmer in the workaday coastal village of Quintero. He escaped, moved to the big city, became an artist. It was to be one of *those* kinds of stories.

JJ and I continued to a vegan café he frequents in the fashionable Barrio Italia neighborhood for soy lattes and *alfajor* cookies before strolling onward to a new gallery ostensibly themed around architecture. The significance of the metallic slabs it displayed in the name of art was lost on me, but the place seemed to please JJ, who mused over the objects with a pensive finger to his lips. When we tried to cap off our tour with a walk up Cerro Santa Lucía – an ornate hilltop park carved out of a decommissioned fort – we found ourselves shooed away by a harried policeman whose olive-green guise was more befitting of a battlefield than of the hip Lastarria neighborhood.

"Happy hour?" I proposed, too enthralled by our own blather to give the policeman a second thought. "*Claro que sí*," JJ agreed, swishing his Aladdin pants down the street in the direction of The Singular, where we find ourselves now.

The afternoon sun casts a harsh spotlight on our table as we toss back stuffed olives, waiting for the long austral dusk to daub the sky in cotton candy hues. Between bites, we discuss plans for the weekend, dreaming up lavish Saturday night activities that we don't yet realize couldn't possibly occur.

I call Felipe, my partner (in love, not business), to join us for a drink, but he's having trouble getting into the metro. "*Aye*, it's completely shut down," he complains. "I've been so busy today getting ready for the new exhibition, I haven't looked at the news. Have you?"

I haven't. I have no idea. I rarely comprehend what's going on in this foreign metropolis of seven million people on a good day. I've only just, in recent years, gotten comfortable reading and conversing in Spanish – though both still feel like brain torture when I need to grasp or convey complex ideas.

"I think I'll have to walk over," he says, his voice muffled by street noise.

Felipe grew up in Santiago and now works for a cultural center underneath the presidential palace, La Moneda, where a lavish new exhibit from the Asia Pacific Triennial of Contemporary Art has been all-consuming. The show is on loan from Australia, where Felipe and I lived before Chile, and features several works from New Zealand, where we met a decade ago, so it feels as if the bizarre timeline of our irregular journey together is suddenly on display.

Over the phone, Felipe says crowds have begun to gather outside the neoclassical walls of the presidential palace, fighting for space amid its pageantry of Chilean flags. The sight isn't entirely unusual given the unpopularity of billionaire business-man-turned-president Sebastián Piñera, whom Felipe loathes, but we agree we'll figure out the cause when he arrives.

I hang up the phone and order another round of champagne, keeping an eye on the floppy-hatted German woman as she wriggles underneath a parasol for a cigarette. Walking past her toward the bathroom, I catch the eye of the Englishman, who's re-emerged from the elevator with a hefty camera around his sunburnt neck. I quickly avert my gaze and watch as he sidles up to the bar, roping the hapless cocktail slinger into a slideshow of images from the famed Patagonian park Torres del Paine.

Back at the table, JJ has become enraptured by the Brazilians, who are now knee-deep in the pool, engaged in an advanced level of groping that soon rivets me, too. We begin to narrate the action, launching into a running commentary of invented translations.

"Do you like it when I slip my hands up your shorts in public?" I ask.

"You know I do," JJ responds, batting his eyes.

"And, ooh, what if I go ahead and stick this scratchy tongue in your ear?" I add. "You like it when I slobber all over you, right?" We bowl over laughing.

When the sexed-up telenovela has thoroughly grossed us out, we turn our attention to JJ's upcoming move to Portugal.

"I don't know, I just feel like I need to remove myself from my comfort zone and find some new inspiration," he says. "New ideas. New outlook. New everything."

It'll just be for a year, but he's dreamed up a local art project to take place in his absence.

"I'm tossing out most of my belongings, but I plan to leave a few items that are dear to me with some of my closest friends," he says. "The idea is that you'll have to photograph the object with your phone over the coming months, doing whatever you want, wherever you want." He winks.

I'm to receive a tin bird from his childhood in Quintero, he says, "since you're always flying all over the place in search of god knows what." I tell him I plan to cart the toy around on my work trips like a Japanese tourist with a Hello Kitty doll, snapping photos of it in front of everything I see. "Perrrfect!" he squeals.

The air around us suddenly grows thick and noxious – like the toxic afterglow of New Year's Eve fireworks. The German tourist removes her sun hat to fan away a growing cloud of peppery air. The Grand Patagonian Explorer shoves cocktail napkins into his nostrils. The Brazilian lovers retreat into the elevator. By the time Felipe arrives, it's clear: the air has been laced with tear gas.

^~^

Foreign tourists at The Singular are now in panic mode, waving waiters over to ask questions in exaggerated English, as if this baby talk is the key to being understood abroad. After five and a half years in the city, I've hardened into an outsider who's more blasé about the passing protests, inexplicable bureaucracies and regular earthquakes that, quite literally, rock my world.

Felipe has read some news about school kids jumping the turnstiles on the metro to protest a rise in fares. It's been going on all week, but it seems today was particularly volatile. Perhaps that's what this is all about? After all, authorities in Chile have been quashing student protests with tear gas and water cannons for years instead of fixing the broken education system, which leaves the students without pesos to spare.

Whatever the reason, we decide it's best to call it a night and find our way home. JJ lives about a mile away in the Providencia neighborhood, but Felipe and I are on the far side of the city closer to the Andes. We devise a plan: We'll walk JJ to his apartment while searching for a taxi, bus or anything with wheels moving east toward El Golf. First, of course, we need to get out of The Singular.

We scrunch together in the mirror-lined elevator, a bit tipsy on our feet, and descend into the splendorous lobby. Its walls have been slathered with the most gentlemanly of art: a sepia-toned polo player, a parrot in silhouette, a dandy reading a book.

Outside, on the far end of the grand foyer, it becomes immediately clear that Santiago is smoldering. Red-eyed protestors are running full force away from Plaza Italia, the roundabout two blocks from The Singular where citizens regularly gather to mark the nation's highs and lows.

Rather than head straight for Plaza Italia, we reverse course down Lastarria, passing the street's swanky wine lounges, pisco bars, seafood restaurants and third-wave coffee shops – all of which are tossing customers out and locking up. At the end of Lastarria we hit GAM, a multi-block performing arts center that's sheathed in a perforated copper façade. Its exterior courtyards are typically abuzz with green-haired teens choreographing dance routines to reggaeton or K-pop. Nobody is dancing tonight.

We round the corner to Alameda, the city's main east-west thoroughfare, which has been turned into a veritable warzone. Fiery barricades block its eight lanes with the detritus of modern civilization: wooden diner stools, guardrails, street signs, share-bikes. Everything's ablaze, bonfires of discontent.

Nightfall sneaks in as we dash across Alameda, avoiding both the olive-green cops and the angry mob howling at them. We find shelter behind a crescent-shaped museum – one of my favorites, dedicated to Violeta Parra, the mother of Latin American folk music and the first female from the region to stage a solo art show at the Louvre. The place offers momentary respite from the inferno of Plaza Italia, but it, too, will be on fire in a matter of days.

We decide it best to push east toward a sinuous strip of green grass known as Parque Bustamante. Surely on the other side there's a clearer route away from the impending chaos? Just as we're about to reach the park, cops blaze down the street in our direction, a blur of green amid clouds of rancid smoke. Crowds flee left and right like stampeding wildebeest, bandanas wrapped over their teary-eyed faces as they duck into bushes, hotel lobbies and half-shuttered convenience stores.

"Run!" they shout, and we do, but not before a puffing canister lands right at our feet.

Tear gas hisses out of it, snaking across the air and seeping into our pores. It crystalizes on our eyes and chokes the backs of our lungs.

"I feel like I can't breathe," I whisper to JJ.

"You'll get used to it," says Felipe.

He was born into a dictatorship and raised to fight for a better country than the one he was given.

"Just try not to blink," he adds.

Tears race out of my eyes and stream down my face, curving around nostrils to land in the creases of my mouth. Soon, the back of my throat tightens. My nose tingles. It's almost as if I've snorted a bottle's worth of broken glass.

The shock of it all makes me laugh.

It's a funny thing to cry when you don't mean to, when you aren't happy or sad, just confused. But I barely have time to make sense of my emotions before we slip into a cobblestoned alley, slowing our gait under the orange glow of arched streetlamps. Residents appear on balconies above, banging pots and pans in a *cacerolazo* protest. It is to become the soundtrack of a long and labyrinthine walk back home.

Felipe and I say goodbye to JJ near the gate of his apartment block, promising to check in as soon as we arrive at our place. Public transportation is suspended, the roads are paralyzed and we've got another four miles to go. Our journey will be like an urban adventure through a city that's newly feral.

"Stay safe out there," JJ says, slinking away into the shadows. He takes just a few steps before turning around. "Welcome to the new Chile," he adds, a smirk in his moonlit eyes.

The streets east of center are abuzz with commuters who, like us, are marching homebound, watching the city morph from a place they recognize into one that will surely be different tomorrow. We meld into the masses, trudging forward in a zigzag pattern past the high-rise apartment blocks, leafy avenues and palm-lined plazas of the middle-class Providencia neighborhood. All the while, pots and pans clank, stoplights flicker, fire trucks wail and warble.

Peaceful protestors have gathered at key intersections, so we stop momentarily to join them. I don't quite know why. I can't figure out what I'm being swept into, but Felipe says it's important. It already feels historic.

We continue one mile, then another. Still, pots and pans clank, stoplights flicker, fire trucks wail and warble.

Our apartment lies on the other side of Providencia, in the shadow of South America's largest skyscraper, Gran Torre Santiago, a 62-story phallus of steel and glass that lights up each evening to puff its own ego. It's an emblem of the greed and hubris of Chile's billionaire class – built by the nation's second-richest man, Horst Paulmann – that remains largely empty years after its completion. But, hey, at least it's useful for navigation when you're stumbling home in the murk of the night.

We reach the final stretch along the typically hectic Tobalaba, an ample tree-lined avenue split by a flowing canal, which has thinned of cars but thickened with humans. We melt into its heated crowds as pots and pans clank, stoplights flicker, firetrucks wail and warble.

Felipe and I don't have a TV, but we do have a projector. So when we finally arrive at our tiny 13th-floor apartment, we beam a live stream of the news across a barren white wall. The scenes that set our dark living room aglow are incomprehensibly grim. Astonished reporters loop footage of one metro station after another engulfed in flames. Public busses, splayed across familiar roads, are charred to their bones. The headquarters of Chile's largest electricity company appears as an incandescent blaze against the ink-black sky. Looters race past a reporter pushing a shopping cart. It overflows with microwaves, flat-screen TVs and six-packs of Cerveza Cristal. Two men waddle across the screen moments later with a washing machine. President Piñera, absent thus far, is finally caught on camera at a pizza party in Santiago's ritziest neighborhood, Vitacura, blissfully ignorant of the fact that the rest of the city is simmering.

By the time the conservative president returns to La Moneda, rumors are percolating that he will order the military out on the streets to contain the billowing crisis.

"They can't do that," Felipe pleads in disbelief as we sit together on a purple couch watching the slow-motion nightmare unfold. "You have no idea the anger that will cause. We overthrew a dictator to get the military *off* our streets."

A soldier once put a gun to the pregnant belly of Felipe's mom, just to mess with her. It's one of those indelible images from the dark days of dictatorship that she's shared, more than once, during our Sunday lunches, tears welling in her eyes. "Imagine the trauma this will cause her generation," Felipe says.

Just after midnight, sufficiently stuffed with overpriced pizza, Piñera addresses the nation, looking feverish. "My dear compatriots," he begins, fumbling with the microphone. "There will be no room for violence in a country with the rule of law at..."

The news comes quick and hits hard: Santiago is to enter a 15-day state of emergency, effective immediately. The government now has additional powers to restrict our freedom of movement and right to assembly. There will be a nightly curfew.

Then, he says what he wasn't supposed to say, does what he should have known not to do. The president of the republic sends soldiers out to patrol the streets of the capital for the first time since the end of the brutal dictatorship of Augusto Pinochet. Back then, in the 1970s and 1980s, thousands of suspected leftists were killed or "disappeared." Tens of thousands more were tortured while hundreds of thousands fled into exile. This reactionary maneuver, too, will have unimaginable consequences.

^ ~ ^

The metro is Santiago's engine. It's also its pride and joy. Seven color-coded lines whip 2.5 million daily riders through snaking subterranean tunnels, which intertwine at 16 key junctures, including Plaza Italia. Yes, you might be smushed up against a pole with your lips in a neighbor's ear, but the Chilean capital, unlike nearly every other Latin American hub, doesn't become a total trap at rush hour; it rattles away to the electronic beat of its workaholic trains. Some stations are veritable masterpieces, blanketed in the works of renowned Chilean artists such as abstract expressionist Roberto Matta and muralist Mario Toral. The MetroArte foundation, which commissions the art, also sprinkles train cars with poems and short stories that elicit passing grins as riders rumble across town. And so, it is with great sadness that Chileans wake up to the news that 20 stations have been torched beyond recognition. Another 57 are seriously damaged. The city's engine will surely sputter for years to come.

The metro has become a flashpoint in a growing crisis that

began, as we had supposed, with a nominal fare hike. Prices for peak-hour travel increased from 800 to 830 pesos. That led to a mass turnstile evasion, promoted across social media as #EvasiónMasiva, which spiraled out of control. This seemingly insignificant change, about US$0.04, comes at the end of a string of similar price increases in basics like water and electricity, pushing working-class Chileans over the edge.

Chile has – at least from afar – been heralded as a regional success story, with workers from across Latin America flooding over its porous borders in search of the "Chilean Dream." The nation's free-market model drove down poverty from around 40 percent at the dawn of the new millennium to under 10 percent two decades later. It also turned Chile into the second-richest country, per capita, in South America.

Scratch beneath the surface and you find a murkier picture. Fifty percent of Chilean workers earn less than US$550 per month, making a small change to public transportation costs a plausible breaking point. Meanwhile, the richest 1 percent of the population earns a quarter of the nation's wealth.

Of course, it wasn't always so unequal. That outcome took some creative engineering.

After the military teamed up with the CIA to overthrow the democratically elected socialist president Salvador Allende in a 1973 coup d'état, Chile pivoted to an economic system inspired by the libertarian teachings of economist Milton Friedman, an advisor to both Ronald Reagan and Margaret Thatcher. A group of Chileans known as the Chicago Boys flew north to study under Friedman and fellow economist Arnold Harberger at the University of Chicago, returning to high-ranking roles where they could import their teachings to the far end of the Americas. This neoliberal model was written into law in a new constitution approved in a controversial plebiscite during the military rule of Pinochet, which followed the coup. Growth came to Chile in the ensuing years, sure, but it certainly didn't reach all Chileans.

Four decades after the neoliberal model was put in place, the promise that free markets would lead to prosperity and prosperity would take care of all other problems appeared to be failing. Chileans aren't nearly as shocked as I am by the rioting and unrest. Many see the chaos as part of a reckoning. *Chile despertó* (Chile woke up) becomes the rallying cry of those who say they've been taken advantage of by the system for far too long. And the metro debacle? That was just the start.

^ ~ ^

The irony of sipping champagne at a swanky hotel while youth revolt against inequality is not lost on me. Truth is, I never saw any of this coming. I should have, of course. I ought to have glued my eyes open to the reality, to the flames simmering beneath the surface. I must have known that it only takes a tiny spark to light a fire. But perhaps my thinking was skewed?

When you're a privileged foreigner from a high-income country, it's far too easy to become emotionally trapped by the things that don't work as smoothly as they do back home, by the gears of the government that don't crank along like they should. Spend enough time in any expat group and you'll become surrounded by grumps from somewhere else griping about everything that's wrong with the place. I chose from the start to chalk Santiago's cons up to the growing pains of development. I'd focus instead on the pros: the panorama of monster peaks on a smogless day, the warmth of a Chilean gathering, the lazy, wine-fueled meals, the perennial sunshine.

I didn't love Santiago upon first sight, but I needed to like it. It belonged to someone who meant everything to me. It made him who he is, and so I willed it to become a part of me too. It's the only city we ever found where we could both have thriving careers, so I became a cheerleader for the place, warts and all. But every cheerleader questions the value of their role when the game doesn't turn out as planned...

^ ~ ^

A popular movement begins to coalesce in the days immediately following the unrest of October 18. Painted in broad strokes, it encompasses a wide range of grievances that affect not only the poor and disenfranchised, but also the debt-burdened middle class. The demands: an overhaul of the privatized pension system, a raise in the minimum wage, a reform of higher education (where university tuitions are among the highest in the world). Any idea is welcomed into the fold if it promises to alleviate the deep-seated frustration Chileans feel with the nation's entrenched inequity.

Meanwhile, President Piñera struggles to find his footing. After deploying 10,000 troops onto the streets – and arming them with generous rules of engagement – his message oscillates wildly. First, he declares that the nation is "at war against a powerful enemy." Then, he goes on television to solicit forgiveness, saying there is, in fact, no war. He offers cosmetic policy changes that do little to quell the unrest. When his approval rating plummets to 14 percent, he acquires a nervous twitch. When protests get bigger not just in Santiago but across Chile, he expands the state of emergency from the fjord towns of Patagonia to the desert cities of the Atacama.

The nation's capital is all but shut down amid the increasing volatility. Museums close, fearing vandals, and Felipe, like many other white-collar workers, starts logging in from home.

Grocery stores reduce hours and hire security guards, while restaurants and bars shutter under the nightly curfew. Evenings become long and lonely. Time, too, goes all topsy-turvy; it expands one day and contracts another. I don't know it yet, but this experiment in home isolation is to become little more than a preview – an early glimpse of a life lived in lockdown.

^.^

Three clear groups have now emerged on the streets of Santiago: the rioters, the yellow vests, and the non-violent protestors. The rioters wreak havoc on the city, using the situation as an excuse to burn, loot and destroy. Quaint little cobblestones become, in their hands, aerial weapons that can smash through the windows of towering office blocks. Rioters topple streetlights to make Santiago Centro an obstacle course. Even churches are fair game, their wooden pews converted into the fuel for fiery barricades that light up the night.

One day, Felipe gets a call from an employee with some rotten news. Her father had enlisted his newly minted Polish son-in-law to help him stop looters at their local supermarket in a riot-struck barrio on the west side of town. By the time the night was over, the son-in-law was dead, struck by a stray bullet in the heat of the action. Felipe's employee not only lost her husband; her dad was the accidental killer.

Similar events take place across the city. One supermarket chain reports that 128 of its stores have been either looted or burned. Meanwhile, the metro adds a dozen new entries to its list of damaged stations. Nobody quite knows who's behind these acts – or if some nefarious organization has been orchestrating them – but the rioters serve to muddy the waters for those with legitimate hopes of peaceful defiance.

Yellow vests, on the other hand, are the rioters' equal and opposite: neighborhood vigilantes whose actions often mimic those of the rioters they're out to suppress. One afternoon, as a rally heats up a block away from my apartment, a yellow-vested man approaches an unarmed protestor. They get into an argument. A shot is fired. I hear a scream and run outside to find a girl in her early 20s in a puddle of blood on the sidewalk, struck in the leg. The cops, instead of helping her, form a circle of protection around the middle-aged man, swooping him and his yellow vest away in an armored car. They charge the man with only a minor infraction. The incident goes viral, fueling calls that the police are protecting the vigilantes.

In the upscale coastal resort of Reñaca, yet another yellow vest incident becomes the talk of the town. An American economist who founded a libertarian compound near Santiago called Galt's Gulch – named for the fictional capitalist haven in Ayn Rand's *Atlas Shrugged* and aimed at attracting "liberty-loving people from all over the world" – is captured on camera firing five bullets into a crowd of demonstrators, one of whom is hospitalized. He then goes home to upload a self-aggrandizing video about it to YouTube, taking selfies with the police officer who eventually arrests him. The chumminess of this encounter between perpetrator and supposed protector enrages the public.

Between the rioters and yellow vests is the final group: the non-violent protestors. Through largely peaceful actions, they're demanding a revolution, congregating in large numbers by day and seasoning the crisp night air with evening *cacerolazos*. They make up the majority of Chileans, including Felipe. He has become swept up in the long-elusive promise of real policy change. JJ has, too, designing protest art and uploading free stencils anyone can download to decorate the city with his surreal social justice imagery.

We attend a few family-friendly protests together in Plaza Ñuñoa, where the atmosphere is more festive than furious, but now Felipe wants to go back to Plaza Italia for a gathering that promises to draw a record number of demonstrators. More than a million people could be there, he says, and it would be wrong of us not to be among them. Problem is, we can't get anywhere near it in a taxi, and the hobbled metro has once again shuttered its graffiti-covered gates. So we resign to making the long walk back, retracing our steps from a week ago. This time, it will be a more conscious pilgrimage.

We set off in the early afternoon, zigzagging along the eerily quiet side streets between our apartment and Gran Torre Santiago. This zone, a financial district, is often referred to as Sanhattan, an ironic sobriquet used to lampoon its small menagerie of shimmering skyscrapers, whose tenants seem to have fled their offices early ahead of the anticipated disruptions. Sanhattan is, in truth, green and pleasant and highly livable, though it does lack a sense of vibrancy beyond its monumental towers, with most of its shops and restaurants trapped in one of Latin America's biggest malls.

We follow the contours of the mud-brown Río Mapocho west from Sanhattan toward the Parque de Las Esculturas sculpture park, then onward past the embassies of Avenida Andrés Bello. Others are marching along the same path in a growing procession. Among them is our friend Carla. We link up with her near the Fuente Bicentenario, a preposterous dancing fountain whose geysers light up like the Las Vegas Bellagio's.

Carla was a backpacker traveling around New Zealand with Felipe when we first met, a decade ago. The three of us arrived on working holiday visas and somehow washed up in Franz Josef, a tiny South Island hamlet known for its colossal glaciers, which drop from the Southern Alps into a temperate rainforest before dribbling into the Tasman Sea. Carla and Felipe worked in the restaurant of the Scenic Hotel. I manned the front desk, where multiple buses arrived each day to disgorge tour groups from around the world. We lived together in an abandoned motel nearby, which boasted views over the wide bed of a small river that would one day, a few years later, swell and swallow the place in a flood.

Felipe was a surprise find in a town of 444 people. We hit it off right away. Our first kiss was in a glowworm cave and our first sleepover on a blanket by the river, dozing off under a speckled dome of unfamiliar stars. At night, we danced at the town's only bar, the appropriately named Blue Ice. On free days, we hiked the meandering rainforest trails of Westland Tai Poutini National Park, losing ourselves amid fuzzy ferns. Those months together in Franz Josef were so dreamlike, so sprinkled with New Zealand's fairytale magic, that I was led down an unsuspecting path to where I find myself today.

Carla, too, got swept away by the magic of Franz Josef. She picked up another Scenic Hotel employee and moved with him to the antipodes, settling on the edge of Swedish Lapland, where the winters are lightless and the summer sun never sets. In time, their breezy international relationship became as icy as the surroundings. In an unexpected plot twist, she divorced, returned to Chile and was now dating Stephanie, an athletics instructor and fellow soccer fan from the working-class Quinta Normal neighborhood.

Stephanie has become deeply involved in the protest movement. She's also a fantastic planner who shows up for demonstrations the way a soccer mom does for picnics: with a bag full of treats. These include rainbow bandanas, snacks and a soccer ball, plus spray cans filled with a bicarbonate mixture she says will neutralize the tear gas. As we push onward to Plaza Italia, she appears eager to share her thoughts with anyone who'll listen. Namely me.

"This protest is not about 30 pesos, but 30 years," she says, echoing a common phrase circulated amongst demonstrators. "It's 30 years since the return to democracy, but we have preserved a constitution made under the dictatorship. It's 30 years of a pension system that impoverishes our elders. It's 30 years of rising prices and stagnant wages."

Stephanie believes there's no other way to emerge from the shadow of the Pinochet regime than a complete rewrite of the constitution. It would be a first step toward a new social pact, she says, and perhaps the citizens could play a leading role to ensure that Chileans have a constitution that actually belongs to the people.

"After all, the last one was drafted by a small group of supposed experts and signed off by a dictator," she adds. "This one could be the product of a truly democratic process."

We stroll together in the direction of the 34-floor Torre Telefónica, a hideous tower designed in the mid-1990s to emulate the blocky mobile phones of the era. Flying stones have busted open its lower windows in recent days, a sign that we're fast approaching the action.

Stephanie says that she, like so many others marching alongside us today, owes millions of pesos (thousands of US dollars) to the bank to pay off a university degree that may have gotten her a respectable job but will never pay a high enough salary to cover rent, living expenses and high-interest loans. As a result of this trap, she still lives at home with her mother. "We've gone to the streets to ask for our dignity," she fumes, "and this won't stop until we get it."

Hers is a demand echoed far and wide. Dignity becomes a

buzzword on news broadcasts of the protests. Google has even changed Plaza Italia to Plaza de la Dignidad (Plaza of Dignity) on its map of Santiago.

We continue in the direction of this newly christened landmark, but it soon becomes clear that we'll never actually reach it. There's now a torrent of attendees. Many are tossing back street *cerveza*, holding up hand-painted signs and waving flags of the long-oppressed Mapuche community, Chile's largest Indigenous group. Some blow the traditional *trutruca*, a twisted bamboo trumpet, while more still thwack pots and pans as they dance, working themselves into a trance.

There's a sea of bobbing protest signs, many of which declare: "Chile woke up." Other posters call for Piñera to resign, for a new constitution, for the military to get off the streets. "We are not at war," they clap back, emphatically.

Joker lookalikes with unnerving red grins dot the crowd, inspired by the recently released Todd Phillips film, which has made Batman's enemy an inadvertent symbol of the oppressed. Many have latched onto the film as a cautionary tale: neglect society's most vulnerable and you can expect horrific consequences in return. One Joker holds up an ominous sign that reads, "I'm here at the bottom so be careful what you do next." Another stands near a cement wall that's been defaced with the message "We are all clowns."

We settle into the crowd, far from Plaza de la Dignidad but entrenched enough to feel a part of the action. A street vendor pushes his way through with a cooler of beers; another hawks bottled water and Super 8 candy bars. We call the beer man over and order four Escudos. They've no taste and are barely cold, but we're thirsty and amped up and drinking on the streets. The *pacos* (cops) are nowhere to be found.

"*Salud*," we say, clinking beers and bobbing heads, easing in to the long afternoon.

A stereo off in the distance blasts the song "El baile de los que sobran" (the dance of the leftovers) by Los Prisioneros, pioneers of Spanish-language rock and one of Chile's biggest musical exports. I first heard this song at an impromptu dance party with Carla and Felipe back in our abandoned motel in New Zealand. An important protest anthem in the twilight years of the dictatorship, it speaks of how Chilean society sets the poor up for failure from the moment they're born.

Everyone in the crowd knows the lyrics. They roar along, singing about the dance of the leftovers. The dance for all those whom society let down. Stephanie, Carla, Felipe and I are all in motion, howling the words in unison and lubricating our vocal cords with tepid beers.

The song's pulsating beat has the crowd undulating. More like it follow. Any lingering fears of danger or confrontation fade into the background. The massive protest party rages on, sewn together by a feverous cause. Felipe leans in for a kiss as the dancing subsides, relishing what is certain to be one of those moments forever etched into the timeline of both his country and our lives.

"There have been protests in Chile for years," he says, recalling how citizens have taken to the streets to demand everything from better education to woman's rights, gay rights and social security. "Somehow, this feels different."

"It feels like, for the first time, we're getting together for a common cause," Carla adds. "We're all complaining about the same stuff. It's like, even if I went to private school, and you went to public school, we both know the system isn't fair."

"That's the thing," says Felipe. "The system tries to make you feel like, if you follow the private path of education or health care, you're safe and nothing wrong will happen to you. But at the end, you realize that it's not like that."

"It's just the message they want you to believe," Stephanie interjects. "But today does feel like a statement. It doesn't matter what class you come from, we're all in this together."

There are many more people who want to be here right now, but who are afraid because they're still haunted by the past, says Felipe. "They agree with the demands, but are scared to be on the streets. Can you imagine if my parent's generation were with us, too?"

We've all been depressed since the city became an inferno, but the joy of today feels like a turning point. Stephanie pulls out a soccer ball and we begin passing it around our tiny patch of pavement. We order another round of tasteless beer. Minutes turn to hours. The amoeba of dissenting voices grows.

News organizations beam drone shots of the crowd out to the nation. None can capture the immensity of it. Five percent of the population turned up. One out of every 20 Chileans is here. Citizens regularly gather in Plaza Italia to mark the nation's highs and lows. Today will be the former. That much is clear.

^_^

Small glimmers of hope begin to emerge as dust settles on the largest public gathering in Chilean history. Piñera says he has heard loud and clear the voices of more than a million marching Chileans. He announces a nominal welfare package and sweeping changes to his cabinet, sacking the interior minister, whom many blame for the government's strong-armed response. Most importantly, there is talk of a possible referendum on a new constitution. My magazine editor, eager to revive the sullied

Santiago story, asks me to resume work. I begrudgingly oblige, as does my next subject, Carolina, a local historian.

Carolina and I meet right where I left off with JJ in Lastarria. The street, one of Santiago's loveliest, is unrecognizable. Overlapping graffiti tags blanket the facades of its trendy restaurants. A barrage of security guards patrols the grounds of The Singular. The storybook Iglesia de la Veracruz church, a popular wedding venue that dates to the 1850s, has been charred like a piece of toast. The street buskers, art hawkers, antique traders, booksellers, tarot card readers and clandestine marijuana dealers who typically crowd its thin sidewalks are nowhere to be found. The gay tango dancers – who draw a larger audience than the art-house cinema they perform in front of – are also gone. So is the smiley man who entertains kids for a few coins with his mechanical diorama, or *lambe lambe*, whose theatrical shows lie behind a tiny peephole.

"This might be a weird tour today," Carolina says with a nervous chuckle.

"You think?" I say, chuckling back.

Weird can't begin to describe it.

I suddenly feel incredibly stupid for asking her to join me on a doomed mission. We're glorifying Santiago with a puff piece while the city blisters. I should have canceled. I should have known it was too soon. But here we are, tethered together on a fool's errand, blithely tiptoeing around army tanks to have a go at sightseeing.

I've never met Carolina before. She comes off as tough – intimidating, even – with a bandana over her head and a black T-shirt that slinks around the curves of her prominent belly. Yet, behind the hardened veneer, she's actually a warm soul and great storyteller with a keen interest in local history.

"Where we are right now is at the southern edge of the Inca Road," Carolina begins, pivoting into tour mode. "The legendary Spanish conquistador Francisco Pizarro sent his emissary Pedro de Valdivia to settle the lands south from Cuzco, Peru, in 1540. He built Santiago on top of an Inca settlement with the support of the Indigenous Picunche people, who would eventually grow tired of their foreign visitors and plunder the place."

The goal of this section of my story is to highlight Santiago Centro, expose its history and find Carolina's connection to it. But as we walk away from Lastarria, I become entranced by all the protest art along the way. At Parque Forestal, the eyes of all figures carved into the Fuente Alemana fountain have been painted over with blood-red tears. A sculpture of Daedalus and Icarus in front of the fine arts museum contains crimson eyes, too. It's a commentary on how the police have purposely aimed for the pupils when firing their pellet guns to disperse crowds.

Santiago's historic core appears to have been spared the damage of other parts of the city, giving us a small window in which to momentarily ignore the embers smoldering on the periphery. Its heart, the stately Plaza de Armas, contains the bulk of our mid-morning itinerary. It was here that Valdivia's master builder, Pedro de Gamboa, instituted a grid layout centered around a grand plaza for the new capital of Nueva Extremadura, as Chile was known back then. Thirty-six endangered Chilean wine palms shade the square today, as does a towering repository of Spanish colonial architecture.

Carolina admits that Santiago was never a crown jewel of the Spanish Empire. More of a historical backwater, it only had 45,000 people when Chile declared independence in 1818. Accordingly, it doesn't quite arouse the same time-warping allure of Lima or Mexico City. But around Plaza de Armas, it comes close. There's also a good excuse for the relative paucity of historic buildings elsewhere: earthquakes.

"Chile is one of the most seismically active countries on earth, thanks to the fast-moving Nazca Plate," Carolina explains. "We had the strongest earthquake ever recorded, in 1960. It was a magnitude 9.5 that struck near the southern city of Valdivia and killed thousands of people. The most recent earthquake was a magnitude 8.8 in 2010, which was the sixth-strongest on record and killed about 550 people between Santiago and Concepción."

"Of course, we've had plenty of others since then," she adds, "but we don't call them earthquakes. They're merely *temblores*."

Carolina brought me here, in part, to show me how the city's historic core evolved over nearly 500 years of regular tremors. The first laid stone in the colossal cathedral in front of us, for example, dates to the 1500s, but it's been rebuilt a half dozen times over the years, giving it a decidedly eclectic look. Many of the other buildings standing today date to the early 1800s, including an old jailhouse that's now the municipal office, a royal court turned history museum, and a former presidential palace masquerading as a post office. All have been remodeled endlessly, though they're more resistant to seismic activity these days, thanks to some of the world's strictest building codes.

To find the current presidential palace, we walk south past more neoclassical buildings in Plaza de la Justicia. The old customs house here is now a distinguished museum of pre-Columbian art, while the former home of the *El Mercurio* newspaper is an upmarket shopping arcade. The presidential palace, La Moneda, occupies an entire city block nearby, with flag-filled plazas on either end and the sprawling subterranean cultural center where Felipe works down below. Sensing a theme of creative reuse, I am barely surprised when Carolina tells me that the palace inhabits a colonial-era mint.

These timeworn buildings, battered by countless earthquakes, speak of the city's perpetual cycle of chaos and rebirth. Old things fall, new things rise, the city moves on. That gives me hope.

^ ~ ^

One month before Chile became a madhouse, I celebrated my solidifying adulthood by doing several things I believed one should have done already by the age of 35. First, I got a credit card. Then, I signed up for an insurance plan. Most significantly, Felipe and I poured our life savings into a condo in a building that was breaking ground in the residential Ñuñoa neighborhood.

The area had just become accessible by two new metro lines and was in that frenzied phase of blossoming. We wanted to play witness to its growth, so we splurged on an aspirational top-floor two-bedroom unit with a view east toward the Andes from its sizable terrace. The building would have a pool, gym, bicycle parking, space – everything our current rental lacked. Plus, it wouldn't be ready for another 16 months, giving us enough time to acquire additional funds.

Look at us, we thought, as we signed and fingerprinted the contract (whose Spanish legalese I couldn't possibly comprehend). Who would have guessed these guys who'd lived most of their adult lives out of bloated backpacks would one day invest in their future? Certainly not the old us, nor anyone we knew. But there we were, in a sales trailer beside a giant hole in the ground, nervously toasting a promising future.

After a dozen itinerant years without living in the same country for more than 18 months, I was finally settling down. In Chile, of all places. It felt monumental.

Now, two months later, I'm questioning the value of planting roots. Not only is Chile, the prime object of my cheerleading as a writer, falling apart, for better or worse, but the wider region I cover is tumbling with it.

In Ecuador, mass anti-government rallies have paralyzed Quito, with citizens angry over President Lenín Moreno's decision to cut decades-old fuel subsidies and implement tax and labor reforms. These austerity measures are all part of a deal to obtain credit from the International Monetary Fund, but the people aren't having it. The unrest becomes so intense that the government is forced to flee the Andean capital for the steamy southern city of Guayaquil.

Meanwhile, Bolivia's first Indigenous president, Evo Morales, flees to Mexico City seeking asylum after weeks of protests over the disputed results of a presidential election that, many argue, he should never have been a part of in the first place. Angry supporters of the socialist leader clash with security forces in the high-altitude administrative capital of La Paz as the deputy head of the senate, a bleach-blonde conservative named Jeanine Áñez, declares herself interim president by right of succession.

In Colombia, anti-government demonstrations erupt over possible changes to the minimum wage, pension and tax reforms, as well as alleged corruption. The protests are some of the largest in recent history, luring hundreds of thousands of Colombians out onto the streets, with residents of the political capital, Bogotá, and salsa capital, Cali, put under nightly curfews as a result. All the while, the socioeconomic crisis in neighboring Venezuela grows stormier than ever, with skyrocketing hyperinflation, food shortages and a new opposition leader trying to topple the presidency of Nicolás Maduro.

Analysts are connecting the dots and calling it a Latin American Spring akin to the Arab Spring of the early 2010s. The so-called Forgotten Continent – which, in his book by that title, author Michael Reid says is neither poor enough to inspire a moral crusade, like Africa, nor as explosively booming as Asia – feels as if it's once again being condemned to failure while the global news cycle scarcely registers a blip.

When the unrest in Chile does make headlines abroad, it's almost always in relation to its direct effect on foreign dignitaries. Santiago has been gearing up to host an Asia-Pacific Economic Cooperation (APEC) meeting in November, where US President Donald Trump and Chinese President Xi Jinping will sign a historic trade deal. Teenage climate activist Greta Thunberg is on a boat voyage to Santiago to attend the UN Climate Change Conference (COP25) in early December. None of them will ever set foot here, of course. The events become yet another casualty of our so-called *estallido social* (social uprising).

One key figure monitoring the protests closely is the UN High Commissioner for Human Rights, Chile's ex-president Michelle Bachelet. The left-leaning politician first rose to power in 2006, buoyed in part by her powerful story of enduring torture under the Pinochet dictatorship. During her first term as president, she played an integral role in founding Santiago's Museum of Memory and Human Rights, an architectural blockbuster and leading cultural institution that ruminates on the human rights violations committed by the Chilean state between 1973 and 1990. Her second term, which ended in 2018, was less memorable, as she failed to push through many of the reforms protestors are still demanding today.

Bachelet, now stationed in Geneva, sends a team of officers to Chile to investigate allegations of physical and sexual abuse at the hands of the police and military. What they uncover is concrete proof of the stories that have been circulating in the news for weeks: there have been 24 cases of sexual violence, 113 cases of torture and ill-treatment and 350 cases of eye trauma from pellets fired by security forces – not to mention more than two dozen deaths and thousands of detentions.

These, it seems, are the excessive costs of an elusive path toward dignity.

^ ~ ^

The momentary high of the million-person march fizzles into the Santiago smog as November rolls into December. Curfews are, thankfully, a thing of the past, making protests possible well into the night. Yet the movement never quite coalesces around any unified demands, much less a clear leader. Instead, it becomes sporadic and disjointed. Demonstrations continue – often ecstatically – but they never quite reach the same level or intensity as before. The rioting, too, becomes scattered and desperate; the disenfranchised carry on with their unbridled destruction of public infrastructure in poorer neighborhoods that need it most.

Weeks pass in a blustery cloud. I meet friends for pisco sours, dine out on ceviche and attend the usual calendar of events. Life goes on, but in a kind of warped version of the way it used to. When I venture into the city center, there's an inevitable brush with cops, a quick dash out of harm's way, an air of anything goes. I never quite know if the metro will get me to or from home, or what stations might be closed for repairs. The mere thought of seeing the city I've planted my roots in look so unpleasant depresses me to the point that I have to amp myself up – with coffee, music, alcohol – just to leave the apartment.

Plaza Italia, epicenter of Chile's social earthquake, is now downright apocalyptic. Vandals have made a mockery of its central statue of General Manuel Baquedano, draping the former army chief in protest clothes and even attempting to decapitate him. Baquedano's namesake metro station is in a pile of rubble, and there is not a working stoplight or streetlamp or pedestrian signal anywhere in the vicinity. To cap off the surreal scene, the walls of all buildings within eyesight of the plaza have been scribbled over so thoroughly that they look like the psych ward doodles of a feral child.

My cover story on this bruised city goes on a permanent hiatus. Other work has dried up, too. There is a lack of interest in travel to South America, and who can blame world-weary tourists for avoiding a mess?

I comfort myself with signs of hope on the horizon. Lawmakers representing nearly every political faction have agreed upon rules for a path toward a new constitution, one that, for the first time in the nation's history, will give all citizens a voice in outlining their future.

In a referendum in April, Chileans will answer two questions. The first: Do you want a new constitution? The second: Should it be drafted through a citizens-only constitutional convention or a mixed constitutional convention, which would include citizens alongside members of congress?

It's not a panacea, of course, but it's a promising start. Only problem is, the world as we know it will be flipped upside down by the time April comes around. And the vote? It will be but one of the many casualties of what will come to be known as the Before Times.

^ ~ ^

The year 2020 arrives and, with it, the start of the austral summer. Like clockwork, residents flee Santiago for the countryside in their annual migrations. I, too, depart for sunnier shores, seeking out peaceful pockets of South America where I can file stories for my editors now that Chile is off the table.

Felipe is to attend an opening night reception at the MALBA museum in Buenos Aires to scope out a new exhibit from Brazilian installation artist Ernesto Neto that Felipe's co-workers will bring across the Andes to Santiago. I tag along so we can relish a few days of momentary peace amid the crumbling opulence of Argentina's seductive capital.

We hunker down for a long weekend in an apartment in the bohemian Palermo Soho neighborhood, tossing back Malbec on the balcony and strolling leafy boulevards lined with more bookshops, per capita, than anywhere else in the world. We dream up ideas for our new apartment in the antique markets of historic San Telmo, then get drunk on the toothpaste-like spirit *fernet* in a gay *milonga* in Villa Crespo, seduced by the romance of tango music. The weekend is as needed as it is enchanting, but I have to cut it short on the final night to catch an overnight bus north to Mercedes.

Mercedes is the dusty gateway city to the world's second-largest wetland, Iberá, which has just become a new national park. I've sold a feature – a rare good-news story in global conservation – so I set off with a local ranger to learn about the ambitious plans to revive this swampy patch of Argentina to the level of biodiversity it had before the rice paddies and cattle ranches munched it up. Rewilding Argentina, a group backed by American philanthropist Kris Tompkins, has already reintroduced five locally extinct or endangered native species to Iberá, including the pampas deer, giant anteater and green-winged macaw. In the coming months, the project will enter its next phase when jaguars return to these wetlands, where they've been absent for nearly a century. I've arrived just in time to play witness to a miraculous new chapter.

One article down, I catch a ferry over to Uruguay for a trend piece on the newfound cool of its Atlantic coast. I interview billionaire businessman Alexander Vik about his trio of ornamental hotels, each of which is stuffed with more contemporary South American art than you'll find in any Uruguayan museum. The hotels lie in the whitewashed beach town of José Ignacio, a onetime fishing village that's now something of an austral Hamptons. Nearby, I investigate Uruguay's push to become a reputable wine country at Bodega Garzón, one of the most lavish wineries anywhere on earth, with impressive eco credentials and decent bottles of the nation's signature red and white grapes, Tannat and Albariño. Finally, I meet with celebrity chef Francis Mallmann in the ghost town of Pueblo Garzón to try and fathom why a man known for his primitive open-fire method of roasting meats thinks he's the maverick to release a vegan cookbook.

Back in Santiago three weeks later, as I write up these stories, I feel as if I've found my groove again. The unrest has largely subsided, the city is empty, the sun is blazing and a referendum is on the horizon. The protests will surely reignite once the summer ends, as they should, but it looks as if the earth that has cracked from underneath me is solidifying. I feel a sense of optimism. *Old things fall, new things rise, life moves on.* Chile could come out on the other end of this a more equal society and I a more conscious member of it. My confidence balloon fills up and floats high until one day, suddenly, it pops.

^˷^

You know how sometimes life seems to get a tad more sinister as you age? And you begin to wonder if it's just like this for each generation, as you move from one stage to the next, or if the times we're living in are a bit more extraordinary? That's how

I feel about Covid-19 when it goes, splat-fast, from an abstract problem affecting someone else – in some world far removed from my own – to a concrete reality fucking up my present.

There's a moment when I guiltily, unconscionably, relish the fact that there are people in other parts of the world living through shitty times while Santiago carries on in relative peace. When Covid-19 arrives in the United States, I think, *finally*, my friends and family – who've struggled to understand what's going on here – will see what it's like to deal with a bit of hardship. It's *their* turn.

Chile is geographically isolated from the rest of the world by the Pacific Ocean to the west, the Andes to the east, fjords down south and an inhospitable desert up north. I naively thought this meant that a pandemic would be slow to arrive and quick to die. Of course, borders mean nothing when planes land in your city each day from every corner of the globe, bringing with them more baggage than what's spit out onto the carousel.

For a while, as Covid-19 finds its footing in Santiago, life isn't so bad. I'm buoyed by the fact that I'm not alone. That I have a rare opportunity to slow down. That I can virtually connect with family and friends, some of whom I haven't spoken with in years because, until now, we didn't have an icebreaker to bridge the rift of time. I take comfort in watching everyone fortify themselves under lockdown, as I am for the second time in so many months. There's also the twisted thrill of living through history, of being a part of something you know you'll still be talking about decades down the line.

By the time the austral fall trudges into winter, however, I feel sure that everything is unraveling again. With strict quarantine measures extended for a fourth month, then a fifth, the future becomes a fog with no end. Days merge together. Depression hovers and then attacks. *Why get out of bed when it's cold and I've got no work? Why change out of my pajamas? Will anyone even see me today?*

Editors I work with send emails, one by one, announcing their departures from the publications that pay my bills. Other employers have frozen their budgets, closed offices or folded altogether. I'm not asking for tears. I don't expect pity. I am incredibly privileged to do what I do. But it still feels like a kick in the gut. My onetime dream job, which took a decade to build, has suddenly ground to a halt. I know it's not just me; it's a storm that's toppled millions of others, many of whom are far less fortunate that I am, but that doesn't stop me from stewing for a while in my own grief.

Coronavirus cases in Chile simmer while North America and Europe rage. Then, they explode into the highest, per capita, on earth while other nations begin to reopen. It feels cruel to have endured an extended lockdown and have nothing to show for it.

Instead, we have places like the hotel across the street from my apartment, which has been turned into an isolation ward for those exposed to the plague. Sirens blare at all hours of the day as ambulances arrive to cart people with deteriorating conditions over to hospitals which, the patients will soon learn, don't even have room for them.

A sensation of entrapment creeps in as the world outside my rented walls becomes a new kind of bleak. I lose all desire to leave home. I shouldn't leave anyway. The government ensures I can only do so twice a week – and for just two hours each time – with permit in hand and mask over my face. I do everything possible to keep the outside world out. It's for the best, I tell myself, though it goes against every grain in my body to be this still.

Meanwhile, everything I love about Santiago – the perpetual

sunshine, the agreeable temperatures, the silhouette of the cordillera – disappears in winter. Most apartments, mine included, don't have heat beyond what you can plug into the wall. As I shiver in the cloudy depression of a pandemic winter, I start dreaming of somewhere warm and liberating I might escape to once tiny pleasures become possible again. Somewhere with wide-open spaces and infinite skies. Somewhere close enough to home, but also far enough away to expand my horizons after months of urban imprisonment. I begin fantasizing about the Atacama.

A day's drive north from Santiago – and spanning the entire upper third of Chile, which is the world's longest country by latitudinal extent – it is the very definition of arid. Popular legend has it that there are weather stations tucked into its thirsty core that have never once recorded a single drop of rain. Its landscapes are so alien, so not of planet Earth, that NASA uses them to test instruments for Mars. And yet, the Atacama is anything but lifeless.

Sprawling geoglyphs and perfectly preserved mummies attest to thousands of years of human occupation, while snowmelt from the Andes and fog from the Pacific support an array of exotic animals. This superlative-rich land is home to earth's loftiest volcanoes, highest geysers and clearest skies. It's also freckled with lithium, the mineral of the moment, which has prospectors abuzz. In short, it's a place I might purposefully wander without considering myself lost.

In my greying state of melancholy, after a roulette wheel of twisted fortunes, I convince myself that the Atacama is the answer. It slowly colonizes my mind, emerging ever more mythically as an antidote to numbing emotions. Perhaps the Atacama could lift me out of my fog. It could retool my mind. More importantly, it could help me understand the place I live in.

All these years I've felt like an indifferent visitor in Chile; being here through a social uprising and a pandemic has made me invested. It's forced me to dive deeper into the stories of my partner's homeland, to contextualize things I've long taken for granted. If I'm going to understand Chile on a deeper level, then what better place to start than the Atacama, the place most Chileans don't even understand themselves?

Maybe it could remind me why I've settled here. These past months, I've been schooled in the subjects that make Chileans tick. What more might I discover if I ventured to the part of the nation that fuels its mineral-based economy, yet remains an enigma to the Santiaguinos who reap the rewards? Surely there's more to the Atacama than dusty mines and broken dreams? I want to find out.

So I plant the seed and let it grow over the long winter of urban isolation.

2 A MESSAGE FROM ABOVE

(CULTS, STARS AND SIGNS:
HOW DESERTS MESS WITH MINDS)

The cabin lies on a rocky ridge above the Puclaro Reservoir, 325 miles (523 km) north of Santiago. It's a rickety one-room structure, colored in mustard and maroon, with a sliding glass door that frames a cerulean cove. Its pros: the rainbow beach chair on the balcony; the kitchen where I cook my meals; the vista of khaki mounds snaking across the horizon. Its cons: the sour aroma of backed-up plumbing; the mattress that folds around my body like a hotdog bun; the linoleum floors, which make me feel like a mouse on a glue trap. The place also groans like a haunted house when the wind blows through, which it does at nearly every hour. It's so blustery here it feels as if the cabin could fall off the stilts that bolt it to the parched earth and tumble into the water below.

If it did, it wouldn't be alone.

On the far side of the reservoir lies the town of New Gualliguaica. Signboards call it "the first 21st-century village in Chile" on account of its rebirth on January 1, 2000. New Gualliguaica sits on a hilltop overlooking the dam that destroyed Old Gualliguaica. Other than the 18th-century church, which was planted at the heart of the new village, the rest of Old Gualliguaica lies almost exactly as it was – a quaint, old-timey town congealed in a desert fishbowl. Scuba types sometimes dive down to the decaying village, but most visitors to New Gualliguaica these days come to windsurf atop it.

I've come here, to the start of the Elqui Valley, to enjoy the last gasp of fertility before the Atacama completely dries up. I've found myself in this second-rate wind box thanks to – of all things – a faded roadside billboard. More specifically, the image on that billboard of Joakin Bello, an Osho-like apparition kneeling in a glass box stuffed with instruments.

"*Conciertos y cabañas*" (concerts and cabins) the sign read, with an arrow pointing up a dirt path above the reservoir. Because I like both of those things, I took the bait and flicked on my blinker. I was greeted at the entrance by a woman named Shalom, which I found both fitting and peculiar. Fitting because I know that, at least idiomatically, it can mean "hello" in Hebrew. Peculiar because Chile is a country where it's easier to come across the descendants of hiding Nazis than immigrant Jews.

Shalom is a gorgeous bleach-blonde of pre-retirement age. Her flowing blouse and form-fitting jeans give her a metropolitan air I wasn't expecting here. I think, upon first glance, that she may have been a model in her youth. She confirms, soon after we meet, in a frenzy of introductions, that she does, in fact, have Jewish ancestry. She moved back to Chile a few years ago after a three-year stint in Woodstock, New York, trying to make it as an artist. There was a time a few decades before that when she was in the Israeli army, but she says she left that country after "the war," as if I'd instinctively know which one. Now, she tends to these plywood cabins overlooking the first 21st-century village in Chile – mostly, I suppose, to cement her connection to that desert deity on the billboard.

I see him – Señor Bello – long before I meet him. Days before, actually. Or rather, days before he sees me. When you live behind glass walls, as Joakin does, and serenade the stars, as he's apt to do, you ensure that you will always be seen.

I like people who like to be seen, mostly because I myself prefer the role of wallflower. So that's how I find myself lured down a dirt path on my first night in the Atacama by a sound that's almost like a whale call beaming from star to star across the obsidian sky. The noise – poetic and sorrowful – seems as if it's coming from a violin or viola, except it doesn't really register as either. It sounds as if a fiddle has been snapped apart and Frankensteined back together so as to create an entirely new instrument that swoops up and down octaves, always landing on the somber edge of each note. If at first the music wails, soon after it warbles.

The man from the billboard entices the moon out from behind the Andes like a storybook snake charmer. It rises ever higher into the sky until its milky-blue spotlight penetrates the glass walls of his lonely studio. That's when I first catch a faint silhouette of him, of his wavy grey hair, which flows down an angelic face to rest upon the upper half of a long white robe. Basking in the moon glow, he looks for all the world like a Sunday school image of Jesus – or rather, an image of Jesus if, say, he went missing for a few decades and the police re-released his photo with modern face-aging technology. *That* kind of Jesus.

Joakin seems to sense my presence on the periphery of his studio, but he pays me no mind. I'm one of only two guests staying at his cabins right now. The other is a ponytailed Mapuche musician who's traveled here all the way from the south-central La Araucanía region with one of those *trutruca* instruments I saw at the protests in Santiago.

The man tells me later that evening, as the moonlight turns the rippled reservoir into a pool of glitter below, that he hopes to record a song with Joakin. He wants to pair the brash and severe noise of the *trutruca* with the swooping melancholy of Joakin's "bellectra" – the homemade fiddle he's been fiddling with all night. But the man hasn't been able to get an appointment to see him for two days. To meet Joakin, you must first deal with Shalom.

^ ~ ^

I link up with Shalom the following morning at a small café she runs along the main road. I order a coffee; she brings me some hot water and a sachet of Nescafé. As I swirl the acidic little crystals into a porcelain teacup, we get to talking. I tell her I'm a writer. She says that, in addition to being a classically trained musician, Joakin is too.

"He's written 23 books," she boasts, "mostly poetry, but also history and philosophy."

"So that's in addition to playing all those instruments?" I ask, pointing to the billboard above the café, the same one that lured me here.

"He also speaks four languages," she continues, "including Quechua, the mother tongue of the Inca."

"He's quite the virtuoso," I remark, cocking my eyebrow.

"You should meet up with him and chat about your writing," she adds. "I'm sure he'd love to tell you about his."

I suddenly feel incredibly nervous, as if my true purpose in the Elqui Valley has been exposed right from the start. I've come to this arid outpost not only as a baby step into the Atacama; I want to understand the kind of people who are drawn into a desert – and what this landscape does to their minds. I'm hoping, also, for something of a leap outside of myself – a mental hop into the mindset of people much freer than I'll ever be.

The Elqui Valley is renowned across Chile as a place of dreamers and dropouts. It's an austral Sedona, where New Age types take quartz baths, hippies join cults and UFOs are more fact than fiction. The place is teeming with Joakin Bellos, and I've come here to see what I can learn from them.

"Yes," I tell Shalom. "That would be wonderful. I'd love to meet with Joakin."

^ ~ ^

Twenty-four hours pass with no news from Shalom about a potential meeting. So I busy myself exploring the area, starting with the main hub of Vicuña, where everything seems to be named after Gabriela Mistral. She has a restaurant, a hotel, a library, a plaza, a museum, even a pisco brand.

In 1945, Mistral became the first Latin American author to receive a Nobel Prize in Literature. The disconsolate poet was born here in Vicuña and had a bit of a rags-to-riches tale, growing up in poverty but dying in New York City as one of the most famous poets of her time. An educator at the Museo Gabriela Mistral tells me that, in her early work, she wrote often of the Elqui Valley as a place of both punishment and despair, but also as a verdant lifeline in an inhospitable land.

Mistral long lived in the shadows of the nation's second Nobel Prize–winning poet: the rabble-rousing Pablo Neruda. Yet 21st-century readers have been kinder to the staunch feminist, who's now viewed through a modern lens as something of an anti-establishment lesbian icon. Meanwhile, Neruda is seen by many as a male chauvinist and sexual predator due to his many affairs, as well as a lurid description in his memoir of raping a maid when he was a diplomat in Ceylon (modern-day Sri Lanka).

To the east of Mistral's birthplace lies Diaguitas, a time-stuck town of adobe homes lining a solitary cobbled lane. On a dusty side street, I find the aging potter Fernando Mahuad at his open-air studio, which is shaded by a droopy willow tree. He tells me, in less boastful terms, that he's single-handedly preserving the artistic heritage of the village's namesake Indigenous group, which lives in the semi-arid transverse valleys between modern-day Chile and Argentina.

The Diaguitas get little attention compared to Chile's other Indigenous communities, but their ancestors left behind the kind of pottery archeologists swoon over. Respecting ancient traditions, Fernando covers most of his pieces with black, white and red patterns. Some take on amorphous shapes, while others depict the haunting faces of birds, felines or reptiles.

The hills beyond Vicuña and Diaguitas are lined in the *Eulychnia breviflora* cacti, whose spikes are so white and girthy they almost entirely obscure the green branches they do such a good job of protecting. I stop at a small roadside stand to try a juice made from its fruit, called *copao*, which a sign informs me has as much potassium as a banana, as much vitamin C as an orange and is as hydrating as a coconut. The bulbous green fruit, which has firm white pulp, fueled journeys across this hostile land during the time of the ancient Diaguitas. Now, like so many South American products that find their way into gourmet grocers abroad, it's billed as a superfood – one that, to my tongue, tastes of kiwi and melon.

The oddness of talking with strangers – the artist in Diaguitas, the educator in Vicuña, the owner of this juice stand – creeps up on me throughout the day. It's been more than eight months since I've left Santiago. It's been less than a month since I've left home for socially distanced social gatherings. I've thrust myself back out into the world for the first time, and I'm not quite sure how to behave anymore.

You start to lose your sense of identity when you don't have an image of yourself reflected back at you in the way that others react to your words and actions. Plus, this brave new world seems to have different rules for all of us – problem is, none of us really know what they are yet. The normal intimacy of a Chilean meeting is out. There are no cheek kisses or shaken hands. We're all, by law, wearing diapers over our faces and mumble-talking from a predetermined distance. We're simultaneously weary of each other's presence and happy for the normalcy of it.

When I get back to my cabin there is a pair of grey New Balance sneakers next to my bed. They're not mine, and they weren't here when I left. Yet, somehow, I'm not particularly bothered by their presence. I take this as a good sign that my aspirational metamorphosis is kicking in. The old me – the stressed-out-in-pajamas enduring-lockdown me – would not be okay with this. The new me – the one aligning my mental mood ring with the whims of the Elqui Valley – is much more carefree.

Shalom never gave me a working key to this place, so I've just been leaving the door open. I'm trying not to complain. I'm trying to soak up the atmosphere. I use the sneakers as a barometer of my ability to let go of the stress and worries of the last few months, of the joblessness, of the ongoing pandemic. I'm glad the sneakers arrived. And I'm gladder still that I don't care.

^ ~ ^

Shalom sends me a WhatsApp message around lunchtime on my fourth day at the cabin. She wants to see if I can meet with Joakin later that evening, at 7:15 p.m.

I respond immediately to confirm.

She texts me again at 7:05 – ten minutes early – to say that Joakin is ready.

Walk down the hill and turn at the little bridge that goes up to his studio. Knock on the door, and then take off your shoes.

I do as instructed. Minutes go by in silence. I take note of an axe lying on the ground near the door. There's also a rottweiler glaring at me from the crawl space between the studio and the dusty terrain beneath it. After I've had sufficient time to worry about both of those things Joakin finally opens the door, which is in the only wall of his studio that isn't made of glass.

He appears in front of me in the same white robe I've seen

him wearing the previous evenings. It's the kind of thing you might acquire at an ashram in India – a place he's clearly visited, given the sitars and sarods hanging from the wall. There are also violins, guitars, panpipes, keyboards, bongos and other instruments of curious shapes and origins unknown to me.

"Welcome," he says, leading me over to a black leather sofa on the glassless edge of the studio. He gestures for me to sit on it before pacing in a semicircle around the room, opening the sand-colored curtains covering three lake-facing walls. With each swoosh of a curtain, more evening rays blaze through.

"Do you know why I chose this spot?" he asks after an uncomfortably long silence, gazing out the wall-to-wall windows. "Because it has the four elements in abundance. You have untouched earth. You have water in the valley. You have a strong sun that burns like fire. And you have air that makes itself known through wind."

There's another prolonged pause as he strokes his tangled beard.

"When did you move here?" I ask, breaking the silence.

He says he's been in the Elqui Valley much of his adult life, but it was 1999 when he purchased this particular piece of land. He watched as the valley flooded, and he's continued watching as it slowly dries up in an incessant drought.

"Do you see that?" he says, pointing to the remnants of Old Gualliguaica re-emerging on the reservoir's edge. "Those are the foundations of abandoned homes."

They're a running jump from where we're at right now. It's unnerving to see them so exposed, as if the ugly secret behind this handsome lake is coming back to haunt the valley.

Joakin turns to join me on the couch. I notice that he's shuffling around in Crocs, seemingly eliminating him as the mysterious visitor to my cabin. It doesn't feel like he leaves this place very often anyway. Maybe he never wears socks, or even underwear? I haven't seen him set foot outside of the studio since I arrived. And then there's his complexion, which is shockingly pale for a man living under the desert sun.

"So what do you want to know?" he asks, staring directly at me (or through me?) with kind, soulful eyes.

I quickly realize I don't have a great answer. I've come, more than anything, to soak up his aura.

I know from Shalom that he's prolific; there are 30 albums, 23 books and 5 DVDs bearing his name. She pointed me to his website, where I learned of his formal education in the USSR and his globetrotting stints based in Spain and California. He claims acquaintance with everyone from Robert Redford to the Dalai Lama. I want to see if living like he does now, locked up in a glass house in the Elqui Valley making books and music, is as alternately brilliant and depressing as it sounds.

"I plan to spend the next few weeks exploring the Atacama," I tell him.

"Oh yeah," he says. "Why's that?"

I want to know what it is about the desert that clutches on to people like him. How does this abundance of absence mold them over time? How does the radiant light tinker with their brains?

"I guess I needed to escape Santiago," I explain, poorly. "So I turned that into a mission. I've never lived anywhere else as an adult as long as I've lived in Chile. But I still don't understand the country. The past year has made me realize how little I've tried, and how much I still have to learn. So I figured the best place to start was the place that Chileans themselves don't even understand…I don't know if that makes any sense," I add, trailing off.

"It does," Joakin says. "But only if it makes sense to you."

"Maybe if the people of the Atacama can help me figure out Chile, then I can begin to understand why I can't seem to leave this place," I continue. "Maybe I'll discover the ways it's already changed me."

His eyes widen and then shrink again into tiny saucers.

"Shalom says that you're something of an expert on local history and languages," I say, embarrassed, changing the topic. "I'd love to hear about some of your work."

"You know, the Atacama starts right on the other side of that lake," he says, pointing across the Puclaro Reservoir. "It really is a magical place full of untold stories."

"Like what?" I ask.

He encourages me to seek out the writings of Fresia Castro, a Chilean mystic who traveled through the Atacama unveiling seven documents that she says (and he agrees) are key to both accessing universal truths and unlocking the secrets prophesied by ancient cultures.

"No one else has discovered the power of the Atacama Desert quite like her," he assures me.

"And what about you?" I probe.

He gets up and, without warning, strikes a gong. It startles me out of my stupor. He then goes to a room downstairs for a few minutes and re-emerges with one of his latest books, *Of the Matrix and the Void*. Its purple cover has a few clip-art images – the sun, the moon, some stars, plus a human ribcage. He flips it open and reads me a sonnet. It's so madcap I can't even begin to make sense of it. Perhaps I misunderstood the Spanish? Maybe it got jumbled in my head in some overly literal translation, I tell myself, but by the time it's finished, I'm pretty sure a cosmic word bomb has just exploded across my brain.

I wonder if I'm allowing myself to fall prey to a guru's vagaries.

But I decide that I'm still intrigued enough to let the act run its course.

It strikes me, sitting there with Joakin, how deserts can become oases for outcasts. Nothing human seamlessly fits into this environment, and so you can choose to stand out as you please. You can let the nakedness of the land strip away society's facades, filling the static-free space with philosophical fantasies.

Later, Joakin tells me he's capable of moving his eyes to the back of his head to ruminate on the beginning of time. Then, "speaking of the beginning of time," he encourages me to seek out some stone engravings that an old friend of his, Javier Cabrera, claims are proof of ancient knowledge of dinosaurs by Indigenous groups in the Atacama.

As the evening wears on, I realize that the line between genius and madman is terribly thin. I excuse myself to go back to my cabin and watch as another self-delusional genius-madman (this one with more nefarious causes) tries to steal the American election.

^ ~ ^

Chile's plebiscite happened the week before I set off into the Atacama. It was six months overdue and, thanks to the pandemic, landed on the 2020 calendar just a few days after the social uprising's fiery anniversary. Perhaps it was this contentious date that helped Chileans channel their discontent into an overwhelming condemnation of President Piñera and the neoliberal policies he embodied.

Catchy jingles and flashy campaign videos flooded Chilean airwaves in the leadup to the vote, but the *rechazo* camp – those fighting to reject a new constitution – never really had a chance. When the results came in, some 78 percent of Chileans had voted *apruebo* to approve a new charter, with roughly the same amount opting for it to be drafted not by politicians but rather by a soon-to-be-elected gender-balanced body who would have nearly two years to mold the shape of the nation.

Felipe was one of the everyday citizens who counted the votes. Chosen to man a table at a schoolhouse polling station in our future neighborhood, he spent the better half of the afternoon pulling paper ballots out of a plastic bin, announcing either *apruebo* or *rechazo* to an anxious crowd. Stephanie had the same job on the far side of town. So Carla and I met up to watch the count play out on a live stream projected across my living room wall. If things went according to plan, we'd march back to Plaza Italia triumphant.

Carla told me before she came that she was nervous. It showed on her face, which slumped down as if to personify those fears. But they proved to be entirely unfounded. Her eyes were like glossy marbles by the time the votes came in exactly as she'd hoped. With just 20 percent of the ballots counted, it was already clear that *apruebo* would whisk Chile into a new, though as yet unwritten, future.

"I just can't believe it," she said in disbelief. "I can't believe things are finally going our way."

Piñera, though visibly disheartened, made a speech on television in the early evening. He congratulated the nation on a record turnout and peaceful show of democracy.

That meant it was official: Chile would get a new constitution.

We popped a bottle of champagne in celebration. The bubbles went down faster than bubbles rightly should, so we packed another bottle for the road.

Carla, newly animated, unfurled a purple *apruebo* flag – a twin message of feminism and constitutional change – and we flapped it in the wind as we set off for Plaza Italia. I bought a rainbow flag from a vendor along the way so that, by the time we joined thousands of other flag-bearers, I could participate in a kind of color guard activism. There were other gays holding hands and waving rainbow flags, proud patriots hoisting Chilean flags, and Indigenous Mapuche draped in their tricolor flags as they beat handwoven drums. It looked like the multifaceted country we all wanted it to be.

Felipe joined us at Plaza Italia just as the clock neared midnight. His brother and nephews showed up too. Moments later, we popped our second bottle of champagne. I launched the cork into the air in that frenzied way they do in cheesy movies, and raised a toast to new beginnings.

I was happy to be there. I really was. But if I'm honest, it was also strange to be so entrenched in that moment when I felt like it didn't really belong to me. I couldn't vote in the plebiscite. I had no hand in its outcome. But, I told myself, no one really plans to be in another country during the defining moment of a generation; it just kind of happens. And without realizing it, you find yourself invested. So you celebrate the end of a chapter with everyone else even if you only showed up for the climax.

The vote for a fresh constitution was like a definitive goodbye to an ugly era for many Chileans. The last ashes of Pinochet had finally been stamped out. The word *renace* (reborn) was projected in all caps across a building above Plaza Italia – and that's exactly how the city felt at that moment. Fireworks crackled in gold and silver across the dark sky, music blasted out of apartment blocks and citizens danced atop confetti-littered streets. The Virgin Mary – arms outstretched, eyes weary – watched from her perch atop Cerro San Cristóbal as a new kind of spark flew through the October air.

^\~^

Felipe and I sit cross-legged atop quartz pebbles inside a gold-framed pyramid, which overlooks the emerald-green waters of Río Cochiguaz. The pyramid is an "energy vortex" where we can do yoga in the morning, meditations in the afternoon and gaze up at the darkening meadow of stars by night. There's quartz in it because, well, that's the "most powerful healing stone in the mineral kingdom," a sign explains. There's also a waterfall spilling into the river where you can take a "purification bath" under the watchful eye of a baby Buddha. Just up the street is a Buddhist temple – the Stupa of Enlightenment – where multi-colored prayer flags radiate out from a pearly white monument. Apparently, if you dig a hole deep enough, you'd end up in Tibet. If you squint a bit, you can almost imagine you're there.

Felipe likes to dabble in the realms of spirituality. I'm curious about the Atacama's mystical allure. So, after a hellish winter, we figured a retreat like this with contrived relaxation stations was just what we needed.

He took a long weekend off work, flew up to the airport in La Serena, and we drove to the end of the Elqui Valley where it splits in two. First, we took the right fork toward Alcohuaz ("house of light" in Quechua), stopping along the way in the artist village of Horcón, where bright fuchsia bougainvillea spill over mudbrick walls. The road got slimmer the higher we climbed. It was ostensibly one lane beyond Horcón, though traffic flowed in both directions as best it could.

Alcohuaz was the tiny town at the end of the terrifying road, just past the part where it became a solitary lane hacked out of the cliff's edge. At its heart was a ketchup-and-mustard church that looked, to me, as if it were designed by a giant toddler armed with truckloads of Play-Doh. On one edge of the remote village was a small gallery filled with outsider art from a recluse named

Juan Carlos Silva who retired here from the capital a decade ago. On the other was a gravity-defying vineyard – Viñedos de Alcohuaz, one of the highest in Chile – where a gonzo enologist planted Syrah, Grenache and Carignan up to 7,300 feet (2225 m) in altitude.

Taking the left fork later that day, we found Cochiguaz ("house of water" in Quechua), where we got a simple cabin by the river and planned for a few days of mystical tranquility before I finally set off into the Atacama proper.

It's now our second evening together but, in all truth, our first attempt at anything remotely spiritual. From our meditative perch inside this open-air pyramid, we obsess over how the Andes appear remarkably soft, as if drawn in pastels. They're beige here instead of brown, round instead of harsh. They're packed with so much quartz that they shine by day and shimmer under the moonlight.

Latticed vineyards line the riverbed below our pyramid, providing a stark contrast to the arid hills above. Their grapes are only just beginning to bud. In a few more months they'll get picked, crushed and distilled into Chile's signature brandy, pisco, which is the pride and joy of the Elqui Valley.

The village of La Unión, just around the riverbend, was even renamed Pisco Elqui in 1936 in a *nanny nanny boo boo* sort of way to vex Peru, which also claims pisco as a national drink (and, to be fair, has an older port city called Pisco). These days, it's full of distilleries like Mistral, Fundo los Nichos and Doña Josefa de Elqui, where one can get a pisco cocktail blended with ginger, basil or *ají verde* peppers.

Pisco Elqui is a curious place, managing to blend a strong Andean aesthetic with splashes of Asian iconography. Its small collection of slender streets holds pottery shops and empanada stands alongside yoga studios and Ayurveda centers. In the central plaza, sellers hawk an array of New Age souvenirs – therapeutic crystals, glowing salt lamps, powdery rainbows of conical incense – together with alpaca sweaters and Catholic rosaries.

We've been sipping pisco in Pisco Elqui all afternoon, treating potent sours as if they were as innocuous as lemonade. Now, we're paying the price for it as the sun in Cochiguaz slowly extracts alcohol from our pores, twisting our heads toward the painful end of indulgence. We relish the moment when it finally dips behind the barren hills, leaving in its wake a cinnamon sky.

The moon rises, as if on cue, not long after. I can't help but feel it's casting an eerie glow over the valley. Our meditation spot is certainly more alien than before. Or perhaps I've just got aliens on my mind. Their bugged-out faces and sinewy green fingers have been sneaking cameos in my daydreams, mucking up every attempt at serious concentration.

Aliens are ubiquitous in Cochiguaz; they appear on signs endorsing everything from herb baths to sonic healing with Tibetan bowls. Of course, an obsession with all things extraterrestrial is common in the gaping skies of deserts – including the Chihuahuan wilds of Roswell, New Mexico – where the boundary between *here* and *there* feels exceptionally thin.

The local craze traces back to a cult that formed in Cochiguaz in the 1970s. A religious zealot in a white tunic called Madre Cecilia preached that spaceships would come to the hilltops to rescue the righteous from a global disaster. As guru, "Mother" Cecilia Rodríguez initially followed the New Age teachings of a Parisian writer and astrologer, Serge Raynaud de la Ferrière, who founded the (still active) group Gran Fraternidad Universal in Caracas, Venezuela.

She told residents of this valley that Earth's magnetic center would transfer from the Tibetan Himalayas (at the 30th parallel north) to these Chilean Andes (at the 30th parallel south) during the forthcoming Age of Aquarius (the exact date was always TBD), imbuing it with an unparalleled energy force. As the years progressed, Madre Cecilia began forbidding mainstream medicines, practicing the fiery Vedic chanting ritual of *agnihotra* and mandating early morning baths in the chilly Río Cochiguaz – all the while collecting millions of pesos from her devotees. They all basked in so much sunshine that they burned deeper into the dream, equating their mounting delusions with a weightier state of bliss.

Talk of extraterrestrial guides and multidimensional portals grew over the years as Madre Cecilia crafted her own UFO-tinged brand of Andean Hinduism. By the late 1980s, she was sure the end times were near. The date of her promised rapture came and went with all the high hopes and dashed destinies of an apocalyptic fever dream. Then it came and went again. Trapped in a spiral of despotic dogmas and missed deadlines, she simply disappeared rather than face her aggrieved followers.

Despite everything, the legacy of Madre Cecilia very much lives on in the atmosphere of Cochiguaz, which remains the mystical hotbed of the Elqui Valley. Legend has it that a bunker she created for the end times still exists, hidden far beyond the end of the road in a place that only a few aging muleteers know how to access. Extraterrestrial contact groups regularly come to Cochiguaz for spiritual gatherings. Others here claim to be developing methods of interplanetary communication. Unsurprisingly, the area is rife with UFO sightings.

The 1998 crash of some unidentified flying object on the top of Cerro Las Mollacas, near the neighboring town of Paihuano, lured ufologists from around the world, sparking wild theories.

Chief among them was that NASA officials covered up the incident before layfolk could investigate. As with so many UFO stories, there are lots of memories and little evidence of them.

You can also find traces of Madre Cecilia's lingering New Age philosophies – which fused elements of Eastern belief systems with alternative therapies, meditative practices and supernatural experiences – in the works of her former followers, including Elqui Valley's most prolific living writer: Joakin Bello.

Madre Cecilia was but one in a series of cult leaders to call the Elqui Valley home. Before her, the most famous false profit was Domingo Zárate Vega, better known as the Cristo de Elqui (Christ of Elqui). Felipe actually worked on a debut opera about Cristo de Elqui at his previous job at the Municipal Theater of Santiago.

"Cristo de Elqui was the Chilean messiah," he tells me, smirking.

We've given up all pretense of meditation at this point. If we're being honest, we were far too tipsy to have attempted it in the first place.

"I think it was like the 1920s or something when he started having these divine visions and began baptizing people in the Río Elqui," Felipe continues. "Then, for the next two decades, he traveled around Chile with 12 disciples. He wore a cloth robe and sandals and had a big beard. He really looked the part."

Christo de Elqui was infamous in his time, alternatively jailed or sent to mental institutions on several occasions throughout the 1930s and 1940s (once after falling from a fig tree while attempting to levitate). Yet he never seemed to stay long, returning to the streets to preach theology, pen books on popular wisdom and grow his posse of disciples. He claimed to be immortal and told the newspapers that breathlessly followed his travels that his body functioned without food.

Like Madre Cecilia would decades later, he predicted an imminent end of the world. Our sitting here in an energy vortex, very much alive, is proof that no such event ever happened. But it's also evidence that he irrevocably shaped the outlook of this place.

"Do you think..." Felipe utters and then pauses, looking up to the sky. "Do you think they're the connected ones, and we're just so disconnected we don't even realize it?" he asks, referring to the dreamers and drifters drawn to this valley.

It's easy to see how this landscape can twist minds, posing those lonely questions deserts ask us about life and death, despair and ecstasy.

"What's that saying again," he adds, searching for the right translation. "Who are the mad ones? The mad ones or us?"

We've spent the entire day snickering at all the hippies here, thinking about how passé they seem, like walking nostalgia. Long-haired and rabid-eyed, they're like cliches of what they want to be, their cures self-fulfilling prophecies. I guess we envy them for their freedom, but we also kind of despise them for it.

I keep reminding myself that I've come here because I want to walk in their shoes for a few days. Some hippie even left me his New Balance sneakers back at the Puclaro Reservoir. I want that kind of freedom bottled up like a potion to cure my neurosis. Felipe wants it too. It's silly, we know. But after all the anti-anxiety pills that got us through five months of lockdown, we're open to a new set of remedies.

Speaking of which...maybe this healing quartz *is* working its magic on me? Sitting alongside Felipe in a new setting after so much time in our tiny apartment does feel rather revelatory. Perhaps it's the lack of ambient city noise, the big gulps of smogless air, the flittering stars and sensational sky? Maybe it's simply the momentary release from the stagnant torture of not knowing what comes next?

We lie back on the quartz and admire the stars and satellites, planes and planets. We talk about how they're always there right above us, but we fail to see them so much of the time – how it takes a place like this, with such a palpable connection between earth and sky, to actually make the effort to look up. We talk about how incredible it is that mankind has all sorts of bits and bobs floating around up there, but how it's even more astonishing, still, that we know very little about what lies beyond the edge of Earth. Who knows, maybe there are aliens up there? Maybe the prophets of the Elqui Valley were onto something after all?

^~^

The following morning, Felipe and I wake up early and bring blankets down to the riverbank. We sprawl out in the shade of a willow tree and watch as its branches flop in the wind like lazy pompoms. The plan for the day is to have no plan, which is a plan I'm not very good at. But I fight against my nature, channeling the aura of Cochiguaz.

Felipe knows far better than I how to tune out; he's a collector of idle moments, always throttling my action on trips to schedule enough time for musing. He opens up a book about how to write a new constitution. So I pull out a book of essays on self-delusion. Every hour or so we follow the shade to a new quadrant of the riverbank, talking a bit, but mostly reading and observing.

The sun in the Elqui Valley is so strong it's like a character you share your day with. You negotiate with it. You do your best to block and avoid it. But in the end, it's unavoidable. It drowns you in light and, like it or not, you have to play by its rules. You have to wake up with it and live your day with it until it finally creeps into the evening oblivion.

When it becomes clear that there will be no more shade on this stretch of the river – that the sun has won – we make the natural decision to strip down and jump in.

The glacial meltwater that rumbles into this valley gives us instant chicken skin. Yet we overcome the initial shock and spend much of the next hour splashing around in an emerald green pool. We wade across slippery rocks and sink into surprise mud traps.

"There's something about swimming in a river that feels more exotic than swimming at a beach," I tell Felipe.

"It's less obviously fun," he adds.

"Which makes it that much more exciting," I interject, "when you realize that it is."

Since we're already wet, we decide to go over to the waterfall for our "purification bath." On the way over, I'm reminded of what the owner of this place, Gonzalo Mariqueo, told me when we arrived: "Some people come here and they say: 'Where is the mysticism? I don't feel anything.' But if you're not open to it, you'll never find it."

I let that thought bounce around in my head as we walk. Maybe he's right? Maybe I'm not opening up to the possibilities of this place. I take his words as a challenge to feel something, *anything*, when we set foot beneath the waterfall.

This stretch of the river pools in jacuzzi-sized pockets, and each one seems to have its daily denizens finding their version of mysticism amid dense clouds of pot and patchouli. We pass several groups and a few camping tents before reaching a hanging bridge between two larger pools. We cross and enter a small ravine before emerging at a cascade spilling down a rocky precipice. Foxtails accentuate the small pool at its base. We step in and close our eyes, letting the falling droplets pound the pressure out of our heads.

The hydromassage is certainly soothing, but a feeling of defeat slowly creeps up on me. Maybe this forced spirituality isn't my thing? Perhaps none of the Elqui Valley's mystical cures are? I'm somehow incapable of being open to concepts I find flaky right from the start, and so I'll never find whatever it is I'm looking for here.

Or, perhaps I'm just searching in the wrong place...

^~^

The Atacama Desert is a relatively inconsequential place for most of Earth's eight billion residents. Yet there is one group for whom it is the epicenter of their entire vocation: astronomers. Atacama is ground zero for innovation in the field. Thanks to its high altitudes, low population density and near-nonexistent inland cloud cover, it has transformed over the past 50 years into a hive that buzzes with two-thirds of all global infrastructure for ground-based observations.

Massive billion-dollar projects debut across the desert every few years, including in the Elqui Valley, which already contains three major observatories. All lie in the Cerro Tololo Inter-American Observatory campus. This sci-fi-esque facility was one of the earlier places to probe the mysteries of stars quadrillions of miles away when it launched in 1965. Part of the US National Science Foundation's NOIRLab and run by an international consortium of governmental agencies and academic institutions, it includes giant telescopes surveying the night sky from between 7,000 and 9,000 feet (2135–2745 m) above the valley floor.

The Víctor M. Blanco – named after a Puerto Rican astronomer who discovered a new galactic cluster in the 1950s – is a 13-foot (4 m) aperture optical telescope that was the largest in the southern hemisphere between 1976 and 1998. The nearby Southern Astrophysical Research Telescope (SOAR) is a slightly larger 13.5-foot (4.1 m) optical and near-infrared telescope that opened around the turn of the century. The award for biggest beast on campus, however, goes to Gemini South, a 26.6-foot (8.1 m) giant that, together with Gemini North in Hawaii, provides almost complete coverage of both the northern and southern skies.

The Vera C. Rubin Observatory – named for an American astronomer who pioneered work on galaxy rotation (and advocated for more women in science) – will be the next megaproject to debut here in the years following my visit. It will house the Simonyi Survey Telescope, a 27.6-foot (8.4 m) wide-field reflecting telescope that's tasked with an unprecedented decade-long optical survey of the visible sky – auspiciously titled Legacy Survey of Space and Time.

This revolutionary telescope will have the capability of photographing the entire available sky every few nights, with images recorded by a 3.2-gigapixel digital camera, the largest ever built. The project's goal is to enable scientists not only to catalog the solar system and explore the changing sky but also to better understand the enigmatic non-luminous materials known as dark matter and the mysterious forces behind dark energy, a wonderfully ominous term for the great unknown.

Felipe and I can see all of these futuristic telescopes high above us as we lumber down a dusty road south of Vicuña. Shiny and metallic, beaming in the sun, they look a bit as if Madre Cecilia's promised UFOs finally landed on these desert hilltops.

We're driving this way because we want a taste of the astronomy action. Of the dozen or so smaller observatories scattered across the Elqui Valley, the best amateurs like us can get our hands on is Pangue, which has a 25-inch reflector telescope. That may be miniscule in comparison with the Vera C. Rubin, but it's of a scale far grander than anything else publicly available. It's certainly worlds away from the tiny tube on a tripod I used growing up.

The road to Pangue runs parallel to the one you'd take to get to the Cerro Tololo Inter-American Observatory campus, so we can almost pretend those Jetsonian marvels on the horizon are our true destination. There are no longer grapevines or willow trees along the road here; it's just bush, bramble and dust as we snake up a winding path to an altitude of 4,000 feet (1219 m). The setting sun paints the desert in a reddish hue as we race higher, hoping to reach Pangue at the violet hour to start our star search before the moon mucks up the evening sky.

We're a half hour outside of Vicuña now and, though we spot the town in the distance from a small overlook, there are otherwise no signs of life anywhere in sight, save the observatories. It's my first real taste of what lies ahead in the greater Atacama. I know landscapes like this – barren hills topped with shiny objects pointing toward the sky – will follow me for the rest of my journey.

Further north, in the Chajnantor Plateau, is the Atacama Large Millimeter/submillimeter Array (ALMA). It's the largest ground-based astronomical project on the planet, with 66 high-precision radio telescopes that pivot in harmony like ballet dancers, probing for answers to questions as seemingly unanswerable as the origins of the Universe.

The US$1.4-billion project, completed in 2013, lies at a lofty 16,600 feet (5060 m) for maximum elevation and minimal humidity, which, when combined, equals reduced noise and signal attenuation from Earth's atmosphere. Its workers travel so high to get to their jobs they need to hook up to oxygen just to survive the day.

I know this because I visited ALMA the year before it opened. It was my first big foreign reporting gig during a momentary stint in Brooklyn. Felipe and I were falling in and out of a long-distance relationship at the time, unsure how to make love last across borders, testing how long we could bend before breaking. I worked at one of those digital news sites that hardly paid employees unless they earned enough "clicks," and he was contemplating a career in photography. I was determined to find a story that could take me down to Chile.

Despite the publication having zero interest in hard reporting – and despite my complete lack of knowledge on science or engineering or Latin America – I convinced an editor to let me have paid time off to document the arrival of ALMA's antennas. "I have a photographer on the ground who can arrange everything," I explained. "I haven't seen him in six months, but I know him well from my time in New Zealand."

And so it was that I came to Chile for the first time. Felipe and I were giddily reacquainted after months of separation, brimming with ideas for how to relaunch a life together but unsure where or when to do it. I met Felipe's family in Santiago, though we didn't have a common language to communicate back then. His mom, instead, showed her love through food, making all of my meals bigger than everyone else's at the table. They were plates so heaping I could never finish them, and they had ingredients so foreign to me – giant briny ribbed mussels, wheat berries floating in a syrupy peach nectar – that I often didn't quite know what to do with them.

The first place Felipe and I saw together outside of Santiago was this desert. I told him when the plane landed that it looked like another planet. I'd never seen anywhere like it. Chile cast its spell on me, and I had a hunch I might come back one day.

ALMA was the headline-maker of a decade ago, which is how I justified that seminal journey to South America. But the two largest ground-based astronomy projects of the 2020s will also debut in the Atacama – both a bit further north from here.

The Giant Magellan is a segmented mirror telescope consisting of seven 27.6-foot (8.4 m) primary segments arranged in a flower pattern to form an 83-foot (25.4 m) light-collecting surface. It's expected to have a resolving power – which is kind of like image resolution – ten times greater than the Hubble Space Telescope's (and better than anything achieved to date).

Meanwhile, the Extremely Large Telescope is slated to become just that: the world's biggest eye on the sky. It'll have a staggeringly large 129-foot-diameter (39.3 m) segmented mirror – so extremely large that there will be no other optical telescope even close in size, save the smaller Giant Magellan.

Instruments like these could completely revolutionize our perception of the Universe in the years to come, answering big questions about the fate of our galaxy and the probability that we're not alone. They may also make discoveries so unfathomable that we can't even imagine what they might be just yet. It's mind-blowing how fast the technology is advancing. And it's wilder, still, that this inhospitable stretch of northern Chile is playing such a starring role.

^~^

Felipe and I are not particularly enthralled by science, but it's easy to get swept away by the philosophical questions posed by astronomy. There's also something weirdly grounding about looking at the stars. They sky becomes an ideal canvas for introspection when you have no obligation to make any sense of it – to try and comprehend the differences between a dwarf galaxy and a globular cluster – which is why we're both so eager to arrive at the Pangue Observatory.

Its director, Eric Escalera, greets us at the entrance, opening a heavy metal gate so our dust-covered Chevrolet Onix can enter.

Eric is a Frenchman with wire-thin glasses and a timid demeanor. He boasts a PhD in astrophysics from the Université Paul Sabatier in Toulouse, as well as the textbook recall to prove it. A resident of Chile for over a decade, he has the ascetic look of a man who found his destiny in the desert. What he prides himself on most is opening up the skies to simpletons like us with the most powerful publicly accessible telescopes in the region.

Beyond the 25-inch (635 mm) telescope we'll enjoy tonight, there is also a 16-inch (406 mm) computerized reflector that he uses for school groups. On a smaller hilltop just below the main facilities lie two white domes holding 20-inch (508 mm) and 28-inch (711 mm) reflectors. All are powered by solar energy, and the latter two are reserved for high-level astrophotography.

"They're actually being operated remotely right now by scientists in the US and Europe," he says, which we find quite impressive until he tells us about an even wilder project he has on the edge of Vicuña.

"It's called the Great Solar Observatory, and it's entirely dedicated to daytime observations of the sun," he says.

The specialized telescope blocks out the sun's extreme luminosity so you can safely search for dark spots, local plasma eruptions and long, serpentine filaments that dance outward into the atmosphere away from the boiling solar surface.

"There's nothing else like it anywhere in the Atacama," he boasts.

Our focus tonight will be not on the sun, but rather the full moon. We're going to try and capture the moment right when it rises from behind the pre-Andes and lights up the evening sky. But before that happens, we have about an hour to see what else we can find.

We start with what turns out to be a natural choice: Alpha Centauri. It's the closest star to us, at about four light-years from the sun, and it's most visible in the southern hemisphere, where it's the third-brightest star in the night sky after Sirius and Canopus. Well, technically, now I see that Alpha Centauri is three distinct stars, including the two bright sun-like stars that appear as one and a faint red dwarf you can't see with the naked eye.

Eric gets a bit giddy telling us what we'll be able to see next: Saturn and Jupiter. The rings of the former have a supernatural glow – almost like a neon frisbee caught around a giant Gobstopper. On the latter, we focus in on a massive anticyclonic storm known as the Great Red Spot. Eric explains that it's like a permanent hurricane twice the diameter of Earth itself. It's been around for at least 200 years, though it's likely much older than that.

Felipe and I have never seen anything like this. We went to ALMA all those years ago, sure, but we didn't actually look through any telescopes. These images are like proof that all those solar system charts we studied as kids weren't a complete work of science fiction.

"Saturn really does have crazy rings," I say to Felipe.

"And did you see Jupiter?" he replies. "It's huuuuge."

We laugh at how dorky and childlike we sound.

Eric tells us that, in a month's time, the two largest planets in our Solar System will actually come within 0.1 degrees of each other, having their closest visible alignment in 800 years. This rare courtship is called the Great Conjunction, though Eric says some this year are calling it "the Christmas star."

The Moon is now shining on Cerro Tololo, whose glassy observatories reflect light back in our direction. We decide it's time to prepare for its imminent rise, aiming the telescope at the very spot where Eric predicts it will crest above the hills. He's got all sorts of gadgets that tell him when and where to look, but in the end, we just have to wait patiently for it to happen.

I can't remember another time in my life when I've deliberately traced every second of a moon rise. Certainly, I've never approached it with the same vigor as a sunrise. But the spectacle proves more than worthy, particularly when you've got access to a spyglass like this.

Felipe and I, still behaving like juveniles, bat each other away from the eyepiece to get the best views. All the while, the pock-marked moon climbs remarkably fast in and out of frame. It's incredible, we discuss, how textured it seems, and how many shades of grey it has. There are whiter patches that are unbelievably radiant, and darker ones that seem to harbor unshared secrets.

The moon rises faster than we can keep up with. Plus, Chile's nightly coronavirus curfew is fast approaching. So we thank Eric for a great evening and begin walking back to the car. Along the way, he says something that takes us aback.

"Everything you see around here, all these minerals in this desert, had their beginning in some cauldron of hydrogen many light-years in the past," he notes.

I've been cataloguing all these items in the sky as things that are very much apart from the Earth. But in reality, we're all intertwined in something much bigger and more complex than any of us earthlings will ever truly understand. I realize in that moment that the universe is not just up above; it's all around us. And every day, researchers here in the Atacama Desert are shining lights on its darkest secrets, chipping away at all the unsolved mysteries.

^~^

The time has come for me to head off on my own into what a cartographer would consider the *real* Atacama, the one with far fewer creature comforts than the fertile Elqui Valley. The sun and stars will surely follow me for the rest of my journey, but there will be no more pisco vines, wineries or waterfalls. I'm putting the healing stones, natural therapies and false prophets in my rearview mirror, too.

My brain has stopped racing at an unhealthy speed, which I suppose I can attribute to the mystical mood of this place. But I will never, myself, be at ease in the mystical mind. It's just not for me. It's not who I am at my core. Yet I know now why poets, prophets and dreamers are called to Chile's arid north. I appreciate its ability to absorb outsiders. I like how it fosters big thinking. This desert gets under your skin, even threatening to make you a little cuckoo. You don't have to believe in aliens to feel like one here.

The Atacama is vast and foreboding, so I'm a bit anxious about my journey ahead. Felipe assures me I'll be fine.

"You always act like you're nervous for a trip, but the second you get out there into the unknown, you feed off that energy," he says.

It's true. Even still, I'm glad he came to see me off. These past few days together have helped make the thought of voyaging into the desert while the world goes to hell seem less reckless than it sounded at the start. And I may have changed his outlook on the Atacama in the process.

"I'm starting to reconcile my feelings for the north," he tells me on the drive back to the airport in La Serena.

He's always been a fan of Chile's greener half. He couldn't understand why, during our long lockdown, I was dreaming so desperately about going north from Santiago instead of south. Why, he wondered, would I prefer such soul-sucking emptiness over woodlands, lakes and fjords? The south is where we've long gone to recharge. It's the imagined setting of distant retirement plans where, as old men, we'd drink tea by a wood-fired stove and read books the size of bricks and wear woolen ponchos and hike to the araucaria trees, which pop like umbrellas over primordial rainforest. The north, by contrast, has always been more of an enigma.

"I get it now," he says, surprising me. "I get why you wanted to come here. I get what you see in this place."

He seems strangely convinced. But to be honest, I'm not so sure I am yet.

There are more than 1,000 miles of lonely roads ahead of me. And I've no idea how mad this desert will get or what effects the ongoing pandemic might have on my journey. Perhaps I'm just afraid of the Atacama's emptiness, of the solitude and extreme introspection that landscapes like this require. I don't know if I'm ready for that.

I kiss Felipe goodbye at the airport, turn north onto the Pan-American Highway, and then invite the Atacama to completely absorb me.

3 SEA TO SKY, PART ONE: SEA
(COASTAL GEOGRAPHIES)

There's this broody miasma of ashen clouds and blustery air called *la camanchaca* that hovers over Atacama beaches during the breakfast hours. Often, the ominous weather phenomenon dissipates in the midday heat. Occasionally, it'll last the entire day. The *camanchaca* I'm traveling through as I drive north from La Serena, however, hasn't budged for nearly a month straight. Thanks to a strong climate pattern known as La Niña, which cools sea surface temperatures across the eastern Pacific, this freak cloud has ballooned over recent weeks into a nebulous ink blot tinting small fishing villages grey while obscuring the desert's most predictable attribute – the sun – from the fisherfolks' view.

Camanchacas are a bit like coastal California fog, draping both beach and valley in a fluffy koala-colored blanket. Head a bit higher up, or inland, and the gloomy skies vanish, almost as if they were always just a slippery mirage. Head back down to the coast, however, and the air becomes thick and damp. I wouldn't call the moisture *camanchacas* produce rain, but when fog smashes against my windshield on the 75-mile (120 km) drive north to Punta de Choros, it does form small droplets that wiggle, worm-like, down tempered glass.

Run-of-the-mill *camanchacas* can happen any time of the year. In fact, their presence along this otherwise arid coast has made it possible for locals to collect freshwater in *atrapanieblas* (fog catchers). These massive nets tower over coastal hilltops, capturing incoming moisture which, over time, swells into droplets that fall as water into canals below. Most use this rare *agua dulce* for irrigation, but there's one guy in Peñablanca who, like a Biblically inspired brewer, turns fog into beer.

For some, the *camanchaca* is a blessing. For others, it's a morning nuisance. I, for one, find it a welcome change from the sweltering heat of the Elqui Valley.

The reason I've wound my way through the *camanchaca* to Punta de Choros is to learn about the animals that call the edge of the Atacama home. Namely, I want to visit a trio of guano-covered islands offshore that are home to the most important breeding grounds for Humboldt penguins. Pingüino de Humboldt National Reserve, run by Chile's park service, CONAF, is ground zero in the effort to protect these threatened medium-sized migrants, whose splotchy pink patches add a touch of flair to the traditional black-and-white penguin suit.

The population of Humboldt penguins has dropped from a historic high of more than a million to less than 24,000 today. They were nearly decimated in the mid-19th century by the mining of guano deposits for fertilizer – a lucrative endeavor that gave rise to many of the cities now found along the Atacama coast. Synthetic fertilizers developed in the early 20th century put an end to the guano era. While the penguin population has slowly bounced back in fits and starts, illegal trawling and unchecked climate change will likely reverse that trend in the coming years.

These playful penguins share their name with the chilly Humboldt Current that flows north from Antarctica along the Pacific coast of South America. Both bird and current are themselves named after the Prussian naturalist Alexander von Humboldt. He traveled these frigid waters extensively in the early 19th century and, ironically for the then-thriving penguins, was one of the first people to predict human-induced climate change.

The sea here is one of the most productive in the world. There are bottlenose dolphins, sea lions and chungungo marine otters, as well as soaring albatross and dive-bombing cormorants. The reserve is something of a mini-Galapagos on the edge of the desert. Problem is, I quickly realize that CONAF hasn't allowed boats to visit since the onset of the pandemic.

Local fishermen say they're prohibited from taking me to the islands, even though they appear so close – like shadowy fortresses on the horizon – I could almost swim to their rocky shores. The dock at Caleta San Agustin, once a local magnet, is now tourism's graveyard. Beached sightseeing ferries lie upside down, their plastic chairs scraping the compacted earth of an empty parking lot. Nearby, the doors of shuttered seafood shacks clack in the wind.

Without tourists, Punta de Choros is just another facsimile fishing village. Bold-colored boats bob in the harbor, birds of prey ride the breeze and men in neon-orange jumpsuits haul buckets of shellfish home to their small, stout *señoras*. What sets it apart from other places just like it up and down the coast is its odd obsession with white geodesic domes, which lie atop the barren headland like sample space colonies for some future mission to Mars. Apparently, when Chileans visit this place on summer holidays, these dome lodgings are *the* place to sleep.

I can see how regional visitors might consider Punta de Choros cute in a sparse kind of way. But it's clearly seen better days. Now, it's like a shell of its old self, with restaurants boarded up and shops closed. Everyone seems to have a dog watching over their empty businesses, and every dog seems acutely aware of my presence, snarling at me through a tooth-lined muzzle.

I'm not really sure what to do here if I can't visit the pink-tinged penguins. Thanks to the *camanchaca*, the wind-whipped beaches surrounding the headland read flat and lifeless, with grey sands blending into grey clouds. The water is too rough to swim in – too cold, anyway – and choppy in a way that makes it gnarly for surfing. I've already paid upfront for several nights in a small room attached to a small home south of town, so I wander around wondering what it'd be like to spend a lifetime on this barren coast.

I can't tell if I'm just depressed about my missed date with the penguins, or if I need to face a harsh reality: that neglected towns like this are what much of the Atacama will be like from here on out.

Costa Bahía is the only restaurant open in Punta de Choros. It's as colossal as a banquet hall, with wood-carved dolphins at the entrance and thatched mermaids hanging from the rafters. I settle into a plastic chair at one of the rickety outdoor tables, where my view is not of the ocean but rather a road of hard-packed sand, one of a dozen or so just like it that intersect to form a semblance of town.

International borders remain closed, so my presence in a place like this – made plain by my stilted Spanish – which I only started learning at age 30, studying the strange intonations of Chilean newscasters – is a shock to the waitress, Marisol, whose long black hair curves around a chubby face. How did you get here, she asks, and where are you coming from?

My answers – car, Santiago – aren't nearly as exciting as she'd hoped, so I add that I'm from the Washington, DC, area originally.

Privately, I lament that, no matter how long I live in this country, I'll never be seen as just another local out for a drive. A Chilean who immigrates to the US at least has the hope (if not always the reality) of being woven into the multicultural American quilt, but an American in Chile will always be inescapably American no matter how long they stay, constantly asked to identify with some city in the homeland they haven't lived in since they were a kid.

We turn our attention to my order, *paila marina*, which Marisol says is the house specialty – a shellfish stew served in a terra-cotta bowl. "And why don't you add a pisco sour," I mutter, feeling defiant of the early hour (and in a sour mood myself).

Marisol needs a name for the order.

"It's Mark."

"Mac?" she asks.

"No, Mark."

"Like the burger at McDonald's?"

I laugh.

"I'm sorry. It's Big Mac, right?"

We both laugh.

"You're so close."

"*Aye*, okay."

"It's Maaarrrrk."

"Maaaaxxx?"

I hesitate for a minute.

"Exactly."

Pleased with herself, she scribbles *Max* on her notepad.

The doormen at my building in Santiago call me Max, too. They've done it for years now, handing me packages that clearly say otherwise. Only one, Marco, gets it right, presumably because he knows we share the same name from the same Bible, just a different translation.

Marisol brings my pisco sour almost an hour before the stew, so I'm half-drunk by the time I find myself slurping mussels, clams and crabmeat onto my sugar-tinged tongue. As I scoop up a few unidentifiable sea monsters that bathe in the salty broth amid specks of floating cilantro, I begin to wonder if my presence here is wanted or not. Am I helping the local economy? Am I a health threat? Marisol seems to want Max – to need Max's tourist dollars – but I can't be sure. This place doesn't get the kind of traffic the Elqui Valley does. It looks like it's been abandoned by the world for months, and it's hard to decipher if I've come too soon or not soon enough.

At least for Santiago transplants Salomé and Daniel, my arrival at their property south of town seems as if it's the most exciting thing that's happened all year long.

"Oh my god, welcome," Salomé says as I pull in after lunch, guard dogs chasing at my heels. "It's so, so nice to have a visitor."

Salomé and Daniel are in their mid-30s and have that kind of flowing unfussy style that city folks adapt when they go rogue. The pair left behind white-collar jobs in Santiago two years ago to try off-grid life in the Atacama. They built a simple home, put some solar panels on top of it, set up a greenhouse, dug a well, and crafted a few detached rooms for travelers like me.

"Honestly, it hasn't been easy," confides Daniel, who used to work in academia. "Everything is a challenge here. And with the *camanchaca* this past month, our solar panels can't charge enough to power the place. But you know what? It's so quiet here, and we love that."

It really is. The only sound besides our voices is the wind and waves off in the distance.

It's clear that the couple likes being king and queen of their own arid kingdom, but they also miss the human interactions they gave up to move here. The Atacama is a lonesome landscape, and it takes a foolish kind of bravery to adapt to its mental demands later in life.

"Please, ask us if you need anything," Daniel says, waving goodbye. "Anything at all," he adds, almost as if to ensure we'll have a reason to chat again later on.

After settling in, I do just that, seeking advice on where to commune with the Atacama coast. Salomé convinces me to forget all about the *camanchaca* and take a walk down the long and nameless six-mile (10 km) stretch of sand in front of their property. It's an odd place, full of round lumps of evenly spaced bush, as if the beach came down with some form of arboreal chicken pox. There are also velvety red succulents poking out of the sand that are so shiny and plasticky they look like the fake flowers you'd buy at a dollar store.

The beach reminds me of a forlorn stretch of the west coast of New Zealand's South Island where Felipe and I used to stroll when we first met, inching out conversations in broken languages – his and mine, which would soon become a hybrid ours.

Being at home in Chile so much this past year has forced me to face the realities of my relationship to both my partner and this country – *his* country – we live in. It's made me realize that I don't really understand either as well as I should. This trip feels like my chance to remedy that. I've convinced myself that, to understand Chile, I need to go to the part of it nobody understands. And if I can understand Chile better, maybe I can understand those cultural chasms that make an international re-lationship like ours such a tough puzzle to crack.

I'm sad that Felipe is back home, but also relieved of the con-stant need to please and entertain, to make sure he's having a good time. I don't know why I get so anxious when we travel together; it didn't used to be like that. When I'm alone, I never feel bored or restless; I feel free. I miss his presence, miss the warmth and comfort of his body next to mine. But I need this kind of freedom to figure out who I am without him. I wonder if my periodic absences are actually the reason our relationship has lasted as long as it has, allowing us to constantly microdose on the highs of loss and renewal. Yet it does get lonely sometimes.

Other than me, there's just a solitary dog on this beach, racing back and forth down a mile-long stretch, terrorizing every sea-bird in sight. We become fast friends, walking together over to the grey-golden sand dunes that rise along the northern edge of the shore.

Waves thrash and birds squeal. Soon enough, I find myself in the desert of popular imagination, where rippled sands flitter across momentary mountains, where getting lost is inevitable. I take off my shoes and walk, then run, then leap over the edge of a drooping dune, following the lead of my feral friend. I go deeper, walking, running, leaping into the abyss.

It's such a shape-shifting sandscape that I can hardly leave my mark on it; footprints last just seconds before being bulldozed by the breeze. It's as if I can roam these sands without touching them or letting them touch me. The thought spurs me to action. I bolt further into the dunes until, minutes later, I'm completely lost and epically disoriented. In all directions, there's a total lack of solid ground. I've no idea which way is east or west, home or away. I don't care.

^ ~ ^

Salomé and Daniel wave goodbye in the rearview mirror as a red dawn sets distant cloud banks afire. They know that I may be the first and last guest they see for a while. And they've been ridiculously hospitable, helping me plot a route north that eschews the highway for unpaved coastal roads all the way to Bahía Inglesa.

"Watch out for the potholes!" Daniel yells as I pull out of their long, sandy driveway.

"And call if you get lost," adds Salomé, before realizing how absurd that sounds. "Actually, you probably won't have signal most of the way…"

They've told me that Caleta Chañaral, the other portal for Pingüino de Humboldt National Reserve, about 14 miles (23 km) north, will be the last sign of life for the first hours of my journey. I quickly realize that it's a much scrappier place than Punta de Choros, with rusty homes sandwiched between menacing boulders and prickly cacti. I'd hoped to find a bite to eat, but it seems even more abandoned than where I've been the previous days, with wild burros roaming desolate streets. I loop around town, endure uncomfortable glares, and decide it best to push onwards.

The rutted road north is made of granular bischofite (a sea salt concentrate) and anonymously named C-494. It turns inland from Caleta Chañaral for a long monotonous stretch past ochre and tawny hills. To pass the time, I count the power poles that line the way at predictable intervals. It's both hypnotic and hazardous, putting me into a complete daze as I swerve around the forewarned potholes that threaten to entrap me.

This neglected backland is like a big brown blur for much of the morning until, unexpectedly, I reach the emerald-green valley of the Río Huasco. I haven't seen a proper tree in days, but here, there is a vast corridor of mesquites and willows. There are wizened Chilean pepper trees (which are so ubiquitous in California that most in the state think they're native). There are orchards of olives and cherimoya, a heart-shaped fruit Chileans use to tang up yogurts and ice creams.

Places like this are an oddity of the Atacama. The Nazca tectonic plate, which lies off the Pacific coast, jams up against the South America plate and lifts the immense Andes at a rate of about an inch per year. These geologically young mountains have gotten so tall that they don't permit humidity accumulating on their eastern edge to pass through to the west. Meanwhile, any precipitation that manages to barrel across the largest expanse of water in the world typically gets sponged up by the cool Humboldt Current.

This may create a hyper-arid landscape, but because of the fortress-like Andes to the east, there exist lateral oases where snowmelt flows west toward the Pacific. Most rivers never reach the ocean, but the Elqui, Huasco, Copiapó, Loa, Camarones, and Lluta do. These verdant valleys are the lifeblood of the desert, home to most of its residents and much of its wildlife.

The Atacama carried a fierce reputation among early European explorers as a formidable place that lacked humans or habitable land. Yet legends about this desert have always outstripped the reality on the ground. It may have been one of the last parts of South America surveyed in much detail – beyond the jungles of the Amazon – but the truth is, people have lived alongside river mouths in places like the Huasco Valley for thousands of years.

I follow the Río Huasco to where it dumps out into the Pacific. Nearby is the valley's namesake town, Huasco. It's larger than I'd imagined and more lived-in than the fishing villages further south. Houses spill down a hillside along latticed streets. Most overlook a busy dock and a small phallic lighthouse whose red rocket tip seems purpose-built for local jokes.

I head to an empanada shop by the dock with high hopes and a famished belly. The chef, a stout old lady with chubby cheeks and protruding lips, tells me, inexplicably, that there's just one option: an empanada of *lapas*. I have no idea what *lapas* are but I order one anyway. A football-sized empanada arrives a few minutes later. It's deep-fried, packed with rubbery grey bits and leaking an acrid cream. I force a smile and try to make a dent – Felipe always tells me it's impolite to leave food on the table in Chile – but it tastes like the vomit of the sea.

Lapas, it seems, are limpet-like sea snails, and they have an exceptionally chewy texture. I thank the chubby-cheeked lady for introducing them to me. I also apologize for my inability to finish her empanada, raising my shoulders into the *whoops* position, chalking it up to being a hapless foreigner (even if, deep down, I'm desperate for Chileans to stop seeing me that way).

Having abandoned the idea of an empanada by the sea, I go instead to the plaza for a *completo*. *Completos* are basically hot dogs masquerading as something haughtier, with mashed avocado, fresh tomatoes and relish on top. Chileans extol them like they're some sort of national treasure. But every time they do, it just makes me sad – both for them and for me as an American, given our similar reverence for this insipid meat garbage.

^~^

It's spring, and purple and banana-yellow flowers are poking out of the sandy soil alongside the coastal road north of Huasco. These tiny stars and trumpets swaying in the breeze are the last remnants of the *desierto florido*, or flowering desert, a sporadic phenomenon that carpets this southerly quadrant of the Atacama in a kaleidoscope of colors. The year 2020 wasn't the best for the *desierto florido* – or anything, really – but there was a small bloom along this stretch near Llanos de Challe National Park.

It defies logic that this ethereal, monochromatic landscape could morph into a florid pallet of pinks and periwinkles, ambers and golds – like a Monet painting come to life. But that's exactly what happens in years when rare winter rains awaken the dormant seeds of desert perennials. These vast carpets of color change gradient by the day as some of the more than 200 species of flowers wither away and others with longer germination periods pop up anew.

In my lifetime, there have been just seven major blooms. Each has had a strong impact on the desert's ecology, with a sharp increase in insects and birds, as well as colocolo wild cats, lizards, foxes and guanacos (the feral cousins of the domesticated llama). Thousands of tourists from across Chile are lured by the spectacle, though this year there is not another tourist in sight.

The park's shuttered headquarters lies in a pretty, boulder-strewn patch of desert where the road inches up against a steep umber-hued hill shrouded in spectral fog. To my left is the splaying ocean, frothing white against rocky cliffs and pebbled beach. Every so often, a two-street fishing village appears atop the rubbled earth with a collection of near-identical tin-roofed homes. I wonder to myself each time what it feels like to live in a place like this, just elemental earth in one direction and a savage sea in the other.

The horizon broadens as I veer slightly inland near Totoral, offering more sand and less rock, more shrubs and fewer cacti. Where it was once a study in the color brown, now everything is blazingly white. The aridity hits me at full force, and it becomes a stupefying drive. There are no dust balls rolling across the road, as in the American Southwest; rather, it's a raw rugged nothingness with only the sunlight to hold things together.

The nakedness of the land makes me recall the cynical ways in which Charles Darwin referred to the Atacama. "It was almost a pity to see the sun shining constantly over so useless a country," he decried on his visit in 1835, adding, "Such splendid weather ought to have brightened fields and pretty gardens." He'd grown "tired of repeating the epithets barren and sterile" in his diaries while traveling "all day over an uninteresting country" that was only "made palpable by a clear, unclouded sky." He seemed stubbornly blind to the splendor of uncomfortable landscapes.

Thirteen miles (21 km) ahead lies one of the Atacama's most comfortable spots, a place Darwin himself would have appreciated: Bahía Inglesa. The desert's finest beach resort, it boasts a serene shoreline where I'll spend the coming week.

^_^

There was a period of time in my early 20s when I spent every waking hour of every goddam day half-naked on a beach. Those were the best years of my life, the years I dream about more than any other. But when I think about them now – think about who I was when I was living them – I can hardly recognize that person anymore.

It was 2008, the economy was tanking and the life I'd always dreamed of in New York City was falling apart. My first long-term relationship fizzled out, as did my job in the art department of the soapy TV drama *Gossip Girl*, which was just becoming a teen sensation when a writers' strike shut down production. Then, I got some mysterious illness that made me incapable of peeing. It was like God himself was taking the piss out of me. Doctors couldn't figure out what was wrong. Maybe I'd taken too much ephedrine lately? Probably it was just stress. To remedy all the shittiness of being 23 and let down by adulthood, I shoved my belongings into a storage unit and bought a one-way ticket to the US Virgin Islands.

I soon found myself living in a wood-and-canvas treehouse on a tropical hilltop on Saint John. It was next to the eco-resort where I worked. I ran the front desk and spent the next few weeks, then months, then nearly two years escaping reality.

It was on Saint John that I met the first gay person who was living his life the way I wanted to live mine. His name was Didier and he was French, though Los Angeles was his latest port of call. He'd spent much of his adult life vagabonding around the world in awe of its wildest corners, hiking from tea house to tea house in Nepal, backpacking the bumpy roads of East Africa, and sailing to the farthest islands of Indonesia – all with the money he could scrape together doing odd jobs along the way.

Ours was a whirlwind week-long romance. We bushwhacked through dense vegetation to beaches I'd never seen. We swam perilously long distances in search of reef sharks. We danced to calypso music in abandoned ruins until the dancing turned to kissing. He was a real adventurer, a gay adventurer, and I wanted nothing more than to be just like him.

Two-thirds of Saint John is a national park, and the island from then on out became my Robinson Crusoe playground, its virgin beaches my nirvana. Every day offered a new hike, dive or adventure. Every night offered a new excuse to disappear gallons of golden rum with my castaway friends. That island set me off down a new path in life, but ever since I left, I've never been able to enjoy a beach quite the same. I don't enjoy anything quite so profusely anymore.

Other than a brief 18-month stint back in Brooklyn, I've lived outside of the US ever since. And I've had to tamp down my American exuberance to match a less overly confident world. But I miss it sometimes. I miss being so loud and carefree, so craven in my need for attention, that I'd do anything to get it. I miss being a center of gravity for those around me, and I think the last time I had that was on the beaches of Saint John.

Most Americans don't realize how uniquely American it is to be so innately overconfident until they feel what it's like to be a person from somewhere else. I suppose, for me, living in a country that doesn't speak my language made me crawl deeper into my shell, to listen more than I speak. But being on this beach – whose turquoise waters remind me of the Caribbean (even if nothing else around does) – makes me long for those older times when the world was a simpler place and I a more vibrant member of it.

This oasis is like a godsend: a rare Atacama beach you can actually swim in, plus a low-key town that's cute enough you want to stick around for a while. Those golden years of my quarter-life crisis may have been tinged in pinks and greens, but here, in this bone-white desert, it feels like taking a beach vacation on the Moon. There are no palm trees or corals – just sand and sea.

The beach – really a collection of pocket-sized beachlets squinched between boulders – gets its name ("English Bay") from the English pirates who once used its rocky coves to hide out while planning attacks up and down the coast. These include infamous privateers like Francis Drake, Bartholomew Sharp and Edward Davis, the latter of whom, rumor has it, buried treasure here.

These days, the place feels anything but savage, with trendy seafood restaurants and sand so soft on my feet it's like walking atop powdered sugar. I spend my first days rolling around on it. When I tire of Bahía Inglesa, I move my ever-bronzer body over to the lengthier Playa Las Machas to the south. Las Machas is home to my thatch-roofed cabana; it's perfectly aligned for the electric tangerine sunsets that become the highlight of my evenings here.

The *camanchaca* is more ephemeral than it was in the south, evaporating by noon. I use the cloudy mornings to hike into the nearby cliffs, exploring the one stretch of the Atacama coast that Chileans swoon over. Tabletops of sandstone rise above the ocean like stacks of wobbly pancakes. Scrambling beneath them, I find Jacuzzi-sized rock pools to bathe in and huge overhangs filled with brittle sea urchin carcasses and mounds of discarded shells.

I think back to my days exploring Saint John with Didier, and how I replaced him with another adventurous spirit when I moved to New Zealand. I remember all the islands Felipe and I went to in Southeast Asia with the money we saved working at the Scenic Hotel. I rewind to the times we hiked out to secret beaches where two gay boys could be just that without anyone watching. I was a different person then. We were different people. I suppose the challenge of aging together is to accept what we've become.

^ ~ ^

When the weekend arrives in Bahía Inglesa, the tranquility of the previous days – all those moments rolling around in memories – completely disappears.

The coastal road to Bahía Inglesa is lined in three-tiered pisco bars and fashionable restaurants. Shut to car traffic, it's filled with tables and chairs and is the liveliest place I've seen since leaving Santiago, largely thanks to its proximity to the regional capital of Copiapó, an inland city made rich by mining.

Folk singers stroll down streets playing bouncy *cueca* tunes for vacationing families and snogging lovers. Each of the previously empty restaurants now has a waiting list. For a moment, everything seems so normal that the pandemic slips from memory. But when I snap back to, the excessive crowds make me nervous. I decide to head over to Bahía Inglesa's more workaday stepsister, Caldera, where I'll feel less awkward eating alone while others eye my table.

Caldera, four miles (6.5 km) north, isn't nearly as attractive as Bahía Inglesa, but it's charming in that way some towns are when you can tell people have pride in where they live. And the citizens of Caldera should be proud; this place has loads of history.

On Christmas Day 1851, a wood-burning locomotive chugged away from Caldera on a 50-mile (80 km) journey east to Copiapó, becoming just the second train in South America to carry both passengers and cargo. The pioneering line was actually built by an American, one with the right kind of name for the job: William Wheelwright. The Massachusetts native had a lion's mane of facial hair that must have left his face a sweaty mess after he arrived in South America in the 1820s. First, the bulbously bearded gringo established a steamship line connecting ports between Valparaíso and Panama City. Then, he turned his attention to railroads, making Caldera a main port of entry into the Atacama.

Caldera appeared prominently on late 19th-century maps, replacing the old port that Darwin visited, Puerto Viejo, which he described with all the disdain he could muster as "an assemblage of miserable little hovels, situated at the foot of a sterile plain." What luster this new port had was lost by the middle of the 20th century. Yet glimmers of the glory days remain. The old rail terminal, for one, has been lovingly preserved; its towering wooden doors now lead to a paleontology museum that holds, among other finds, the jaws of a megalodon.

Nearby is the first non-Catholic Christian cemetery in Chile, which is filled with all the Americans, Brits and Scots who came to work in rails or mines here. The central plaza has a church from the 1860s, painted in dandelion-yellow and cotton-candy-blue, whose old-timey bells clang long-forgotten tunes on the hour. Yet the most attractive part of this otherwise utilitarian port town lies down by the harbor, next to the towering statue of Wheelwright.

The bustling firehouse-red seafood market is a cabinet of curiosities – perfect for educating myself on the larder of the Atacama coast. There are the standard fish one would expect – tuna, sea bass, hake – but also bug-eyed *reineta* and slithery *dorado*. I find the familiar shellfish – oysters, clams, crabs – but also giant *loco* abalones and fleshy *piure* tunicates. I can choose my own epicurean adventure, picking my protein and eating it raw in a ceviche, fried in an empanada or cooked *a la plancha* at any number of stalls lining the boardwalk out front.

Though I'm tempted to order my favorite Chilean dish, *pastel de jaiba* – a cheesy crabcake casserole baked in a terra-cotta bowl – I opt instead for *ostíones a la parmesana* and watch as a chef plucks palpitating scallops out of a display case and bakes them on the half shell with a creamy white wine and parmesan topping. The meal is the antithesis of my seafood empanada in Huasco; it's kingly.

I lick salty globs of cream off the purple shells and watch as a small crowd gathers around a man with a pop-up table and megaphone. He's offering a demonstration on how to shuck oysters. Nearby, kids are feeding seafood scraps to elephantine sea lions while their moms hawk pearl necklaces to passing shoppers.

I once again allow myself to forget that there's a pandemic. I mentally erase all the masks, all the rubber gloves and sanitizers and elbow greetings, and the scene feels so quotidian. But as I drive back to Bahía Inglesa that evening, I notice a sculpture on the side of the road that stops me in my tracks. I pull over and walk up to the sign sitting next to it. Painted in blue on a toppled refrigerator, it reads: *Las Crónicas del Coronavirus: Memoria, Denuncia, Homenaje* (The Coronavirus Chronicles: Memory, Complaint, Tribute).

The sculpture is a tangled web of rubber tubes, metal wires and broken flagpoles that's about 50 feet (15 m) long. Caught within are pots and pans, baby dolls, boxy computers, microwaves, bicycle tires, a beach chair, a pink bow, a knife, a teddy bear with a knife. A second sign on the far end describes the work as *Minimas Ofrendas: La Procesión de las Cosas* (Minimal Offerings: The Procession of Things). It's a tribute to the lives lost in the pandemic, an *animita* writ large.

Animitas are roadside shrines to the dead. I've become morbidly obsessed with photographing them and trying to understand why Chileans build them. Many lie at the sites of traffic collisions, but others honor victims of murders, mining accidents and other tragic untimely deaths. There are thousands of them all over Chile, but I've never seen them so omnipresent as in the desert, where they brighten up the colorless roads every couple of miles.

The word *animita* is a diminutive of *ánima* (soul). It's said that the "little souls" of those who lost their lives in tragic circumstances wander around the area where they were killed. When family and friends build these roadside dioramas, they're offering a place for them to rest, but also for loved ones to light votive candles, leave flowers, reflect and commune. Of course, bodies aren't buried at *animitas*; rather, they mark the spot where the body and soul were separated, and where the soul can linger for a while and still be reached (often to act as an intermediary for the living when they need favors from God or the Virgin or whomever they hope to contact in the great beyond).

Though generally set up by working-class Catholics, they're not exactly sanctioned by the church. And while you see plenty of crosses, the themes are not always religious. Many are filled with soccer trophies or empty beer bottles (Corona seems to be a favorite). Some are shaped like churches, others like small homes. In the desert, they're often painted in bright neon colors with flags flapping in the wind alerting you to their presence.

I find the *animitas* more joyous than sad – like time capsules of what the person loved at the moment they left this earth. One little girl's bubblegum-pink *animita* is filled with giant stuffed animals. A tattooed teenager's shrine has a mosaic of his favorite soccer team, Club Universidad de Chile. Another teenager's memorial has a trippy photo collage set against a backdrop of US$100 bills – presumably a wish for riches unfulfilled.

The Coronavirus Chronicle in front of me now is like a giant *animita* for the times, with all the ordinary bits and pieces that make up life woven together into something much more evocative than the sum of its parts. It represents all of this year's untimely deaths. It's tragic and it's beautiful. It's a very 2020 kind of memorial that's both a tribute and a complaint.

4 SEA TO SKY, PART TWO: SKY

(ANDEAN GEOGRAPHIES)

"What the hell are you driving?" barks Ercio Mettifogo, a legend in the local mountaineering community, clearly unimpressed with my wimpy, low-riding Chevrolet Onix. "You know Chile is a four-wheel drive country!"

"I know," I say, ashamed to admit that I couldn't afford one. "Do you think I'll be able to make it to the *refugio*?"

I've traveled to the interior city of Copiapó to meet up with Ercio and learn more about the high Andean plateau that rises on the eastern end of the Atacama. A friend in Santiago put us in touch because he runs a small, off-grid mountain hut on the edge of the lagoon-filled Nevado Tres Cruces National Park. It's two hours east – and a killer 12,400 feet (3780 m) above – where we're standing right now. There's nothing around it for miles.

"Getting to the *refugio* won't be an issue," he explains. "Moving away from it to visit other lagoons will be more challenging."

Ercio is a big guy with wild grey hair and a white face reddened under the desert sun. He fumbles around in his appropriately giant truck for a pen and paper, and then draws me a crude map of the largely dirt road up to Laguna Santa Rosa, my base camp. He scribbles two wobbly ovals and labels one Laguna del Negro Francisco and the other Laguna Verde.

"If you need to bathe one day, there's a pool of thermal water here," he says, drawing an X next to Laguna Verde.

"If you want to see more flamingos than you've seen in your life, go here," he notes, adding an X by Laguna del Negro Francisco.

"Now, here's what you're going to do," he continues. "You're going to go to the gas station and get an extra tank of petrol. Then, go to the grocery store and get enough food and water for a week, just in case you get lost or go down the wrong road, because if you get stuck in a rut up there, the customs house is the only thing around, and it'll be a good two- or three-day hike to reach it."

I nod, wondering if I'm preparing for the ultimate adventure or my dramatic demise.

"Have you got a good sleeping bag?"

"I do."

"Propane stove and mess kit?"

"Yup."

"Winter jacket?"

"Uh huh."

"Power bank?"

"There's no electricity up there?"

"Just a bit of solar power for emergencies."

"Right. Of course."

"Don't worry, you'll be fine," Ercio continues. "You're going to love it up on the altiplano. It's just you and the flamingos – and maybe a fox chasing the flamingos. And then at night, it's just you, the flamingos and a sea of stars."

^ ~ ^

When flamingos appear on neon bar signs, they're almost always alert, their gangly necks craned over two matchstick legs. In the wild, they're typically face down, ass up, like fuzzy balls of pink tiptoeing across shallow pools. They rarely lift their heads even to walk. Instead, they comb the water, picking at the brine shrimp and beta-carotene-rich algae that will make their skin blush.

Most envision flamingos as tropical animals, but they're actually fixtures of the high-altitude lagoons of the Atacama, where they seem apathetic to the harsh conditions. Even at night, when shorelines freeze over, the birds simply wait it out in the ice, trapped but unfazed, knowing that daylight will unlock them once again.

There's the rare Andean flamingo, which has yellow legs and black-tipped wings, and the slightly smaller James's flamingo, which has brick-red legs and a bright yellow beak. There's also the pinkest flamingo of them all: the Chilean flamingo, which, despite its name, is the most common across South America, found from Argentina up to Ecuador.

All are present at Laguna del Negro Francisco, a cloud-hugging lagoon within Nevado Tres Cruces National Park. They're joined here by other waders (such as the Andean avocet) and fastidious nest-builders (such as the horned coot) among 17 bird species that make this Ramsar wetland home.

Laguna del Negro Francisco is a shock of color on this otherwise monotone landscape, with milky-blue waters that never drop below three feet (0.9 m) in depth. It's a near twin of the park's other lagoon, Laguna Santa Rosa, which is even more prismatic, surrounded on one side by spiky orange-yellow *paja brava* plants and on the other by the crusty white Salar de Maricunga, the southernmost salt flat of the Atacama.

The road between the two lagoons is awful, like a giant sand trap. Yet miraculously, I avoid getting stuck or having to hike out for help on what would no doubt be a suicide mission. I breathe a sigh of relief when I see my *refugio* at Laguna Santa Rosa off in the distance, its khaki walls just barely visible in front of the khaki hills behind them.

It's my second day on the altiplano, but I'm already gripped by the powerful invisible forces of altitude. I'm blowing scarlet blood into perfectly white tissues. My eyes feel heavy and dry, bulging with extra weight. I can hear the veins in my brain going *thump, thump, thump*, trying to make do with 30 percent less oxygen. I am, suddenly, a less capable version of myself; a young man prematurely aged.

My *refugio*, unlit and unpowered, lies at 12,340 feet (3760 m). To travel over to Laguna del Negro Francisco, I had to climb to 13,485 feet (4110 m). To go to Laguna Verde tomorrow, I'll climb higher still up to 14,200 feet (4330 m). My head wasn't made for this elevation. I have a slight headache, shortness of breath, a dry cough – all symptoms that might otherwise lead me to believe I had the current plague.

Tibet is often called the roof of the world, but the title is just as fitting for the altiplano of South America. It's the second-most extensive area of high plateau on earth, fanning out north from here across Argentina, Bolivia and Peru. An area of extreme contrasts, it's the place where arid desert meets fertile oasis – and some of its most dramatic features lie just east of Copiapó, within reach of this remote *refugio*.

Most of the Andean peaks out my window are between 16,000 and 20,000 feet (4876–6096 m), their domes frosted like wedding cakes and massaged into curvaceous knobs by the notorious altiplano wind. But Nevado Tres Cruces, the grey volcanic massif that gives this park its name, has three summits that are higher still, including Tres Cruces Sur, which, at 22,139 feet (6748 m), is the sixth-highest mountain in the Andes. Like Tres Cruces, many of the tallest peaks here are volcanoes, and their ancient eruptions have filled in valleys, forming an extensive high-altitude flatland.

If this were a normal year and the borders were open, the bare bunks at this *refugio* would be filled with mountaineers acclimatizing for an ascent up the highest volcano of them all, which lies just out of sight behind Nevado Tres Cruces. Ojos del Salado is not only the second-highest mountain in the Andes, after Aconcagua, near Santiago; it's also the highest volcano in the world, at 22,615 feet (6893 m).

I set off to reach its base on my third morning, following another restless night worming around in a sleeping bag as temperatures plunged below freezing. I warm up under the blazing mid-morning sun, driving alongside the edge of the Salar de Maricunga. This 56-square-mile (145 km²) salt flat lies in a closed basin between the Domeyko and Claudio Gay ranges of the Andes. Yet, as harsh as the background seems, I find it oddly painterly. The *salar* is like a Rothko of fuzzy-edged white, teal and chocolate blurred across the horizon. The hills above it have swirls like oil slicks, as if brushed by Van Gogh.

I pull over, briefly, and take off my glasses, as I often do when a landscape startles me. Bare eyes give my surroundings a soft glaze, like a cinema camera. It's not the stuff of photographs, which often surprise me when I see them afterward, all sharp and sculpted to unnecessary perfection. To me, landscapes always feel more heroic in my own myopia.

About an hour into my trip, I link up with the paved Ruta 31, which climbs over the Andes to Argentina via the little-used Paso de San Francisco. As I rise in elevation, I follow a trickle of a river – the Lamas – which carves an impressive canyon to my right, like water poured atop a sand castle. The border up ahead is closed to through traffic, so if the raging wind knocked me into this canyon, no one would be around to notice.

The altitude is clearly messing with my mind, while the radiation is zapping me dry. A recent study published in the *Bulletin of the American Meteorological Society* proved that the Chilean altiplano has the world's highest surface irradiance, making it, in other words, the sunniest spot on earth. Its authors equate the radiation here to what you might experience standing on Venus. Perhaps that's why the sun is turning my lips into a thousand Grand Canyons and my skin into an itchy network of spider-webs. I push onward with the knowledge that my first "bath" in days lies up ahead.

An earthen amphitheater with spiky white snow sculptures appears on my left. I pull over to hike into its core. These long, thin blades of hardened snow pointing upward toward the sun are known as *penitentes de hielo*. Apparently, they got this name because they evoke the tall, pointed habits and hoods worn by penitents during the Holy Week procession. This Catholic reference is lost on me; what I see up ahead as I climb the mocha-colored hill looks more like a bunch of ghosts gathered for a rave.

Penitentes de hielo were long thought to be a result of the altiplano's strong winds, but they actually form when the sun turns snow directly into water vapor without melting it first, a process called sublimation. This spiky ice is only found in desert environments above 13,125 feet (4000 m) – at least, that's the only place you'll find them on Earth. Apparently, NASA has spotted them on Pluto as well as Europa, one of Jupiter's 92 known moons.

Back in the car, and closer to the border, Ojos del Salado finally appears on the horizon. Fittingly, there is a UFO-like lenticular cloud right above it. The massive volcano has a more muscular look than the lower hills around it, like a bunch of grey biceps fused together, its white veins filled with perennial snow. Somewhere out of sight, 20,960 feet (6389 m) high on the eastern edge, lies a permanent crater lake believed to be the highest body of water anywhere on earth.

What I love is that a theater critic (Jan Alfred Szczepański) and journalist (Justyn Wojsznis), both members of a Polish

expedition to the Andes, were the first to see it on their landmark ascent up Ojos del Salado in 1937. These days, only about
500 people climb the volcano each year. It's not that the hike
itself is super technical – only the final push to the summit re-
quires rock climbing skills – but the long acclimatization period
and harsh weather (punishing winds, temperatures in the nega-
tive double digits) make it a formidable challenge.

Nuclear-orange poof balls of vegetation line the rubble road
up to its base. I try to set off on a small hike to channel my inner
mountaineer, but the wind makes it almost impossible just to
stand. Even the parked car is jerking around like one of those
coin-operated kiddie rides outside American dollar stores.

I'm fast realizing something that should have been obvious
from the outset: the Atacama is no place for humans. It's freak-
ishly unforgiving. But if I've learned anything about myself in
these past years, it's that I nihilistically seek out uncomfortable
places because they're so often the most complicated and fas-
cinating on earth – the ones that make you feel something deep
down at your core.

When I told friends in Santiago about my plans to travel the
entire Atacama, many had strong opinions about why it was a
bad idea. *There's nothing in the desert*, they said. *The cities are
ugly. The people are tacky. How many weeks? You'll go mad.* I told
them that was the point. I wanted landscapes like this that would
make me mad, people who would defy stereotypes and places
where I could reconsider what's considered ugly. I also wanted to
prove to them that they were just parroting words passed down
by others who, like so many from the comfortable world, harbor
unconscious fears about the places they can't understand.

Deserts are so often spoken of as cruel and deceptive, plagued
with daily riddles that are never easily solved. *The heat is scorching.*

The sun is a burning disk. The land shimmers in mirages. And yet, to me, deserts are places of utmost appeal, their mind-warping challenges merely foils for those unwilling to put in the effort.

Take the wind right now at the base of Ojos del Salado. It's an element I don't live with every day in my city apartment. I could go weeks without thinking about it. In the desert, I reckon with wind constantly. Every day I think about how it will regulate my temperature and determine my posture, about whether it will prop me up or blow me down. I think about whether I like it (sometimes, when I'm hot) or loathe it (often, when I'm cold). It makes me feel something. It even makes me cry when I don't want to…and then plasters those tears onto my cracking face.

Ojos del Salado is such a fierce vision, but I'm far too cold and manky to appreciate it for as long as I'd like. Just around the bend lies the deceptively named Laguna Verde (Green Lagoon), whose water is so cerulean blue it almost glows like neon under the afternoon sun. It's the kind of surreal blue you find inside a glacier or mint-flavored toothpaste or laundry detergent. On its southern bank lies a small knee-deep pool of thermal water with a waist-high wall of stones protecting it from the ferocious winds. I strip down and ease myself in.

The view from here of patchy clouds caught atop volcanic peaks, of a salty beach and scintillating waves, is as breath-taking as the air itself. I lie back and submerge my body. Unlike the lagoon next door, this lukewarm water actually is green, with an emerald-colored bed of algae I use to exfoliate the sweat-caked dust off my skin. I close my eyes and fade into the landscape.

It's funny; I've come in search of the desert but seem to be spending all of my time next to water. But I guess that's the story of deserts, isn't it? They come alive in oases like these, and so you plan your journey from one to the next, dreaming of sand and ending up in water.

^ ~ ^

Journeying from sea to sky, traveling across the southern quadrant of the Atacama, I've begun to appreciate the geography of Chile and how it's made this desert such a singular place. What I haven't yet grappled with is how the most precious parts of this landscape are constantly threatened by the treasures buried within. It is, after all, this desert that makes Chile rich. Yet the cost of those riches isn't always clear to those of us living in the capital.

To get a better picture, I hone in on another Andean lagoon that epitomizes the challenges Chile will face over the coming decade as the world transitions from gas-powered to electric vehicles. Ercio assures me my car will be useless for getting there. Instead, he links me up with his friend Gabriel Rojas, an entrepreneur about my age with a big red jeep that's up for the task.

Gabriel is a soft-spoken guy who chooses his words carefully – which is to say we don't speak much at all in our first hour together as he susses me out. We meet in his hometown of Diego de Almagro, a small city 90 miles (145 km) north of Copiapó that was almost wiped away in a freak 2015 flood.

One of those increasingly frequent "once-in-a-century storms" dumped nearly three inches (7.6 cm) of rain on the city, which normally sees no more than half an inch in an entire year, turning the dust of the desert into mud as thick as fresh-poured concrete as it raced through town. The place has since recovered from the deluge, but I get the feeling Gabriel came away from that experience with a renewed sense of pride in where he lives, as well as the need to show it off to visitors.

In truth, there's not a whole lot to see in Diego de Almagro, which is skeletal in the way many places inhabited by miners are. But there is plenty to love about the hills just beyond.

The early morning sun rises over brown mounds as we bumble down a dirt road east of town. The route runs parallel to a small salt river that Gabriel says is ten times more saline than the sea. Unlike nearly every other waterway I've seen in the Atacama thus far, this one has no life growing up around it. It's toxic. And it starts on the edge of the very place we're headed today: Salar de Pedernales, a high-altitude salt flat with a near-mythical turquoise lagoon.

To reach that lagoon, we must first follow this salt river deeper into the valley. Up above are signposts indicating where the Inca Road crosses our path. I tell Gabriel that it's hard to believe they could've built a highway through this inhospitable desert more than 500 years ago, but he says there's plenty of evidence of their presence. In fact, nearby is El Tambo del Río La Sal, the remains of an old stone fortification that was a motel, military checkpoint and supply hub all rolled into one.

We leave the salt river behind and instead follow an abandoned railway line further east of Diego de Almagro. Soon, we reach the carcass of the copper mine it served from the 1920s through the 1950s. In the hill above is the ghost town of Potrerillos, which once had 7,000 residents, including Gabriel's mother, who was born here. "Everyone was forced out by the year 2000, when the government deemed the area too contaminated for human habitation," he says.

It strikes me as incredibly sad to lose your hometown in such a callous manner, but Gabriel says it's the story of so many places just like it scattered across the Atacama. "It's a fact of life here in the desert. People only see value in this place when there's money to be had. When the mines dry up, nobody cares what happens to the towns built to serve them."

We enter an area called *los jardines* (the gardens) due to the multicolored mineral striations along the valley wall. From here, we zigzag in a near-vertical ascent up to 10,825 feet (3300 m), where we reach the *puna*. This montane grassland has just enough shrubbery to sustain South America's two wild camelids, guanacos and vicuñas, which graze along the side of the road oblivious to our presence. "When you see a guanaco or vicuña, it totally changes your perspective of the Atacama," Gabriel says. "You think it couldn't possibly have life, but it's totally contrary, because life flourishes here; it's just really well camouflaged."

The grasslands give way to a blindingly white patch of crumpled earth as we approach Salar de Pedernales. At 130 square miles (337 km²), this far-flung salt flat is vast and glittery, its gypsum shimmering under an aggressive sun. Pedernales lies in an amphitheater of 16,000- to 19,000-foot (4880–5800 m) peaks, sandwiched as Maricunga is between the Domeyko and Claudio Gay ranges of the Andes. Some of the mountains on the horizon have names, but many more are just anonymous mounds in one of cartography's forgotten corners.

"When I was 18 or so, I finally realized the value of the place where I was living," Gabriel says as we leave the rutted road behind and rumble atop the salt moguls of the *salar*, which gleam and glint in the noontime light. "What I knew up to that point was so little, and what was left to be discovered was practically infinite. That's what motivated me; one experience in these mountains was enough to make me want to know more."

He points to the 16,650-foot (5075 m) Cerro Doña Inés, a dormant snow-capped stratovolcano off in the distance. "To climb a mountain like that widens your perspectives of the land

and makes you want to keep exploring it more and more," he says. "This desire to explore eventually becomes so great it's inexhaustible."

That's how he and his brother Álvaro ended up surveying Pedernales two years ago and finding a circuit of multi-hued lagoons they knew could turn their Andean backyard into a major attraction. They built a small 2.5-mile (4 km) path around the lagoons to ensure their protection and began opening the region up to tourism.

"There are few natural wonders left on earth that haven't already been put on display for visitors, and this was one of them," he says as we park the truck at the trailhead. "My brother and I found it so striking here when we first saw it that we knew we had to show it off to the world."

Pedernales is an endorheic basin of brackish water with a halite crust and dozens of small lagoons – kind of like a block of Swiss cheese with a brie-colored mold. The trail Gabriel and his brother developed leads to a handful of the most spectacular pools, including one tinted blood-red by bacteria and another emerald-green. The star attraction is Laguna Turquesa, a peanut-shaped pool filled with the same Caribbean-colored water as Bahía Inglesa. The big difference is that there's so much salt in this lagoon that, when I lower my body into it, I immediately float like an ice cube in a giant punch bowl.

The water, which tastes of olive brine, is about 60 degrees Fahrenheit (15.5°C) – warmer than the air up here, but cool enough that I can no longer feel my extremities after a minute bobbing on the surface. I shiver and shake for a few minutes more, spouting cheekfuls of water into the empty sky. Then, I decide it wise to get out. Gabriel pours a bottle of fresh water over my body to remove the salt, but I still feel a thousand pinpricks on my skin. My lips taste like movie theater popcorn and my bathing suit, now removed, is solidifying into the texture of cardboard under the blazing sun.

I dry off almost instantly thanks to the altiplano's raging winds and return to my winter clothes. Gabriel and I then sit together by the turquoise lagoon, snacking on cheese and olives and popping open a bottle of sweet *pajarete* wine.

"You know, in my childhood, I never knew the high Andes," he says, pulling an olive pit out of his mouth. "Back then, there was very little access to these areas."

Now, he says, he and his brother are taking advantage of newly built mining roads that snake up and down the cordillera to photograph places even more remote than this – like the Lagunas Bravas and Salar de Gorbea – that previously had no photographic records. The paradox, of course, is that the industry that's opened this area up to deeper exploration may also be in the process of destroying it.

Whereas hillside deposits of iron, gold and copper have long been the dominant minerals of the Atacama, now the *salars* themselves are targets. That's because they hold huge deposits of the latest mineral du jour: lithium.

Chile has, by far, the world's largest lithium reserves (which are the exploitable deposits found in the earth). Unlike neighboring Argentina and Bolivia in the so-called Lithium Triangle – which holds about two-thirds of the global supply – most of Chile's lithium is pure and "economically extractable." Some analysts predict Chile could become the Saudi Arabia of the Electronic Age.

This ultra-light metal is the main component in the rechargeable lithium-ion batteries that power smartphones, smartwatches, laptops and tablets. It's the secret weapon in the electric vehicles, solar panels and wind turbines that may transform our future, ushering in a global transition to a low-carbon economy. And Chile is already exporting more than US$1 billion worth of it each year, scattering bits of its iconic desert all across the globe without most of us ever realizing.

This developing nation – with its melting icefields, disappearing glaciers, gargantuan wildfires, and dire drought – would love to fuel the clean energy revolution. Yet, if that happens, it's places like the Atacama that will pay the ultimate price. Extracting this silvery-white alkali metal means pumping in large amounts of fresh water. Industry experts calculate that it takes a staggering 500,000 gallons (1.9 million L) just to produce one ton (907 kg) of lithium.

Mines need this water to churn up the salty brine sitting beneath the crust. The mineral-rich sludge is then left in large pools to evaporate over a period of 12 to 18 months for processing. Problem is, the Atacama doesn't have much water to give. Its famous lagoons are now shrinking at alarming rates, as are the flamingo populations that depend on them.

"I get sad just thinking about it," Gabriel says, his eyes glossing over.

Chile's state-owned Codelco, the world's number one copper producer, is exploring for lithium at Maricunga. Chinese, American and Australian companies are all scouting Pedernales. Many more have already set up camp at the Salar de Atacama further north, where 65 percent of the local water is diverted for mining activities.

There are already fears that local communities – many Indigenous – will no longer have enough water to grow crops and maintain livestock. Lithium mining also produces large amounts of waste and air and soil pollution, and can create contaminated water, often from toxic chemicals used in the process, like hydrochloric acid. Soon, it may become even harder to eke out a living here.

"It's not that lithium itself is bad," Gabriel clarifies. "On the contrary, lithium is the hope to change the contaminating energy sources we use now. But the cost of that is really high for beautiful places like this and those of us living nearby."

I take a long sip of the syrupy golden wine and consider that most of the electronics in my apartment have elements that can be traced back to places like this. So do the electric buses I ride, the glassware I cook with and the sun cream I just reapplied after jumping into the very place from which one of its ingredients may be sourced one day soon.

"Hopefully something can be done to slow down the process or ensure that the damages won't be so irreversible," Gabriel continues. "But I can imagine a very real possibility that in 20 years, I won't be able to take people to these lagoons anymore because they won't exist."

Millions of years ago, salt flats like Pedernales and Maricunga were vast lakes. They've been slowly, naturally, drying up ever since. Scientists have come to view them and their brethren as key to understanding the effects of climate change, since they've undergone a process that could very well happen elsewhere on Earth as temperatures rise. The great irony of the current gas-to-electric revolution is that, in our attempt to combat climate change, we may irrevocably alter the very places that could have helped us to understand it better.

5 OF MINES AND MEN

(POLITICS, POWER AND MASCULINITY: HOW DESERTS BURY SECRETS)

It's a strange thing when the site of a tragedy transitions into a place for selfies. I suppose it's also strange to be a willing visitor at a site with a dark or complicated history. None of us really knows how to behave at a place like this. Do we walk around in silent reflection? Do we hang our heads in reverence? Do we stretch out one arm and smile for the camera? Increasingly, unconscionably, it seems to be the latter.

Such is the case at the infamous Mina San José, a small-scale copper and gold mine on the northern outskirts of Copiapó that is one of the Atacama's most selfied destinations. There's literally a selfie session in progress the moment I arrive. A waifish twentysomething in thin white slacks and sharp red heels is wobbling across the dirt access road with a pink phone pointed at her face.

Her destination is an orange hill of sand and dirt with 33 flags flapping in the wind. Thirty-two of them are Chilean, with horizontal bands of white and red as well as a five-pointed star in a royal blue square. The other flag is Bolivian, with an Andean coat of arms set against tricolor bands of red, yellow and green. Each flag represents one of the 33 miners who spent 69 days trapped beneath the surface here, buried alive in the deepest stone tomb in human history.

Everyone in Chile knows the story of what happened here on August 5, 2010. It was around two p.m., and the 33 men on A shift were just about to ascend for lunch when a single block of diorite broke off from the rest of the mountain, thundering downward through several layers of the mine. The hungry men in the bowels of the desert were suddenly trapped on the far side of a 45-story rock wall. Try as they might, there was no way out. Worse, the mine was crumbling around them. For the next 17 days, they became like astronauts of the inner earth, completely cut off from the rest of the world like few humans before or since.

Héctor Tobar wrote in his bestselling tell-all *Deep Down Dark* that, to survive, the interned men would need to ration 18 cans of tuna, 24 liters of condensed milk, 1 can of salmon, 1 can of peaches, 1 can of peas, and 93 packs of cookies – the meager and thoughtless supplies left in an emergency cabinet within a small refuge 2,300 feet (700 m) below the surface. Filthy industrial water – used in normal times to keep engines cool – was their only option for hydration. Most would strip down to their underwear to endure the sweltering temperatures, which hovered around 85 degrees Fahrenheit (29°C). As days became weeks, formerly rotund men shriveled like raisins into puttering zombies with savage hair and sunken eyes. Yet they never gave up hope. Neither did their families gathering on the moonscape up above.

The cross where the red-heeled woman took her selfies was the site of a makeshift tent city known as Campamento Esperanza (Camp Hope), where the miners' kids, parents, siblings, girlfriends, wives and mistresses assembled as soon as news of the collapse reached their ears. They traveled from all corners of Chile to hold vigil here, pressuring authorities not to give up on their loved ones even when hope seemed entirely irrational.

Chile's state-owned mining company, Codelco, took over rescue efforts from San José's inept owners at the San Esteban Primera Mining Company, who were known for cutting corners. Meanwhile, Sebastián Piñera arrived on the scene, sensing an opportunity to boost his profile at the start of his first term as president. Operación San Lorenzo (Operation St. Lawrence), named after the patron saint of miners, was soon full throttle ahead.

The Codelco team drilled exploratory five-inch boreholes to make contact with the living dead, but because San Esteban Primera Mining Company had provided them with out-of-date mine maps, the boreholes drifted miserably off-target. The miners below sat in the dark and listened as the mountain moaned with each new attempt. Finally, on day 17, the operator digging a borehole at a depth of 2,260 feet (689 m) heard something that sounded like tapping on the drill. He pulled it up to the surface and noticed a strip of red paint. Then, he found a note taped to one of the drill bits. It contained the message everyone had hoped for: *Estamos bien en el refugio, los 33* (We are all fine in the shelter, the 33 of us).

Ten years later, I walk past a replica of this auspicious note on a rock wall in front of the cross. I then continue downhill to peer into the old mine entrance, which spirals deeper than the tallest buildings in Santiago are tall. As I approach, I notice a figure watching me from a nearby shed. I walk over, unsure if I may be trespassing. He introduces himself as Jorge, Jorge Galleguillos, the 11th man rescued from a sunken hell.

Jorge is an older man with furry grey eyebrows and a white beard twisted into a corkscrew under his chin. While the rest of the 33 men have done everything possible to forget San José, I quickly realize that he sees it as his duty to be the one who remembers.

"This could be nothing right now," he tells me, fanning his arm over what remains of the decommissioned mine. "Someone needs to maintain this place so that its story isn't forgotten."

That someone, of course, is Jorge.

In the first five years after the accident, the veteran miner says he would find himself inexplicably driving over to the San José just to look at it a few times each week. "I don't know why, but I could never fully disconnect myself from this place," he explains.

In 2015, Jorge took it upon himself to become the caretaker of the San José, acting as an ambassador for the diminishing number of visitors who still gave a damn about his personal tragedy. In some ways, he's the last man standing here. And to be that man, he tells me, is a thankless job.

"According to my *compañeros*, I made myself the owner of this place; I took it just for myself and left them aside," he says. "But it needs money put into it, and if you don't put resources into something, you have nothing to show."

Jorge built a small interpretation center and an informal route around the site that visitors can tour. It's a bare-bones one-man operation, with near non-existent funding, but it's given the retired miner a new purpose in life – "even if my *compañeros* think what I'm doing is sad."

Jorge takes me up to show me a freight container he's converted into a small exhibit hall, his prominent belly leading the way as he walks. Just outside the container is a balcony with panels describing a 69-day timeline. On it are the events etched deepest into the story of his life.

"On day two, day three, day four we had hope," he says, pointing to the timeline. "On day five, there was total silence. Death felt close on days six, seven, eight, nine. From day ten, there was a bit of hope again when we heard the drills getting closer."

Yet it would still be more than a week before the miners made contact with the outside world. In that time, Jorge's legs would swell up like balloons while his body would succumb to a fast-spreading fungal infection.

"Food deliveries and a phone connection arrived the day after we sent the note," he says as we hop in his truck for a drive over to the site of the first tubes used to send supplies. "The only thing we had left at that point was two cans of tuna."

Consultants from NASA recommended slowly increasing daily calorie intake to 500, then 1,000, then 1,500 – a cruel realization for the starving men, but necessary to avoid cardiac failure due to their low levels of phosphates and potassium, which the body uses to digest carbohydrates. The first deliveries, Jorge tells me as we stare into the inconspicuous boreholes, carried little more than insipid vitamin-enriched gels.

In the weeks that followed, as an international team numbering in the hundreds raced against the clock to build a shaft big enough to rescue the men, Jorge and the 32 others would become caged celebrities. The cruel particulars of their subterranean struggle fueled nightly news segments. Letters the men sent up to their wives and mistresses got sold off to newspapers around the world. In Chile, the miners became local heroes used to personify the tenacity of the prospering country. The fight to save them also catapulted President Piñera to a level of approval never attained before or since.

Jorge and I continue in his truck over to the site where, after more than two months underground, he was finally winched back to the surface in a rescue capsule constructed by the Chilean Navy using input from NASA.

"The media said that the strongest men came out first, but that's not true," says Jorge, the 11th to depart. Puffing his chest, he adds: "There were men who had one day of experience in mines. Others who had one or two months. I had 46 years."

Few artifacts of that massive rescue effort are left at the mine today. Chilean arms dealer Carlos Cardoen (currently on Interpol's wanted list for his Pinochet-era exports to Iraq) purchased many of the artifacts for his lavish museum in the wine region of Colchagua, while the Fénix 2 rescue capsule sits in the underfunded Museo Regional de Atacama in Copiapó. Nevertheless, the winch platform where the miners ascended from their dark dungeon into the blinding Atacama light remains, offering a clear reminder of the global media event that happened here on October 13, 2010.

An estimated one billion people around the world tuned in that day to watch Jorge and the others escape from their 69-day ordeal. Then, in the above-ground weeks that followed, they continued watching as the men became instant celebrities. Of course, this unexpected international stardom came right at the very moment when the miners were least equipped to handle it.

"Where did you say you're from again?" Jorge asks me as we drive together back to the shed where we met.

"Virginia," I say. "Near Washington, DC."

"That's right," he continues. "Me and my *señora* went to Washington for the opening of an exhibit about all of this. But I don't remember the name of the museum..."

It was, in fact, the National Museum of Natural History, one of the biggest and most visited museums in the world. The Smithsonian put together a show called *Against All Odds* about the story and science of the Chilean mine rescue. They treated Jorge and three of his colleagues to an elaborate ceremony where he was quoted snapping at the media about how uncomfortable he was in their spotlight.

"We also went to Disney World and Hollywood. We flew to Greece and the Holy Land. I met with the vice president of Greece and the mayor of Los Angeles. All of this has been a privilege for me, but it was a lot to take in at the time."

Before the mining accident, Jorge had never seen the world

beyond Chile; he didn't even own a passport. Now, he was being shuffled around like a puppet on all-expense-paid junkets, watching as his story got told and retold until it became like a fable he didn't even recognize.

International travel dwindled over the years. Yet Hollywood brought the miners back into the spotlight in 2015 with a US$26-million blockbuster, *The 33*, loosely based on the book by Héctor Tobar, which had come out the year prior. The film's bizarre cast included Spanish icon Antonio Banderas, Filipino-American Lou Diamond Phillips and French legend Juliette Binoche – all pretending to be Chileans while speaking in accented English.

"The book was all right, but the movie was shit," Jorge says, kicking the dirt. "Between the two I made about US$1,800. That was it. It was nothing. The investors scammed us."

The tragedy brought the men fleeting fame in those early years, but in the end, there was very little fortune. The miners did receive US$10,000 each from an eccentric Chilean businessman. And they continue to receive a monthly pension from the state of around US$550 (400,000 pesos, just above Chile's monthly minimum wage), but it isn't enough for a dignified existence. Many of Jorge's colleagues returned underground, while others struggle with alcoholism and mental health issues. After failed lawsuits to compensate the men for their near-death experience, as well as broken pacts of silence regarding the telling of their story, *los 33* were left bitter and divided.

"Everyone assumes we're rich," Jorge says, "but do I look rich to you?"

A decade on, he doesn't even talk to most of the men anymore.

"All of them are *penca*, they're *callampa*," he says, using Chilean slang for things that are rotten, lazy or foul. "They're *aweonao* [stupid, also Chilean slang], they want everything for themselves and they get angry when someone else is doing better than them."

The ten-year anniversary of Operación San Lorenzo happened about a month before my visit, but the event barely registered, even in the local media. Men like Jorge are propped up as heroes when their stories embody the national narrative of hope and solidarity. But when those heroes are revealed to be humans just like the rest of us – when their miracle fades into a nightmare of trauma, illness and jealousy – they become disposable all over again.

Chile is a nation of rigid class distinctions that's built on the backs of men like *los 33* who risk their lives inside mountains to enrich the comfortable elite in cities far away. Like many of his former friends, Jorge is the son of a miner. He carried his first load when he was just 12 years old. For him to have almost died underground was never such a surprise; it was always possible that his life might end that way. Of course, it didn't. And that's a miracle. And he feels like he's the only one left who thinks that's a story worth remembering.

^˷^

It's not until I'm driving down the dirt road away from the San José mine, back into the nothingness of the open desert, that it hits me: I've actually seen Jorge before in person.

The world premiere of *The 33* took place at the Teatro Municipal de Las Condes, a glass cube of a cultural center two blocks from my apartment in Santiago. Felipe wanted to drool over Antonio Banderas – and I guess I did, too – so we walked over to watch the fanfare. It was a cold Sunday afternoon in August. The trees along the way were naked of leaves. The air was frosty. Yet the greyness of winter didn't stop scores of Chileans from pouring in from across the country.

Banderas might have been the main attraction, but you wouldn't have known it when the miners, dressed in their finest ill-fitting suits, paraded down the red carpet. Hand in hand with their *pololas* and *señoras*, they catwalked around a billowing crowd of hundreds. Everyone roared with applause, ourselves included. When Banderas finally appeared, he gathered the men in front of the theater for a group shot. They waved Chilean flags, waved their hands in the air. News cameras flashed with excitement. It felt like a special moment. I didn't know all the circumstances at the time; I had no idea it wasn't such a Cinderella story after all.

It must have felt like a big blow for Jorge and his companions when the Hollywood remake of their story went on from Teatro Municipal de Las Condes to bomb at global cinemas. The action-packed thriller was, as Jorge himself said, terrible; it was painfully inauthentic, sanitized in that way foreign stories so often are when they're made in English using non-native actors.

Jorge occupies my mind all afternoon as I drive west, and then north, headed away from the San José mine. I think it's because he shared so much of his life story with me but, in return, a lot of what I told him about myself wasn't even true. All Jorge wanted to talk about (when we weren't talking about the mining accident) was girls. Did I think Chilean girls were prettier than American girls? Did I have a nice wife back in Santiago? Any chance I could hook him up with Ivanka Trump?

I told him what he wanted to hear: that I had someone back in Santiago waiting for me, that *she* was beautiful, that *she* had wavy black hair. With guys like this who spend their lives in a hypermasculine hole, who pee on the dirt in front of me as if I'm not there, who invite me into their pickup truck in the middle of the desert where there's not another soul for miles, I'd rather be invisibly "normal." I'd rather try and pass as the straight person they want me to be. And it makes me sick to my stomach every time I feel the need to protect myself that way.

I suppose I've gotten used to code-switching over the years. As a gay man, I've learned workarounds to thrive out of my element. Not being in my comfort zone is a zone I know well. It's a state of being I was born into. All gays have the scars of swung slurs stuffed away in some dark corner of our wary hearts, hidden but not forgotten. And so, I learned early in life how to be a chameleon.

When Jorge and his 32 companions were getting rescued from their subterranean prison, Felipe and I were mapping out a months-long trip around India and Nepal, where, we were told, it was best not to appear as anything more than backpacking buddies, and to accept rooms with two beds when all we wanted was one.

In one very consequential moment, when Felipe and I got trapped on either side of a sliding glass door at the New Delhi airport, we made it very clear that we were, in fact, more than just friends.

It didn't end well.

Felipe got blocked from entering the airport, ostensibly because his flight left a few hours after mine. We pleaded with the lanky security officers to let me leave, to let him come in. We needed to hug each other goodbye. It was the first time each of us was returning to our home countries after meeting in New Zealand and spending a year and a half abroad. We had no idea when or where we'd see each other again. The officers just laughed at us; we cried.

I got on a plane to Washington, DC, a few hours later without ever saying goodbye to Felipe. We didn't see each other – didn't complete that forbidden hug – for six more months.

When, in the years that followed, we flew through South Asian airports or packed into Javanese *bemos* or slept in Alabama motels, we always used an unspoken and outdated playbook: *What they don't ask us can't hurt us. What we do tell may.*

There've been so many times in my more recent solo travels when I'm alone in a taxi in some foreign city in the Global South, and the driver – whom I will never see again – asks me a few loaded questions about my family or relationships. They're probably innocuous; most people don't think twice about how to respond. But if I answer a question like that honestly, it tells them the thing about myself that's a big thing, but which never felt to me like it should be a thing at all. It could take the conversation in a thousand different directions, only I'll never know in advance which one. All I want in that moment is for the conversation to end. All I crave is to be invisible. It's easier that way.

When I ride on the back of a motorbike taxi in the Amazon, knee-hugging the driver, I am invisible. When I sidle up to the bar next to a stranger in small-town America, I am invisible. When I meet up with a miner in the middle of a Chilean desert, I am invisible. And because of it, I'm starting to lose myself along the way.

Perhaps my fears of what I've been taught to fear – about being me in certain places with certain people – are unfounded? Maybe I'm just not brave enough not to care? "The moment of queer pride," Maggie Nelson says in her memoir *The Argonauts*, "is a refusal to be shamed by witnessing the other as being ashamed of you."

I grew up in a generation of gay men perpetually worried about ways of walk, talk or gesture and how they might endanger us. But maybe, these days, much of that residual fear is just rooted in self-loathing rather than self-preservation. I think the next generation will live bolder than I am. I bet – no, I know – they already do.

^ ~ ^

Long before Jorge, *los 33* and all the other copper, gold and lithium workers arrived in this desolate stretch of mineral-rich earth, there was another group of lonesome pioneers: the *pampinos*. They were the original miners of the Atacama and the first to seal its destiny as the driving force of the modern Chilean economy. They came to the desert to extract saltpeter, also known as potassium nitrate, which had its heyday between 1880 and 1925, when some 65 percent of the taxes recovered by the Chilean state came from this precious alkali metal.

Saltpeter is the mineral that first transformed the nation, allowing Chile to carve out railway lines, construct grand government buildings and pave roads beyond the capital. While it's found in many parts of the world, from California to the Far East, it was only in the bone-dry north of Chile that it was of sufficient grade and quantity for large-scale exploitation.

To extract the saltpeter, you needed workers. And to get workers to live in the middle of the desert, you needed towns. And so it was that, in the 1860s, the most unwelcoming tracts of the Atacama began welcoming folks from both Chile and abroad – all lured by the chance to make it rich in the nitrate boom. They settled in *oficinas*, or company towns, where they developed a unique *pampino* culture due to their spectacular isolation.

Useful as both a fertilizer and an explosive, Chilean saltpeter went on to transform the agricultural fields of Europe and fuel its battles. Some 200 nitrate towns had popped up across the Atacama by the industry's height during World War I, when mines here extracted a key ingredient for the gunpowder used on the far side of the Atlantic. It was, in the end, little bits of the desert that allowed Europeans to kill each other en masse.

As with most extractive industries, a boom lured these *pampinos* in and a bust (caused by the creation of synthetic fertilizers and smokeless powder) sent them away, all within a matter of 90 years. The Atacama was left littered with the ruins of a fleeting era.

^～^

I drive north along the Pan-American Highway on a road riddled with bizarre rock-themed pull-offs. The first takes me to a string of coastal boulders sheathed in orbicular granite, an extremely rare rock whose concentrically layered patterning gives it the look of leopard skin or some geological bacteria.

Next is an open-air "rock zoo." A sign claims that it has the world's largest collection of tafoni, a honeycomb-like weathering within coastal sandstone. I step outside for a stroll, but quickly realize that this unmanned roadside attraction has become something of a roadside bathroom for passing truckers; to see the tafoni, you must first tiptoe around petrified poop.

The only attractions on the road further north are the rusty carcasses of decades-old cars, which lie on the edge of the asphalt like lawn ornaments for a lonely highway.

About an hour north of Caldera, I reach the city of Chañaral, a graceless outpost of narrow streets and tin-roofed homes that looks as if it popped up accidentally, like mold on the edge of a dreary coast. Romani women and children beg for money on its main drag, Merino Jarpa, which is filled with *comida rápida* (fast food) and tacky dime-a-dozen discount stores. I exit almost as soon as I enter, pulling off the highway onto a bischofite road that takes me into the more serene landscapes of Pan de Azúcar National Park.

Leather-skinned men comb the empty beaches alongside the road here for a Medusa-like kelp called *huiro*, thwacking the crocodile-colored algae over their shoulders to haul it away to waiting trucks. Those trucks then bring this brown-green gold to nearby ports for shipment to the far side of the Pacific. Once in China, the *huiro* will be crushed into a raw material used in beauty products that are then shipped back out to malls around the world.

The market for *huiro* has become so profitable in recent years that the *huireros* no longer wait for the seaweed to wash up onshore; they now live in tents like nomads, roaming up and down the seaboard with dive equipment and crowbars. In the early morning hours, they plunge into the frigid sea to detach roots from the rocks that keep the kelp alive, irreparably deforesting the Atacama coast as voraciously as the mining industry defaces the inland desert.

^~^

I turn off the highway again at Taltal and immediately regret it.

I've begun to dread reaching towns in the Atacama because they so often shit on the otherwise inspiring landscape. Taltal is no exception. It appears downright apocalyptic upon entering, with trash strewn about grey-brown hills and half-broken homes clinging to the desperate earth.

Mercifully, Taltal has a soupçon of charm down by the ocean, where a long promenade includes towering wine palms and vibrant mosaics depicting the nomadic Changos, who lived in coves like this up until the Spanish conquest (about 5,000 modern Chileans claim Chango descendancy). Late 19th-century homes, painted in birthday-cake colors like dandelion-yellow, lavender, and robin-egg-blue, line the streets just back from the sea. Yet it's the central square, Plaza Arturo Prat, that's clearly Taltal's pride and joy.

On one end of the plaza is the salmon-colored Teatro Alhambra, a grand Georgian-style theater built of Oregon pine. On another side is the gold-and-turquoise Iglesia San Francisco Javier, a three-tiered church and clock tower that dates to 1890. The plaza itself is a lush green fantasy of flowering bougainvillea. At its heart lies a gurgling fountain, which is held up by four chubby-cheeked cherubs – one for each season of the year.

Taltal has a current population of around 10,000, but there were more than twice that number a century ago, when it was the third-largest nitrate port in Chile. Perhaps that's why, for such a small place, it has a colossal cemetery. Most of it is covered in Catholic mausoleums, but I find a section behind a baby-blue fence that's full of Protestant tombstones with English-language epitaphs. There are names like Baker, Buchanan and Burns.

These dearly departed Brits came to Taltal to get rich during the golden age of nitrate. Their legacy is most obvious in the tea time tradition of *elevenses*, which they popularized in English-owned saltpeter mines. Tea time spread from here across Chile, morphing into a wholly unique ritual that now takes place not at 11 a.m., but rather in the late afternoon, between lunch and dinner. Called *once*, it's considered Chile's "fourth meal," with the obligatory tea accompanied by bread (the roll-like *marraqueta* and biscuit-like *hallulla* are the preferred styles), as well as eggs, jam, butter, cheese, meats and mashed avocado.

When Felipe and I go over to his parents' house in Santiago in the evenings, *once* is typically the meal we eat. I always thought it was a kind of twee tradition dying out with their generation, but when I said as much to Chileans our age at a party once, I learned how very wrong I was.

Once is such a staple of Chilean culture that there are regional differences. Here in the north, desert-dwellers pair theirs with empanadas stuffed with candied *alcayota* (a fibrous gourd). In the German-influenced south, forest-dwellers couple their teas with *kuchen* (cake) sweetened by Patagonian berries. In the fertile Central Valley, you'll find strips of fried dough with lemon zest and powdered sugar known as *calzones rotos* (literally "ripped panties"). A fisherman on the coast might cap off a workday with a fried-fish sandwich, while those in the interior prefer *sopaipillas* (fried pastries spiced with pumpkin).

It'd be easy to assume that *once* ("eleven" in Spanish) was simply a bastardized translation of *elevenses*. But the most common origin story is that it was actually coded language for a secret ingredient miners slipped into their tea to be able to work in such an inhospitable environment: the 11-lettered *aguardiente*, a cheap and generic "firewater" swigged across Latin America. Alcohol plays no role in modern *onces*, but the name stuck nonetheless.

Taltal not only nurtured Chile's popular tea time ritual; it may actually be the birthplace of regional mining, too. Archeologists from the Universidad de Chile uncovered a 12,000-year-old iron-oxide mine here that they say is the oldest evidence of organized mining in the Americas. The find, discovered in 2008, pushed the known history of mining in the Americas back by more than 7,000 years.

I book a simple room not far from the ancient mine in one of Taltal's historic homes. I then find a café near the plaza for *once-comida* (a bountiful tea time that doubles as dinner). If it were 1920, I might have gone out to place bets at the horse races or enjoyed an evening of opera. Instead, a century later, I walk the crumbling streets back to my *hospedaje* and fall asleep to the symphony of street dogs commencing their nightly brawl.

^ ~ ^

The titanic multi-tiered ruins at the southern end of Antofagasta are not at all what they seem. They're not, as I'd first imagined, some ancient Incan citadel. They weren't built by any Indigenous community. They aren't even that old. The Huanchaca ruins are, despite their Machu Picchu–esque appearance, only from the turn of the 20th century, and they're little more than the remains of a stone refinery for the Bolivian Huanchaca Company, one of the richest silver-mining operations of the late 1800s.

Antofagasta is, today, the largest city in the north of Chile, with nearly half a million residents. Until the 1870s, however, it was an important port of Bolivia. During the War of the Pacific (1879–83), a minor dispute over taxes led Chile to invade the nitrate-rich lands of Bolivia and Peru. That war, which ended with a Chilean victory, proved extremely consequential for all involved: it landlocked Bolivia, robbed Peru of the northern Atacama and deprived both nations of the mineral bounty that would transform Chile into one of the richest countries in Latin America. And so it was that this desert, much of which didn't even belong to Chile for most of its existence, became the very place that would shape the trajectory of the nation's modern history.

All that mineral wealth surrounding Antofagasta has turned it into Chile's richest city by GDP per capita – though, like every-where else in this divided nation, the gap between the rich and poor is immense and noticeable.

Generally, the haves live down by the beach in shiny apartment blocks overlooking leafy boulevards that make you forget you're just a few dozen miles away from Yungay, one of the driest places on earth. The Playa Blanca neighborhood, in particular, is clean, modern and full of beauty salons. Half of it is low-rise, low-key backstreets, while the other is a high-rise oceanfront avenue that attempts something of a Miami vibe. Its residents all seem to have vastly different opinions of the weather. Some are in bathing suits, others sweaters. This despite the fact that the perennial forecast here at the Tropic of Capricorn is perfectly and predictably pleasant: lows in the mid-60s, highs in the mid-70s, sunshine and zero chance of rain.

The have-nots live in tin-roofed shacks in the barren hills above town, out of sight and out of mind. Many are immigrants from Haiti and Venezuela, and they find work hiding the true nature of this hyper-arid city. Dressed in neon-yellow jumpsuits, they wander in search of places to water, including Plaza Colón, the central square, which has a miniature replica of Big Ben (a rather patronizing donation from Britain), as well as an ornate gazebo (a classier gift from Croatia). Without their hose work, the bougainvillea, Norfolk pines, wine palms and jacarandas that give the place its verdant façade would shrivel up and die.

On the whole, Antofagasta has a surprising charm for a place that friends in the capital told me was *feo* (ugly) and *flaite* (tacky). It's a bit like the Tulsa of Chile: not somewhere you'd seek out, but nicer than you'd think once you arrive thanks to all that money it's made sucking the earth dry.

^~^

There is perhaps no place that evokes Chile's nitrate era more persuasively than Humberstone, a UNESCO World Heritage site that's part ghost town, part industrial graveyard. And there is no one who knows the *pampino* culture that thrived here better than Patricio Díaz Valencia, the director of heritage at the organization that runs the place, Corporación Museo del Salitre.

Born in 1945, Patricio spent 30 years of his life working with saltpeter in the waning era of the industry. That's why it's become his life's obsession to keep the story of the *pampinos* from fading into history – though he's quick to clarify that he doesn't consider himself one of them. "I worked with the type of people who lived this life," he says when we meet in his small office at Humberstone, which is covered in the awards and certificates that earmarked his career. "I learned their personalities, their ways of being, who they were as a people."

To show me what he means, we take a stroll around the old company town, which was founded in 1872 by English chemical engineer James Thomas Humberstone. It's located on a desolate patch of bone-dry desert and once housed up to 3,700 people. Ultimately abandoned in 1960, it now contains only faint echoes of their lonesome existence.

"People from all over the world came here," Patricio remarks as we leave his office. "After one generation, this new society came to be known as *pampino*. A kid who was born here was born not with the culture of their mother or father, or where they came from; they were born into a culture that was their own, which was created here on the pampa."

Aging wooden homes groan in strong gusts of wind as Patricio and I walk along the path back from the entrance. Because the desert is nature's embalmer, Humberstone lies before me in a state of perfect abandon, its empty stores and meeting halls like canvases on which to paint tragic stories. Some are rusty and bleak, with screechy hinges, kind of like the ruins of Chernobyl;

others house vestiges of the era – ceramic jugs to store rationed water in one; wrought iron toys made for kids in another.

Patricio says he spent four years cleaning the town between 2006 and 2010, part of a mandate from UNESCO to make it safer and more accessible to visitors. He removed all the cobwebs, reinforced the slumping roofs and catalogued the discarded relics into thematic rooms, transforming many of the old buildings into dioramas of a lost era.

"There are still a few old folks who lived here as kids," Patricio says as we follow an abandoned train line to a rusting caboose. "They come back every November with their walking sticks to poke around. So we wanted to make sure that we conserved the character of the place right down to the colors on the buildings and the letters on the signs."

The main plaza is lovingly restored and shaded by *tamarugo* trees. I imagine the radio dramas that would blast over loudspeakers here in the evenings. These aural spectacles, which followed the spoken news, would see the whole town gather for nightly entertainment as the heat of the afternoon swung toward the crisp of night.

Towering above one side of the plaza is the pea-green church, whose wooden clock tower determined daily schedules. Patricio says religious festivals were the events that broke up the hard years. These were, he adds, highly devout communities, where survival was tenuous and God was both feared and celebrated in equal measure.

We dip into the forest-green theater on the far end of the plaza. Styled in the Art Deco fashion of the time, it could fit up to 350 *pampinos*. They'd crowd down the red-carpeted isles, file into thin rows of wooden seats and wait for the velvet curtains to fold open with applause. One week there might be a concert; the next a play, a *zarzuela* (traditional operetta) or, in later years, a silent movie.

Most company towns had a theater just like this one. Actors such as Willy Zegarra, who performed social commentary, and singers like Jorge Negrete, who sang Mexican *rancheras*, made it big touring the desert, performing in all the dusty company towns from here to the Peruvian border.

Patricio says the center of activity on the plaza – when there wasn't a show – was the *pulpería*, or company store. Here, you could buy the fabrics to make your clothes, the grains to make your meals and even ice to cool your drinks. The *pulpería* also housed a bakery and a butcher shop – everything you might need to survive another day in the desert.

What you couldn't find at the *pulpería*, you'd look for at the market, which lay on the south side of the plaza. It would bustle with all kinds of products and services, from haircuts to fruits from the oasis of Pica. Adjacent to it was the town's lone hotel, where industry bigwigs would strike high-powered deals in the kind of stiff, starched outfits most *pampinos* could only dream of wearing.

Beyond the plaza we find a now-empty pool made of repurposed iron plates, which were scrapped from tanks used to treat saltpeter. I picture parents sitting on the pine bleachers above it, watching as kids whisk dirt off their faces, splashing away under the piercing sun. Near the pool lie cricket fields (used mostly by men) and a basketball court (used mostly by women) whose net posts now swan dive toward the sandy ground.

Patricio takes me to the one-room San Mauricio schoolhouse. Its floors creak with age as we enter. Kids, many of whom were born to illiterate parents, were able to get a basic education at the wooden dollhouse-like desks here. But that education only

lasted to age 11. "The conditions were tough and the life expect-
ancy was short," Patricio says. "At 12, you became a worker. By 16
you were considered an adult, and by 55 you were dead."

Working in the mines was grueling and physically dangerous.
Company towns like Humberstone were also heavily segregated.
"You needed a special pass to cross from the worker side to the
management side," Patricio says. "And they had living conditions completely distinct from the laborers, who realized, over
time, that the system wasn't working for them.

"The fight for social justice," he adds, "really began from there."

Walking around Humberstone, you can still sense the dreams
and dramas that unfolded here. There were the silent bonds
forged over clanking machinery. There were the friendships
wound tight by isolation, and the kisses backlit by a hostile sun.
You can also sense the sacrifice and struggle that launched the
seminal protest movement of a generation.

The residents of Humberstone may be gone, but they left behind a legacy that would change the nation. At the turn of the
20th century, unrest spread from one nitrate town to the next.
It's remarkable, really, that it didn't happen sooner. Finally,
pampinos across the region were mobilizing, petitioning for
improvements in both their working and living conditions.

Many felt increasingly trapped, earning not pesos but *fichas*
(tokens) that could only be spent in the *pulperías*, markets and
other facilities owned by the mines that employed them. That
ruse had to end, they said. They also wanted a fixed minimum
wage, new safety measures and, more than anything, a system
that didn't leave them helpless when managers laid down laws
to live by with no government oversight. Those who complained
found themselves wandering off into the desert in search of the

next company town – all with little more than the shirts on their backs.

In a massive region-wide strike in December of 1907, thousands of workers converged on the city of Iquique, grinding the nation's most important industry to a halt. They gathered with their wives and children at the Santa María School, asking the government to mediate between them and the nitrate bosses (many of whom worked for firms based not in Santiago but in the faraway capitals of Europe). Negotiations stalled. Tensions flared.

The demonstrations happened at a time when the price of nitrate had dipped, as had wages. Sensing an imminent threat to the nation's economic model, President Pedro Montt sent the military to Iquique to clear out the protestors. However, they refused to leave. The *pampinos* were given one hour to vacate the Santa María School. Otherwise, troops would open fire.

An hour came and went, but these men, hardened under the desert heat, weren't about to back down now. They reiterated their demands. They stood strong. They never anticipated the bloodbath. They never grasped how little their lives meant to the country they'd made rich.

The government didn't issue death certificates. It barely acknowledged anything had happened to the men, who were buried in mass graves. The Santa María School Massacre, Patricio says as we tour a small museum about it at Humberstone, would be swept under the carpet for decades.

It's estimated that as many as 3,600 people died that day, though the real number may be closer to 2,000. A reign of terror ensued at company towns, but the *pampinos* played the long game. Labor unrest persisted, workers shut down more mines, and when little changed, they formed some of the first trade unions in Latin America. These workers of the Atacama birthed the nation's earliest socialist movements, setting the stage for many of the seminal events in modern Chilean history.

It was artists and activists who resurrected the massacre, uncovering bits and pieces of hidden history over time. The stories they learned of the *pampinos*, of their struggle for dignity, would soon echo across the decades, taking on an almost mythical aura.

In 1970, the year Salvador Allende embarked upon his socialist transformation of Chile, the folk band Quilapayún released the album *Cantata de Santa María de Iquique*, written by the Iquique-born composer Luis Advis. It was one of the most influential disks of the Nueva Canción Chilena movement and one of the most lauded Spanish-language albums of all time.

The cantata speaks of the increasingly tense struggle between the miners and their exploiters through song and spoken narration. It became so closely tied to the messaging of the Allende era that, in the early days of the dictatorship, in 1973, the military destroyed all copies of it. The narrative threads unspooled in Quilapayún's music felt less like a historical struggle than a universal tale repeating itself. The band had no choice but to live in exile in Europe for more than a decade thereafter.

Not long after the return to democracy, Quilapayún staged a historic show at the company town two miles west of Humberstone, Santa Laura, performing the cantata in full. Various other Chilean acts interpreted the work for anniversary events in 2007. When the *estallido social* erupted in 2019, the massacre at the Santa María School – and its legacy in popular culture – was fresh on the minds of protestors.

Walking around Humberstone with Patricio, I could draw parallels between what happened here, in this tiny microcosm of society, and what's just happened on the streets of Santiago.

When a million people gathered at Plaza Italia that October day, refusing to leave, that too was a stand against the system. It feels surreal to have been part of that moment, to have been a witness to history.

One of Quilapayún's other songs of the Allende years, "El pueblo unido jamás será vencido," became a rallying cry of the 2019 protests. "The people united will never be defeated" speaks of a collective fight for a more just society. It expresses solidarity and resistance. And I can't help but think of the song as a companion piece to the *Santa María de Iquique* album. It was the deafening chant of the rallies I went to with Felipe. It was the message rattling around in my head back when I was still piecing together what was happening in my adopted home, wondering if it needed to go up in flames to be rebuilt anew.

^ ~ ^

Iquique is a sprawling city of 200,000 people hemmed against the ocean by a wall of suffocating dunes. There's an air of anything-goes that's evident not only in the mood of the place but also in the architecture, with buildings that sprout like sporadic weeds from lifeless soil. The Atacama at its flashiest (or, perhaps, trashiest?), the city aims for glitz, but so often gets trapped up by its ghosts.

The glitz, naturally, is easy to find. There are the skyscrapers that line Playa Cavancha beach, which light up in purple and red each night like Disney castles. There are the nearby reggaeton clubs and pisco bars where women wear very little clothing. I let the city try and woo me for a few days, willing myself to like the place. I even enter the casino, relishing a dark, air-conditioned refuge from the desert. But all I see inside are ghosts.

Off-duty miners and their wives have become transfixed by

the machines, intoxicated by the neon displays, tranquilized with overstimulation. One hand on the screen, the other gripping a drooping cigarette, they forfeit money to a backdrop of generic oldies ("Funkytown" by Lipps Inc., "Beautiful Life" by Ace of Base). All the while, they look, to me, like animals in colorful cages, their zoo upholstered in the kind of dizzying patterns found on bus seats and in bowling alleys. I feel sad as I look on, a silent witness sipping *piscolas* at the bar.

The *zona franca*, the largest free economic zone in South America, is more of the same. It, too, is meant to numb the senses. Called Mall Zofri, this labyrinthine shopping district is filled with jewelry stores, car dealerships, perfume outlets and, more than anything else, shops selling the world's most unsellable name-brand clothing. Mall Zofri is the end of the road for the latter after it's journeyed from factories in Asia to shops in the US or Europe, ending up in duty-free purgatory in Chile. What's not sold at Mall Zofri (or transported onward illegally to the rest of South America) ends up in massive piles in the desert. They grow by up to 39,000 tons (35,000 t) each year, making Iquique the graveyard of consumerism and a tangible example of everything wrong with fast fashion.

There are more visceral ghosts in Iquique, too. Those of the fallen *pampinos* from Humberstone and other company towns. The victims of drug trafficking over the Bolivian border. The immigrants from Bolivia, Peru, Colombia and Venezuela, who live in squalor in the satellite city of Alto Hospicio.

Then, there are the victims of the coup. I stumble upon black-and-white pictures of them atop empty chairs placed in rows for a commemorative ceremony in Plaza Condell. On each photo is a name, plus the location where they were detained and ultimately "disappeared." For some, it was Estadio Nacional in

Santiago; for others it was right here in Iquique. Floating above the chairs are white and red balloons.

The disappeared, sitting on chairs in Plaza Condell, were mostly socialists and communists. They were the people who ushered Salvador Allende to power in 1970 and then suffered repression, torture and untimely death during the brutal military regime that toppled him.

The group organizing today's event is the Agrupación de Familiares de Ejecutados Políticos y Detenidos Desaparecidos de Iquique y Pisagua, or AFEPI, which is kind of a second family for those most deeply affected by the dictatorship era. Everyone in the crowd seems to know each other well, having forged tight bonds over the decades through a shared grief of loss without closure.

AFEPI President Héctor Marín takes to the microphone, describing the events that led these men to join the ranks of the disappeared. "They called on our men to present themselves to the authorities, and they did so voluntarily, even arriving with wives and kids, thinking that this was just a small procedural measure," he says. "None of them had committed any crimes; they only held the ideals and dreams of having a Chile that was fair and just for all."

Later, he says, when the reality of the situation became clear, "a profound sadness spread through our city, through our entire country." So the dissidents united.

"In parallel to the repression – and the climate of terror – brought about by the dictatorship, we were organizing in a clandestine way," Héctor says. "First, it was just to get information and to find out what happened not just in Iquique, but across the country. Since the day of the coup, we've never paused in our efforts to seek justice against those who committed state-sponsored terrorism on our streets."

Héctor then commences a roll call. When he announces the name of a disappeared person from Iquique, the crowd chants in unison, "*Presente*" (present).

"Manuel Araya."

"*Presente.*"

"Nolberto Cañas."

"*Presente.*"

"Pedro Mella."

"*Presente.*"

Héctor dedicates the final portion of the roll call to the men discovered in 1990 in unmarked graves in the prison camp of Pisagua, 100 miles (160 km) north of Iquique. He describes the horrors they lived through, and then the crowd chants, "*Presente.*"

"I'm telling you they are all here," Héctor affirms. "They are here with us right now."

A grey-haired widow stands in the center of the plaza to perform the *cueca sola*, a traditional dance forged in the early days of the dictatorship by the wives of political prisoners and the families of those missing. Back then, it was a symbolic gesture of resistance to Pinochet, with the woman dancing *sola* (alone) when she should be performing a duet. Now, it's a reminder of the injustices of the era – and how most have gone unaddressed.

The widow waves her red handkerchief in the air, twirling in half circles while clomping heels to the ground, her eyes lost to a memory. Pinned to her white blouse are photos of a man who vanished nearly 50 years ago. The lyrics of the *cueca* are haunting and painful. They express the grief, so pervasive in the turbulent climate of the 1970s, of not knowing where your partner was or who might be spying on you or what tomorrow might bring.

They recall an era when Chileans stopped speaking to each other, when nobody knew who was who anymore.

"Day after day, more people are dying without reparations or ever getting justice," Héctor bellows into the microphone when the dance is complete, imploring those in the crowd to release the balloons into the cloudy mid-morning air. "Today we are here in this plaza remembering. We are making memories for the disappeared. We maintain faith, and hope, that with the great uncertainty we face, a new constitution will guarantee all of our human rights – and that, my compatriots, will be the fruits of our labor."

^ ~ ^

The Atacama, like other deserts around the world, has been treated so many times throughout history like the wasteland many believe it to be. It's become a sanctuary for predators, a cage for prey, and a dustbin in which to sweep away unspeakable crimes. Nowhere is the darkness of this desert more tangible than in Pisagua.

Inhabited by the Indigenous Changos for centuries (as evidenced by the ancient midden deposits at Pisagua Viejo, which lie at the mouth of a dry riverbed two miles to the north), it grew to importance in the 19th century as a prosperous nitrate port, changing hands from Peru to Chile after the War of the Pacific. One of the richest cities along the coast at the start of the 20th century, 50 years later it was all but abandoned.

As it declined in importance as an industrial hub – for nitrate and later fishmeal – it gained a new life as a prison colony. Those perceived to have shamed, repulsed or endangered society were locked up between sheer rock walls and the thrashing Pacific, trapped here in a natural cage.

I really, truly, did not want to visit Pisagua. I knew this town would utterly depress me. Parents in Chile used to tell kids to behave or they'd end up in Pisagua. Soccer fans would taunt poorly performing players by shouting at coaches to ship them to Pisagua. Pisagua has become a synonym for hell. But here I am. And I guess I needed to come. If my goal is to uncover the real character of the desert, to understand it better, I know I have to deal with the unsavory and uncomfortable bits, too.

I begin my descent into this cursed port on the pampa high above, navigating a sunny plain of beige hills as the ocean inches closer on the horizon. Suddenly, the road curves into a thin fold between two towering mountains and emerges anew on the narrow edge of a sheer rock face buffeted by thick coastal fog.

The path down to Pisagua is ostensibly two-way, yet it is wide enough for only one car. There's nothing but the angry ocean below to catch me if I slip. Sand patches trick my wheels on impossibly sharp horseshoe bends as I creep around one turn, then another, my feet slamming on the brakes to fight the precipitous decline.

The landscape out my windshield is at once hellish and awesome. There's a sheer cliff to the east and an empty ocean to the west. Sandwiched in between is a small ghost town with faint sparks of life. I can see now why Pisagua has often piqued the darker instincts of despots. It is, after all, nature's perfect prison.

Descending into its waterfront, I find the *huiro* seaweed drying on what's meant to be a public plaza, giving Pisagua a fitting odor of decay. Nearby is the grand old train station, a shell of its former self. The bones of other abandoned buildings are covered in graffiti, their rafters housing packs of vultures.

A few palm trees on the main drag make a futile attempt at cheering the place up. That's because 256 people still live here, down from a historic high of about 3,000. I find a few of them squatting in makeshift homes built behind century-old facades; most live in shabby newer constructions in the hills above.

Many of the abandoned ruins downtown are now covered in street murals. Some depict oceanscapes; others sailors and fishermen, an homage to the only folks brave enough to live in Pisagua in the 21st century. The murals guide me to an old Georgian theater with faded trimmings and collapsing balconies, which sat hundreds at the height of the nitrate era, when opera companies from Europe toured the boomtowns of this faraway desert. Out front is the entertainment of today: a pimpled teenager, drunk on pisco, rapping Latin trap beats to an audience of one.

I stroll from the theater over to the former jail, which is painted a deceptively cheery bubblegum-pink. This neoclassical building dates to 1910 and was one of the main structures used to house political prisoners (others have now been either destroyed or repurposed). It was briefly transformed into a luxury hotel in the 1990s, when right-wing investors sought to gloss over the past by turning Pisagua into a resort town – a tactless idea that failed spectacularly.

The ex-jail stands adjacent to – and towers above – a newer field where kids play soccer, giving downtown a cyclical aura of death and rebirth. Even still, the place feels irrevocably stuck in time. The ornate blue-and-white clock tower, which looms on a hill over the port, seems to suggest as much; it's forever frozen at nine o'clock.

Pinochet spent much of his early military career in the north. He knew its unique ability to sweep away sins. He even oversaw Pisagua for a brief time in the late 1940s, when President Gabriel González Videla turned it into a concentration camp for 500 or so Marxists.

In his memoirs, the then-lieutenant wrote that it was here in Pisagua that he had his first direct contact with communism: "I was much concerned that such pernicious and contaminating ideas should continue to be taught in Chile," he said, calling Pisagua "a true Marxist-Leninist University where people were [despite a ban on political activity by prisoners] trained or would later act as agitators."

A congressional commission came to inspect the conditions at the camp during Pinochet's short reign. He turned them away at gunpoint. Among the commission members present that day was his future adversary, Salvador Allende.

When Pinochet amassed absolute power over the nation three decades later, it was in places like this in the Atacama that he chose to imprison his enemies. The military would often conceal their bones in shallow graves. To this day relatives, like those I met in Iquique, continue to sift through the desert, digging for the disappeared.

Other bones lie right here in the cemetery on the northern edge of town, where hundreds of wooden crosses poke out of the desert like toothpicks in a sandbox. Many crosses don't have names; they rise up a barren hill in anonymity. Other graves don't even have crosses; small sand moguls are the only indications of the bodies buried below.

The cemetery looks like a set piece from some dystopian horror film. Walking through it, I can't help but hear mysterious sounds, like faint unintelligible whispers. Maybe it's just the sea breeze brushing past my ear. Or perhaps it's the lost spirits of Pisagua coming back to haunt the place.

In June of 1990, soon after the return of democracy, two local men (following the tips of ex-prisoners) unearthed a mass grave on the edge of Pisagua's cemetery. Twenty-one bodies had been mummified almost exactly as they died thanks to the coastal salt, making it easy to link them to those missing and executed at the neighboring camp. Many still wore blindfolds and hand ties. Two were mutilated. One was beheaded. The bullet holes were plainly obvious. The discovery made headlines around the world. It was yet another dark chapter in an incredibly bleak era.

The 7-by-45-foot (2×14 m) grave is, today, a big empty hole surrounded by a chain-link fence. I find several fresh carnations woven into its coils. Nearby are a half-dozen memorials to "lives lost in the construction of a free, fair and solidary homeland." Above is an area with tiered seating, like an amphitheater. I walk up and take a seat, stewing over all the trauma buried in the desert here.

Many of the 800 or so dissidents imprisoned at Pisagua were kidnapped from their homes by secret police who denied their whereabouts to anyone who asked. Upon arriving at this forlorn port, usually by ship, they weren't always confined to a solitary cell. Given the natural isolation, Pisagua was at times more like an open-air prison where men wasted away days fishing for their meals and spent cool nights studying the stars.

Death loomed over the concentration camp in the early days, as did the threat of torture. Techniques for the latter may have been imported from Nazi Germany. A mid-ranking SS commander named Walter Rauff – one of the most wanted Nazi fugitives of the 1970s, who made a name for himself developing mobile gassing vans – has long been linked to Pisagua as its torturer-in-chief.

Felipe grew up around stories of Pisagua – the kind that hit close to home. Pepe Caucoto, the father of some of his favorite cousins, was tortured and imprisoned here for several months before being transferred unexpectedly to another facility in

Patagonia (he later fled to exile in Ecuador). Pepe had been an ardent leftist and vocal political activist in Iquique in the early 1970s. Since Felipe's parents and the Caucotos were the only left-leaning members of their respective family circles, they became extremely close – especially when Pepe returned to Chile in the 1980s and became a prominent member of the Party for Democracy (PPD).

Felipe always knew that his uncle had been tortured, but the family didn't talk about it. He was too young to fully understand the dark side of humanity, and his parents gave few details – until stories about Pisagua appeared on the nightly news in 1990. That year, when investigators found the mass grave, they always turned up the television.

There are few photos of the prison camp from the early days of the Pinochet dictatorship. One that does exist – and always featured prominently in those news stories – depicts a group of bare-chested men. They're standing in two parallel lines, their hands bound behind bronzed backs. *That one is Pepe*, Felipe's parents would tell him, pointing to a young man in the middle. Felipe could tell, even at that young age, that his uncle's eyes were different back then. He knew Pepe as a kind man, the family joker. In the news stories, his uncle seethed with quiet rage.

Before I came here, I knew that Pisagua had been used as a penal colony not just during the Pinochet dictatorship but also several times in recent history. What I didn't realize was that the first time it served that purpose was to lock away homosexuals, who were brutally repressed in Chile under the rule of the deeply homophobic dictator Carlos Ibáñez del Campo (whose namesake son was believed to be gay).

Legend has it that he had them – us – rounded up and thrown out of ships into the Pacific with weights around their – our – ankles.

What's certain is that Ibáñez del Campo brought male homosexuals to Pisagua from prisons across the country as a way to
isolate them – us – from the rest of society, just as Pisagua's mass
exodus was taking place. The gays got shipped to Pisagua, and
everyone else fled. The first concentration camp here was born.

^ ~ ^

Everything I represent as a gay man with progressive ideals is
what Pisagua sought to sequester. I think that's why the place
repulses me so much. It's got too many ghosts. They're too close
to home. But traveling here via the Mina San José, Humberstone
and Iquique has helped me to connect some dots. I see now how
the north came to shape the ideology of both Chile's working
class and the political left that represents them. The stories these
places tell may be tragic and uncomfortable, but they feel particularly vital amid the backdrop of a new constitution.

The Atacama, I now realize, is full of tragic stories. There are
the *pampinos* who marched to their death in Iquique, the miners
buried alive near Copiapó, the gays and socialists who ended up
in Pisagua. Each one gets me a little bit closer to understanding
this desert and how it shaped this country.

6 READING THE COCA LEAVES

(THE LIFE AND LEGENDS OF THE LIKAN ANTAI)

A full moon curves across the sky over the oasis of Coyo toward distant mountains made of salt. Carlos Vega and his wife, Sandra Flores, have been expecting this moment. They've been waiting for me join them, preparing a billowing bonfire for a cleansing ceremony at dusk.

At over six feet tall – in a country where the average height is five seven – Carlos commands attention, especially with his red checkered poncho and long black hair, which is tied in a ponytail below a pair of sturdy shoulders. Sandra is much smaller, some strands of her chin-length hair momentarily in the mouth of a grandchild, Gaspar, who's swaddled in a *manta* (blanket) wrapped around her back. She and Carlos are both huddled together next to the fire, standing above a mound of coca leaves.

"We clean ourselves with the coca leaves to clean our body energy, because we believe there are lots of things that are stuck in our bodies, and the only way to get them out is like this," explains Carlos, rubbing the leaves across his wide frame.

I follow Carlos's instructions, reaching down to scoop a pile of leaves into my sun-cracked hands. I then rub them, rather awkwardly, from my toes up to my head.

"Next, we must give them to the Pachamama, the Mother Earth," Carlos continues, gesturing for me to toss them into the flames, where they pop like firecrackers. "In this way we believe we can reach a harmony once again with nature. Because everything we do is about energy, about intentions."

The intention of the moment is a cleansing of the mind and spirit. It'll take place in the Sweat Lodge Carlos and Sandra built in their backyard in this small *ayllu*, or Indigenous-run community, on the outskirts of the resort town of San Pedro de Atacama. Yet, as with most ceremonies here, everything begins with the coca leaves.

Scientists first isolated these leaves' psychoactive cocaine alkaloid in the late 1850s, inventing a range of medicines, tonics and drinks, including the original Coca-Cola and its little-remembered predecessor, a coca-infused wine called Vin Mariani. Pope Leo XIII endorsed the latter in promotional posters; it was equally beloved by inventors (Thomas Edison), actors (Sarah Bernhardt) and US presidents (Ulysses S. Grant).

Sigmund Freud was one of cocaine's loudest early promoters, calling it a cure for depression and sexual impotence and saying that a small dose "lifted me to the heights in a wonderful fashion." People started snorting the substance by the 1910s, leading to an inevitable fall from grace by the 1920s, when it was banned in most countries (and relegated to the underworld).

Here, among members of the Likan Antai community, coca leaves are – and have always been – sacred. They're one of the world's oldest stimulants of natural origin, cultivated in Andean societies for at least 8,000 years and chewed to suppress hunger, pain or fatigue, as well as to fight the effects of altitude. The stimulus is mild and has little in common with the illicit cocaine extracted elsewhere.

Carlos and Sandra have recently welcomed me into their home – and I'll be staying for the better part of a month – so this coca ceremony is to be something of an initiation. It's also, I'm told, a way for me to clear my thoughts. In the Sweat Lodge, I'll release stress and bodily toxins, and open up to deeper contemplation – or at least, that's the goal.

Sweat Lodges are found in Indigenous communities up and

down the Americas – though there are different forms and techniques. In Latin America, there is typically a series of four *puertas* (or doors) to pass through, with each one involving new intentions and a higher level of heat. Here, among the Likan Antai, the rocks for the ceremony need to be from the Licancabur Volcano, which looms large on the lumpy horizon.

"This is our volcano protector," Sandra explained to me earlier in the day during the three hours she and Carlos roasted its fragments over an open flame. "We use these rocks because they're more resistant to burning and then receiving water; others would crack."

Now, Carlos is placing the first stones inside the clay dome. Meanwhile, my nerves are prickling. I'm no fan of extreme heat, but within minutes, I strip off layers, fall to my knees and crawl inside. What I find on the other end is like an earthen womb. There are pillows, colorful *mantas* and instruments: a *quena* flute in one corner, a drum of stretched llama skin in the other. In the center is a steaming pit, my only light. It glows like the innards of that distant volcano.

Carlos arrives to fill the pit with more smoldering stones, a scoop of water, a blast of heat. "Let's begin by thinking about the earth, about the animals that fly above, as well as those who maintain four feet on the ground below," he commands before departing.

Sweat grows from beads to blobs. Soon, it's creeping around my body, forming rivers that flow into cascades. My hair, formerly dry, wilts into a leaky faucet, drip-dropping into my clouding eyes. My mind races to the high-altitude *puna*, that better-watered realm of the Atacama choked with brush. It has become my happy place on this trip. I let its swaying grasses, lanky camelids and hungry raptors lull me away.

Fifteen minutes pass and, like clockwork, Carlos arrives with more smoldering stones, a scoop of water, a blast of heat. Liquid splashes into steam; the pit crackles anew with primal energy. Sandra has infused the water with local herbs: the caramel-like *chañar*, the nutty *algarrobo*, the citrusy *rica-rica*. Their aromas permeate the ever-thickening air.

"Focus now on your friends and family," he implores. "Dive deep into the meaning of your relationships."

I grab the drum and bang on it until my hands find a rhythm. In that rhythm, I block out the world beyond. I use the hypnotic beat to dive inwards, stewing on the friends and family I left to live here. I think about the newer relationships built abroad, and how they were harder won. I wonder where my allegiances lie. *Can you ever really leave home and still keep what you left behind? If not, can you ever really find that same sense of belonging anywhere else again?*

My mind drifts to Felipe and the challenges of sustaining an international relationship. There are the unintended missteps. The accidental miscommunications. The failures at integration. The inherited mores. The added layers of queerness and race. There are the ways we've met in the middle. There is the baggage we're unwilling to change. There are the times we understand so much about each other until, suddenly, puzzlingly, we don't.

I think of our canyons and our bridges and the roads we're building around it all. I wonder if the foundations are sturdy. Are we okay, in the tedium of a decade-old relationship? Or is it possible that we're perpetuating a slow-motion breakup neither of us is willing to admit? Will this trip make any difference at all? Or is it a selfish endeavor in the guise of some search for greater meaning?

Fifteen minutes pass and there's more smoldering stones, a scoop of water, a blast of heat. The pit emits a hissing noise. I surrender my body to the space, acquiescing to a trance-like state, beating away at the llama skin drum as I sway from side to side. The temperature climbs above 100 degrees Fahrenheit (38°C). The floor is now puddled with sweat. My body is as slippery as a seal's.

Breathe in. Breathe out. Breathe in. Breathe out. Keep pushing...

"Who are you?" comes the next, seemingly simple prompt, which throws me even deeper inside my head. Or rather, outside this world. *Why is this question so hard?* I dive inward. *Who are you?* I feel like I've stopped feeling things lately, like my mind went numb for a while. But this trip is making me sensitive again. There's a rekindling. I care more. I'm shedding some of my cynicism. I'm also learning how geography can change a person.

I've now lived in this country long enough to feel like I've dived down the deep end of something and lost the directions back. The more I travel through the Atacama, the deeper I go. I'm unlocking mysteries about myself, even if I don't know what to make of them just yet. What I do know is that this land is starting to leave its mark on me. Each day a little bit more. So I keep journeying, slogging through the desert, searching for meaning in the stories I'm told.

Breathe in. Breathe out. Breathe in. Breathe out. Keep pushing...

My eyes no longer feel the need to stay open. Meanwhile, my breaths are getting longer, harder and more intentional. Time passes. Minutes. Or maybe a half hour? I'm not sure about anything until, suddenly, there is an absence of heat. The cool, dry evening air rushes into the dome, fulfilling the elemental cycle of earth, fire, water and wind. A chill runs up my spine. My eyes go wide. The drumming stops. A bucket of cool rainwater lands atop my head; pores closed, cleansing complete.

^ ~ ^

Foreign tourists love to tick the driest desert on earth off their global bucket lists, but they all invariably go to the same spot where everyone else has gone before them: San Pedro de Atacama. This is the only place in the vast and inhospitable desert that most outsiders will ever see. It's where your classic adventure types go, decked out in two layers of North Face jackets, Columbia pants with zip-off legs and Oakley glasses with lenses that double as mirrors.

Since you can't really be a pioneer anymore (what's left on earth to discover?) they come to role-play the idea, seeking novel experiences, managed suffering and grammable content. They look for authenticity. What they don't realize is that San Pedro is the very place that any local will tell you has simply codified a regional identity – one that never really existed until it became profitable and desirable to outsiders.

The "San Pedro style" is both a description and a prescription, developed over centuries by the Likan Antai until it was frozen in time and co-opted by the government to become a regional vernacular. Whether it's truly authentic or not is probably irrelevant to most visitors; there's no denying the town's aesthetic appeal. It's accessibly quaint, with dirt streets, cobbled plazas and whitewashed adobe facades. Step to the far side of any one of them and you find a riot of colors in the textiles that hang from walls, double as rugs and wrap around every seat cushion. The horizon is alluring, too, with ominous volcanoes to the east and a salt-crusted "moon valley" to the west. San Pedro is, as all oases are, a swath of green in a sea of brown.

Downtown is backpacker central. It's got all the chipper touts, cheap bars and could-be-anywhere coffee shops that make it a key stop on the Gringo Trail, that blogged-about South American circuit whose pilgrims roam foreign lands in pajamas and would like to be known as *travelers, not tourists.*

There are artisanal ice cream shops with local flavors like *chañar*, *algarrobo* and *rica-rica*, but also "artisan" markets with mass-produced goods made in China or across the border in Bolivia. There are restaurants that blast endless panpipe music and serve approachable versions of local llama dishes. Splashed across walls in between these venues are posters demanding an end to lithium mining, which is depleting the area of its precious water. Yet the few tourists here to see them don't seem interested in learning about things that might momentarily bum them out.

Just beyond all this, down the dusty country lanes, are the lavish, Andean-style all-inclusive luxury resorts that cater to in-and-out jet-setters who will never set foot in town. There are a half dozen of these properties, and they cost upwards of US$1,000 a night. Nowhere is the Atacama more prized – and less despised – than here.

This valley's dramatic transformation from an isolated collection of Likan Antai *ayllus* to Chile's largest tourist destination north of Santiago is a recent phenomenon. The evolution took off largely at the end of the dictatorship, with San Pedro growing exponentially in the years up to the *estallido social* and pandemic. Now, however, with borders only recently reopened, it looks a bit like a deserted set piece – like some abandoned theme town at Andean Disneyland just sputtering back to life.

It's only in places like Coyo, about 20 minutes outside of San

Pedro, that you can get a glimpse of how this region looked before it was "discovered." Coyo never really relied on tourism, so it doesn't appear any different today than it would have in 2019 or 1999. It is, as a travel pamphlet might boast, "authentic"... whatever that means.

.^ ~ ^

It's water day in Coyo, and mud-brown sludge is now gurgling through a canal at the far end of Sandra and Carlos's sprawling property. Their teenage daughters, Catalina and Taina, race after it, shovels in hand, with just 90 minutes to flood the entire field. To do so, they need to open and close a series of trap doors, channeling water to the left, and then the right. When gravity sends it flowing all the wrong directions, they build up sand barricades or dig out mud moats to rein it in. They try to ensure that it flows where it's supposed to flow and stays where it's supposed to stay. Then, they adjust the trap doors, move south along the canal and repeat.

It's a valiant effort. But it's mostly in vain. The water drifts as it wants, forming knee-deep pools that linger for days. The family dogs splash around, delighted. I do, too. It feels like a miracle, even though I know this event was entirely anticipated.

There are 18 *ayllus* surrounding San Pedro de Atacama, and each one has a *celador* who controls the water. Every 28 days, Orlando Martínez, the *celador* of Coyo, releases river water from a nearby dam into canals that flow to all corners of town. Families have about 90 minutes each, depending on the size of their property, to make of this lifeblood what they will.

The air in the days that follow has an odd smell (for the Atacama) of dank earth. It cools the property, giving Carlos and me an opportunity to stroll around. He takes me on a tour past the medicinal plants. There's *ruda* (for fever and stomach aches), *malva* (for throat pains), *matico* (for digestive issues), *clonqui* (for urinary infections) and *chilca* (an anticoagulant, which works like a bandage for cuts). He shows me the wild mints like *poleo* and endemic pink peppercorns like *molle*. There are also patches of potatoes, ají peppers and corn. We pass orchards of quince, fig and pomegranate, whose fruits are like pygmy versions of the ones I know, due to their infrequent baths. Carlos explains all the astounding ways you can transform a desert into a pantry.

I use this newfound knowledge to soak the native fruit *chañar* in water until its skin turns soft enough to nibble on, like a gooey caramel chew. I pound the carob-like *algarrobo* pods into a flour to make gluten-free treats, and go to a neighbor's place to try a sweet *algarrobo* drink called *añapa*, which tastes a bit like Ovaltine. The bounty of these two trees, staples of these desert oases, is the base of so many food products here. Then, there are the wild herbs like *cachiyuyo*, a bush that sucks up the salinity of the desert, which I use as a replacement for salt. Or *rica-rica*, which elevates a pisco sour into a citric and minty flavor bomb.

I've been in a bit of a rush lately, so this time staying with Sandra and Carlos is my chance to slow down, to savor the desert, to learn some of its secrets from those who know them best: its Indigenous caretakers. I spend mornings wandering around in the garden, swinging from a hammock strung between two *algarrobo* trees. Then, I wander aimlessly around Coyo, walking down its dirt roads to other small family farms fed by a maze of canals. I notice one day that, in the scorching afternoon heat, *algarrobos* bleed a black resin. It drips like honey onto mud-brick homes and smells like burnt papaya.

I notice, another day, that the roof of the town church is made from the *cardón* cactus, which grows at a rate of just half an inch each month and is only found in the Andes above 10,000 feet (3050 m). Historically, villagers collected it after windy days, when trunks are often knocked over. They then dried it so that its light, latticed wood could be affixed to doors and windows of adobe homes, or the roofs of squat churches, as decorative flair.

One afternoon, I follow a dry riverbed from Coyo over to the ruins of Tulor, which date back to around 400 BCE. This ancient Likan Antai settlement, first discovered in 1958 by a Jesuit priest, was once a thriving oasis along the Río San Pedro de Atacama, with dozens of circular homes made of mud and vaulted ceilings – all surrounded by a hulking perimeter wall. Archeologists believe it was abandoned after the oasis dried up. Then, the dunes moved in, largely burying it from view.

Homes here all faced east to catch the sunrise over the Andes, whose mountains have traits and stories invisible to the casual visitor. Mostly volcanoes, they're so alive with inner turmoil that, according to the site's caretaker, they've been personified over the years.

One legend has it that Láscar – the most active of the group – expelled Quimal from the Andes to the parallel Domeyko Range after his two sons, pointy Licancabur and flat-topped Juriques, both fell for her, leading the former to decapitate the latter. However, the ex-lovers are said to meet again each June. During the winter solstice, the shadow of Licancabur races across the salt valley to fully embrace the summit of poor Quimal (who, as is often the case among the women in these stories, was punished not for her own crimes but for those of the men who loved her).

Despite – or perhaps because of – his notorious temper, Licancabur is the most revered volcano among the Likan Antai. Rising to 19,410 feet (5916 m) above the desert floor, he's visible no matter where you go. He's also, generally, the spot from which the sun first rises over the Andes, leading ancestral Likan Antai to build altars on his upper slopes. His name, in the local Kunza language, even translates to "mountain of the people."

The oases beneath Licancabur have been the heartland of the Likan Antai for generations. Ruins extend far beyond Tulor, including those of *pucarás* (hilltop fortresses) built between the fall of the Tiwanaku Empire (around 1000 CE) and the rise of the Inca (around 1400 CE), both of which expanded into this area.

When the Spanish conquistadors galloped through soon after, in the 16th century, they wrongly referred to this desert as the *despoblado de Atacama*, assuming it was both uninhabited and uninhabitable. Yet groups like the Likan Antai have been here all along, inhabiting this desert and making small swaths of it surprisingly habitable. Though their methods and manners have changed, many still farm alongside the river valleys and herd llamas on the flanks of the Andes, as has been done for generations. If before it was a matter of necessity, now it's a matter of pride.

^ ~ ^

One afternoon, I shadow Sandra as she takes her herd of bucktoothed llamas out to a grazing area called Chalarquiche. This land at the base of the Andes is ideal for the task, as it's shaded by the wizened *tamarugos*, bushy trees in the pea family that were introduced here in the 1950s to save the species from extinction.

Sandra's 17 llamas love it in Chalarquiche because the ground is littered with the *tamarugo*'s legume-like pods, a key source of nutrients. We walk beneath these improbable trees, hopping from shade to shade, when she tells me a story dear to her heart. It's about how she lost touch with the culture of caring for llamas – and how she fought hard to reconnect with it again.

The story begins in 1982, when the Láscar Volcano roared back to life. The shepherding community of Talabre, where Sandra lived, was the closest village to the gurgling giant. In fact, it lay in a flood-prone ravine right on its slopes. With an eruption seemingly imminent, the government was adamant: everyone had to go.

So her family upended their agrarian life and relocated to the regional city of Calama, but her mom soon got sick from all the chemicals belched out of nearby Chuquicamata, the world's largest open-pit copper mine (and a potent symbol of capitalist oppression in Che Guevara's memoir *The Motorcycle Diaries*). They moved halfway back in the direction of the volcano and settled in San Pedro, where Lascar, looming on the horizon, became a permanent reminder of everything they'd left behind.

Eventually they made their way back to the volcano, to a new, government-approved village called Talabre Nuevo, but they were just in time for it to actually blow. That was 1993, when the extended family lost all of its animals.

For several years, they worked as caretakers for other people's llamas. But they were pretty sure that some of their own had survived. Plus, their beloved llamas had recently been marked with identifying strands of wool for the annual *fiesta del floreo* ceremony using her family color, pea-green. This floppy flair, which dangled like pompoms from the llamas' ears, made the animals easy enough to recognize when the family finally caught up with them roaming the *puna* half-feral a few years later.

The descendants of those 12 animals now chew on the *tamarugo* pods in front of me. "If I didn't have these llamas, I couldn't teach this culture to my daughters," Sandra says as we walk. "This culture would be lost. Because I come from a family of shepherds. But when you move closer to San Pedro, people tend to lose contact with the animals."

That's exactly what happened to her. For years, when she was busy raising kids, she kept her llamas in a pen in Coyo, feeding them daily piles of alfalfa. But two years ago, with the kids now teenagers, she decided to raise the animals in the ancestral way, shepherding them across the pre-Andean plains. It was a huge lifestyle change, consuming as much as six hours of every day. "But I feel like I've been able to return to my nature again," she shares.

As we walk the llamas back to their pen, the sun drops down the sky in the direction of the westerly Cordillera de la Sal range. It's a slow-motion descent, with the golden orb not sinking into the hills so much as melting across them. While it disappears, a predicable breeze sweeps across the valley. Carlos joins us at Chalarquiche for the violet hour, and together we prepare a bonfire.

Warmed by its flames later that evening, he tells me the origin story of the Likan Antai. "According to the archeologists, we have about 14,000 to 10,000 years in this land," he begins. "During this period of time, about 11,000 years ago, a meteorite fell here in the Atacama – here in the *salar*, about 110 kilometers [70 miles] from here, in Monturaqui. According to our ancestors, when the meteorite hit the earth, everything went dark."

The Atacama became incessantly cold. Plants and animals died out. And the people did, too, he says. "The ancestors who survived did so inside caves. That's how they passed the time, in darkness and cold. Then, after many days of darkness, the sun returned. When the sun came out, there wasn't anything to eat. Everything was dead."

That's when the visitors from the sky first arrived.

"They taught our ancestors how to sow the earth. They gave them the seed of corn. And they say that, during this time period, our ancestors learned agriculture. Then, the visitors from the sky went away. Our ancestors were scared that a meteorite would come once again, so there was a group of people that didn't want to abandon the caves. They started to build a civilization inside the earth. And the other ones went to live on the land above and sow it like the visitors from the sky had taught them."

The ones who live inside the earth are known as the Pachachos, and the ones who live atop the earth are the Likan Antai. And because that third group lives in the sky, the Likan Antai are constantly looking up, searching for signs.

"I'll tell you about the astrological map of my ancestors," he continues as twilight transitions into twinkling stars. "The Milky Way has two arms, and each one has an interpretation of what it means to be a human. The arm that gets closer to the center of the Milky Way symbolizes, for us, the physical experience of being a human – what we are living now. The arm that goes away from the center symbolizes the spiritual world of what it means to be a human."

The Likan Antai, he explains, believe that everything has a duality. That extends to both the lights and shadows up above.

"When we observe the sky, the light parts are just as important as the dark," Carlos continues. "So we have constellations made of light, but also ones made of its absence. Those constellations – the fox, the shepherd, the llama, the snake – are found in the dark part of the sky."

I poke at the fire with a long stick while prodding Carlos for the deeper meaning of these celestial shadows.

"The fox for us symbolizes problems," he explains. "Then, the shepherd symbolizes work. The llama represents fertility and prosperity. We can interpret our lives by looking for these symbols, especially in the winter months. We can plan out our year. If the fox is really well defined, we know that we can expect some difficulties. If we see the shepherd really clearly, that means it's going to be a year with lots of work. If the llama is really clearly defined, it will be a prosperous and fertile year. When it's time to leave this earth, death is a journey through the snake constellation."

There are also bright constellations. To see them is to untangle the cobweb of quivering stars. I learn of a butterfly who acts as a rain messenger, and a slingshot-like weapon called a *waraka*, which was put in the sky to defend the spiritual world from bad energies.

We lay back on a *manta* with our legs facing south, splaying our bodies into the shape of the *chakana* (a stepped Andean cross), gazing into the light bits and dark bits for a while. Then, Sandra pulls out a bowl, pours some water into it, and tells me to look down into the reflection, instead of up, as way of training my mind to tune in to the messages of the sky. It takes extreme patience to still the water. After a long struggle, I finally stare down into the bowl at the megawatt stars. I trace their contours and try to identify their celestial messages.

I'm reminded again of my first trip to Chile, when Felipe and I visited this very part of the desert to look at these very stars from the ALMA observatory. I was a different person then. We were different people. But these stars, they stay the same. And over time – with age, with guidance – you learn how to see the same stars differently. You discover how to find new meaning in their presence. You begin to mold them into clusters to try and make sense of your life, as well as the lives of those around you.

It's only been a week, but Sandra and Carlos have already opened my eyes to new ways of seeing this desert. They've showed me something so familiar – the night sky – and made me look at it like I'm seeing it for the first time. They've shared so much with me, but I want to be sure they're comfortable doing so. I ask if I'm posing too many questions. I wonder if they're worried about sharing too much.

"There was always an awareness that we were not to share our culture, our beliefs, or our spirituality with anyone," Carlos explains. "That was an inheritance of the Spanish conquests of the Atacama, when they made laws that you couldn't practice your traditions or you'd be killed. From then up until now, people have lived their culture in secret without sharing with anyone. So even archeologists and anthropologists came here and we said, 'No, no, no.' We didn't share anything."

Everything changed in 2017, he says, when there was a sign: a solar alignment that marked the start of the fifth *pachakuti*, or "return of time." This was a period of upheaval and cosmic transformation that heralded a new phase spanning half a millennium.

"We believe there were 500 years where the energy went to the left; it was a dead energy from when the conquistadors came to the Americas. In December 2017, the fifth *pachakuti* began, and the energy began to turn to the right. So now, for the First Nations of the Americas, we are going to receive the energy of the right."

Carlos tells me that, in 2017, when the wise men of the Andes gathered together for the fifth *pachakuti*, they shared a message: Teach all people of the Americas the culture and spirituality of its First Nations, and the great importance of protecting our Mother Earth. Let it be an end to the old ways of thinking about this planet. Help your neighbors to find a higher state of consciousness.

Think not on who we were, but rather who we are becoming.

After centuries of appalling violence and oppression, the world has been turned right-side-up again. Harmony and order can be restored. The cultures of the Andean world, he explains, have the space to thrive. "We can now bloom. We can begin to do the socializing and sharing we haven't done before, and it will influence the cultures of the entire world."

^ ~ ^

It's dawn at El Tatio, and the light is dim, the smoke is heavy and the earthen hellscape comes slowly into view. Sprawling across the altiplano are vibrant multi-hued hot springs, puffing fumaroles and effervescing mud pools. There are perpetual spouters on my left and finicky geysers to my right, which disappear into the earth only to spurt up anew. They're all part of the largest geyser field in the southern hemisphere and highest geothermal complex on earth.

The prismatic pools at El Tatio are absolutely scalding (even though the wetlands on the winding road up here were frozen solid). They belch mud skyward, sending it pirouetting into the thin Andean air. I walk carefully down El Tatio's stone-marked paths; one false move, a sign warns, and I might be cooked alive in seconds. All the while, water sputters in fountains and sporadically snaps like an uncapped fire hydrant. To my ears, it's all gurgles, bubbles and groans.

I later hike five miles (8 km) along the adjacent Río Blanco past rock walls crowded with hurdling vizcachas, large rodents you'd mistake for rabbits due to a fluke of convergent evolution. They bound around boulders by the dozen, hopping past chartreuse cushion plants called *yareta*, which may be thousands of years old but look, to me, like '90s-era Nickelodeon slime dripped across the desert.

This river valley is as devilish as landscapes come. There are pools of ochre orange and emerald green. I find frothing cones that seem to act as portals to the underworld. In parts, the river flows in rainbows, with veins of bacteria that wiggle like the licks of some flamboyant flame.

The scene takes me back to my family road trip to Yellowstone, in 1993, when I penned my earliest piece of journalism. Written in Ticonderoga No. 2 pencil on wide ruled notebook paper, and then stapled together, *The Geysers of Yellowstone* included an 8-year-old's opinions on all the jets and fountains our family saw on that trip. I guess that, since a young age, I've found a profound sense of comfort and joy in uncomfortable and joyless landscapes.

I'm back above 14,000 feet (above 4300 m), where the sun is so close you feel like you could reach up and snatch it out of the sky. The Atacama, at these frozen altitudes, repels the casual visitor. My eyes are once again frog-like. My nose is a bullhorn. My skin is an achy, flaky mess. I creep perilously close to the steam vents, letting them bathe me in their sulfuric moisture, which offers momentary relief. I will regret this in the hours to come, when I find it impossible to rid my body of the smell of rotten eggs.

^ ~ ^

A few days later, I venture down another river, one of the many in this desert known as Río Salado (Salt River). This time, I'm accompanied by one of Carlos's friends from Coyo, Dagoberto Peña, a retired teacher and avid mountaineer, whose mother grew up in Humberstone before its only occupants were ghosts.

Dagoberto tells me as we wade through shin-deep river water that this canyon was actually a popular rest stop on the ancient trade route for llama caravans, which would cross the Andes to exchange goods between South America's Atlantic and Pacific coasts. That's why the ochre petroglyphs we find along cliff walls include monkeys, jaguars and parrots, which aren't native here – and never have been – but were kept alive in desert hamlets as status symbols.

Nearby is an entire rock face filled with llamas – many of which appear pregnant, with baby *llamitas* drawn inside. There are also ovular fertility symbols and hunter figures holding bows. These petroglyphs date back about a thousand years to the time between Tiwanaku and Inca rule. Up above, on the road into the canyon, are signs of the newer travelers, mostly truckers, who've masticated coca leaves into gooey balls and affixed them to a rocky overhang, offering a payment to Pachamama for safe passage.

We follow the river to its confluence with the Río Grande, turning back into a narrow slot canyon with waist-deep waters before re-emerging from the brown froth into a wide valley with a thin rocky beach. We then climb through aggressive grasses into the cordillera, where there is a sweeping panorama of volcanic peaks, before descending back to our starting point at Río Salado, burnt and beat.

Dagberto and I go on several more adventures together. One

day, we climb Volcán Poruña, a parasite volcano to the much larger Volcán San Pedro. The quest had sounded quite exciting when he first mentioned it, but gave me no bragging rights, as it's one of the smallest volcanoes in the world at less than 500 feet (152 m) from bottom to top. It is, in essence, an anthill in front of a giant – though it does boast a five-mile-long (8 km) lava spill, which carves a scar across the desert to the end of the horizon.

We continue from Poruña past giant wind and solar farms to Lasana, a green oasis with canals and terraced fields straddling the Río Loa, Chile's longest river and the Atacama's largest watercourse. This village was, for centuries, one of the most important stopping points for the llama caravans, whose voyagers viewed the Loa as lifeblood. The river walls north and south of it are doodled in even more petroglyphs and pictographs dating back as much as 4,000 years, as well as dozens of bubbling springs that ancient settlers saw as fertility symbols.

The llama caravans stretched in all directions from here, up to modern-day Bolivia and down to Chile's Copiapó Valley. One or two people could herd dozens of llamas, loaded with up to 66 pounds (30 kg) of cargo each, to the remote settlements of this desert, linking places like this to a vast network of exchange. Of course, trade often led to disputes and the need for a good defense.

The towering Pucará de Lasana is a 12th-century fortress built of rocks and mud, with roofs carved from *algarrobo* or *chañar*. To tour some of its 110 buildings, Dagberto and I scramble up stone-hewn stairs, down narrow alleyways and into rooms with crumbling walls that feel seconds from tumbling to the ground. Many, we find, have *trojas* (storerooms), which would have been used for potatoes, corn and *charqui* (dried llama meat). The dramatic setting overlooking the Loa and the distant Volcán San Pedro, as well as its twin Volcán San Pablo, was surely no accident.

At its height, nearly 1,000 people lived inside the *pucará*. Today, there are less than 100 residents, almost all of whom are female and live in new-built homes nearby. They work the land while their fathers, husbands and sons spend weeks down in copper mines. We sleep in their midst at a small campsite by the river. At night, I search the dark parts of the sky for the fox, the shepherd, the llama and the snake. I keep my head outside my tent so I can ease into sleep reading the Milky Way.

^~^

It's often said that tedium is the persistent foe of those who dwell in deserts. But in that tedium, I find a certain kind of peace, as well as an avenue for deeper reflection. Perhaps that's why I'm drawn back to Chalarquiche to walk the buck-toothed llamas with Carlos and Sandra. In a rhythm I've come to expect, we weave our way through the *tamarugos*, the sun plunges, and then the winds roar across the valley. A fire spits blue-tipped flames, and Carlos, invariably, comes armed with a fable:

"I want to tell you a story about the wind, and what it has to do with being a human," he begins. "From the moment humans were born on earth, the wind was always observing. In the mountains here, the people lived with their llamas. But when the wind blew hard, the food of the llama went away. Or the llama, when it felt the wind too hard, wouldn't eat. So the relationship has always been tough. But to be a human was to have your llamas."

Sandra places a grill over the fire and begins to roll some flatbreads. I offer a helping hand as Carlos continues.

"To understand the rest, you need to know that there are very special places where the llamas have their earth baths. These are areas with nice powdery sands and, over time, people started giving a greater meaning to them. The *revolcaderos* is what they're called. In the mountains, there are not many places where the llamas can find *revolcaderos*. They are like small holes, or nests, and you couldn't walk through them because they are just for the llamas, whose space has to be respected."

We toss the first flatbreads on the grill. I grab a beer, and hand one to Carlos.

"Anyway, one day, the wind was tired, so it decided to rest, and it transformed into a small boy. This small boy saw that there was a very good place to take a siesta, and it was a *revolcadero* of the llama, so he went to sleep there. Then, the shepherd came with his llamas to this place in the pasture. When he saw the boy in the hole, the shepherd got angry. He had taught all the kids in the area to never be in this spot because it was sacred. So he took the boy by the arms and yanked him out. He said, 'Why are you sleeping in this place? It's sacred. It is the place of the llama.' He admonished the kid."

A strong gust tosses one of the flatbreads off the grill and into the sand. I wonder in that moment if the wind is listening, too.

"In this act, the kid felt that he was being treated badly by humans. So he started to transform back into the wind. In fact, he morphed into a tornado, and he took the man up into the sky, hit him against the rocks and killed him. From that day on, the wind was angry with mankind, and they were never to be friends again. So when the wind sees that humans are growing food, it comes and takes it away. Or it comes and pushes the clouds away so that there are not any rains. Or it comes and destroys what humankind has created.

"Now, when we see the winds come, when we see that the wind is hungry, we come out to offer it coca leaves, a little bit of food, some water, so that it doesn't destroy our land and our home. In that way we can make peace with the wind."

We put a salsa called *pebre* on top of the roasted flatbreads and sit in silence for a minute, listening to the gusts as they sweep across Chalarquiche in whooshing waves.

"This is just one story. We see every element as an intelligent being: the wind, the fire, the earth, the water. But intelligence is much more than that; it's a form of consciousness."

Carlos looks up from the fire and notices he's emptied his beer.

"Could you grab me another?"

^ ~ ^

This desert used to scare me with its extremes: *All that space. All that nothingness. So much silence to fill.* Increasingly – as I venture further and understand it deeper – all I feel is awe. How could I not at the sight of places like the Salar de Atacama, one of the largest salt flats on earth? It's blindingly white in parts, with crunchy crystals that feel, under my boots, like broken glass. In others, it holds watery lagoons that sprawl like giant oil slicks with swirls of black, cyan or acid green.

There are a few that are safe enough (both for me and the local ecology) to swim in, including Laguna Piedra, which is so saline that, when I enter, I immediately bop to the surface and float like a rubber ducky, just as I did up on the Salar de Pedernales. Try as I might, I can't keep my body vertical. So I hover splat-flat on my belly, laughing all the while.

Carlos tells me later that evening when I spot him in his field that the Likan Antai view a *salar* as the uterus of Mother Earth, where life is born. Historically, people would travel to their shores to meditate. "I always thought this was an odd ritual, but then later, with the rise of lithium, the scientists came," he recalls. "So I asked them if there was something in the *salar* that made you have a hallucinogenic trip."

The scientists told him that they give off a variety of gasses, which can be highly concentrated on the surface during the morning hours at first light. "When I heard that, I went and put myself on the edge of the *salar* one morning and concentrated on my breathing. And it's true; they will give you a little high. So that was the scientific explanation of the ritual, of why people would use *salares* for these ceremonies."

Salar de Atacama lies just south of Coyo. It's the world's largest and purest active source of lithium and the epicenter of the rush for this "white gold." I ask Carlos how he feels about that. He says he believes that all bodies of water are inhabited by a protector spirit. But this spirit is currently threatened by all of the lithium mining as outsiders try to tame and control a desert they don't understand.

"If you take the branches off a tree, it will die," he explains. "So if you take the water out of a *salar*, we believe that it, too, will die a slow death." And because all of the salt flats here are interconnected by subterranean channels, "if you interfere with one," he adds, "you interfere with them all."

^ ~ ^

A shadow in the desert is a gift for the lonesome traveler. Mine has been my constant companion on this trip, stalking me and forcing me to face myself. He used to show up in my photos accidentally, angering me. So now, I've taken to proactively photographing him instead set against a myriad of textured terrains. I like how he gets all tall and gangly in the low morning light, and stout and grumpy by midday. I look for him everywhere I go, or else he finds a way to find me instead – which is why it comes as such a shock when, for several days, my shadow completely disappears.

At first, the unusually grey clouds dribble lazily. Then, a beaded curtain of drizzle swoops across the desert. Eventually, the sky completely falls out and there are three consecutive afternoons with grumbling thunder and pouring rains – all followed by glorious rainbows of splintered light that rise from the Andes to curve over crumpled plains.

I had never, ever, imagined days like these on a journey through earth's driest desert. Yet weather like this isn't entirely unusual. There *are* pockets of the Atacama like greater San Pedro, mainland Chile's easternmost quadrant, that do see annual rain-storms. The reason: high temperatures built up over Argentina, Bolivia, Brazil and Paraguay meet masses of humidity barreling in from the Atlantic Ocean or across the Amazon Basin before ascending onto the Chilean altiplano and unleashing over towns just beneath it.

This rare convergence of meteorological events – paradox-ically known as the *invierno altiplánico* (altiplanic winter) even though it takes place in summer – has left the roads beyond Coyo flooded and nearly impassable. The air is so electric, mean-while, it has my hair tingling with static, even as the house lacks electricity amid sporadic evening power cuts. So I mostly hang around in Coyo, cooking on the gas stove, reading by candlelight and clomping through the wet earth in shoes that are now sev-eral pounds heavier with mud.

I've no raincoat, no umbrella, no waterproof anything. But when you've spent this much time in the desert, all you really want is to run wild, to put your tan, flaky skin in touch with this erratic celestial offering. So I don't avoid the rain; I embrace it. There are moments when I'm swinging in the hammock beneath the fruit trees, massaged by falling beads, where it feels downright Amazonian. The air no longer has the herbaceous aroma I've grown accustomed to. It smells like the absence of something, like a freshness I've been missing.

The one day I do venture out, it's to visit the nearby Valle de la Luna, or Moon Valley. Silver clouds hug the lifeless mountains of the Cordillera de la Sal range as golden lightning bolts thwack the barren plains just beyond. It feels apocalyptic, like some scene out of *Mad Max* or *Dune*.

I take momentary refuge in an abandoned bus left here by salt miners decades ago. It's little more than a tin carcass painted green and white (where it isn't rusty or graffitied). I watch from its missing windows as little mud rivers wiggle around outside. I notice how the water brings the salt to the surface, giving the orange-tinged earth a glistening veneer. Distant mesas disappear behind clouds and then emerge anew.

The storied volcanoes of the Andes have vanished entirely. But they reappear by morning, blanketed in a fresh layer of snow accentuating their muscly peaks. I rush out at daybreak, tiptoeing around puddles to see them. I'm stopped by the arroyo just east of Coyo, which has been bone-dry my entire visit, but now overflows with water the color of molten brick. It has wet edges of cracked earth, like crocodile skin, where an odd latte-like foam floats on the surface. Within 24 hours this river will be gone and the earth dry. The land will look as it did before, smooth and innocent, as if these past days were all just a wild fever dream.

^ ~ ^

The lightning stirs something in Sandra, whom I haven't seen in days. She's been sleeping out at the couple's small shelter in Chalarquiche, tending to the llamas and taking care of her grandson Gaspar. He's once again swaddled around her back in a *manta* when she finally returns to Coyo. She tells me she's been busy keeping Gaspar away from the storms, which has made her think a lot about her own grandparents.

Over a cup of coca tea, which has the musty flavor of cut grass, Sandra tells me the story of her grandfather, and how a storm back in 1940 changed the trajectory of his entire life.

"It was a day just like the other day," she begins. "There was clouds and rain and lightning. The mother of my grandfather, Cecilio, knew the rains were coming and told her son to be home early. But when he set off with the sheep he met a friend in the countryside, and they began to play. When the afternoon came, he realized he'd lost the sheep because he was playing, and when he went to look for them, it started to rain. He was very far away from home by the time the lightning started."

Suddenly, a golden bolt crackled out of the sky and landed atop the wet head of little Cecilio González, sending the 8-year-old boy tumbling down to the muddy earth. The friend, wide-eyed, went into a state of shock. When he regained his composure, he did the only thing he knew to do, running back to tell Cecilio's mother that her son was dead. It was dark by the time he arrived in the village, but the family set out anyway, racing across the Andean foothills with torches in their hands. It wasn't until the early morning, when the sun rose again over Licancabur, that the search party first caught a glimpse of Cecilio.

"He was lying injured on the ground, but they saw that he still had a warm body," Sandra continues. "So they brought him back to town. My grandfather woke up after a few days like nothing had happened, as if he had just had a long sleep. There weren't any visible scars, but there was something different about him, something which nobody else could see."

Cecilio came to realize that he could sense the energy of others. Just by looking at you, he could tell if you were sad, or happy, or in pain. He could hear voices. As the voices began to crowd his head, he became convinced that he was going mad.

"That's why he kept it as a secret just for himself," says Sandra, her eyes lost in the memory. "He was scared to tell his friends or even his parents. So he grew up hearing voices and feeling the nature and the energy of the plants. When he was a bit older, he tried to drink it away to stop feeling all of those strong feelings."

One day, when he was about 20 years old, Cecilio went to a big party where he knew not a soul. An old man saw him there, drunk as usual, and called out his name. "Cecilio," he said, "come over here and speak with me." Sandra's grandfather asked how the old man knew his name, and he explained it quite simply: he was a *yatiri*, a traditional healer. He was one of the Andean soothsayers who, having been called to action by a strike of lightning, play a key role in strengthening (or repairing) relationships with nature, community and ancestors. The man read the coca leaves that night; that's how he knew that Cecilio was a *yatiri*, too.

"He told him that everything he had heard or seen or felt was a power," Sandra continues. "It was a gift he received the day he was hit by the lightning. He told him there was much more to learn and to know, but first he had to accept who he was. Over the next few days, he taught him how to understand this gift, and how it could be used to serve other people. And so, from then onward, my grandfather started to talk openly about what had happened to him."

Cecilio visited his mom so she could be the first to hear the news. Of course, she already knew something was happening to her son. But there had been less and less communication between them following the incident. It took Cecilio another 20 years to fully see within himself that he was a *yatiri* able to heal. Little by little, over time, he began to practice, and to accept that he was never crazy after all. Sandra says he was even recognized by the Chilean Ministry of Health in 2002 as a traditional doctor. His fame grew exponentially from there, spreading to the far corners of the San Pedro River Valley.

"Before he died, in 2016, he was saying all these things that we thought were incoherent, like he was hallucinating," recalls Sandra. "Then, a week before he died, he said that the moment when he was going to pass on from this world it would rain in the cordillera and there would be lightning. It wasn't the time of year for this, but I listened. Nobody believed me. The day it happened, I was putting the animals away and there wasn't even a cloud in the sky.

"He died at about eight or nine that night, and in the morning, there were clouds across the cordillera. In the afternoon, after lunch, we started to have lightning. I had thought this was a power too big for him, but I saw it happen with my own eyes.

"That day, I could finally understand the great power that he had."

^ ~ ^

Tears poured out of the crying sky so fast on the day Carlos joined this world that he almost never made it at all. Or, at least, so the legend goes. His origin story is such a wild and winding tale – not unlike that of Cecilio's – that it's almost hard to believe, with a climax akin to a fable solidified by the passage time.

Sandra tells me that his mom had the misfortune of going into labor during an Atacama thunderstorm, like the ones we've just had. It was the kind where rains turn sand into rivers of concrete. Nevertheless, she rushed to the hospital, but it happened in such a flurry that the driver went to the wrong one.

Somehow, in the confusion, they ended up in downtown Calama, while her doctor was at the shiny new American-built hospital by the Chuquicamata copper mine. It had a reputation as being the best facility north of Santiago. But it was another 30 minutes away. The baby was fidgeting. They rushed to Chuquicamata anyways, but by the time the pregnant woman finally gave birth, the boy she saw was no longer restless; he wasn't moving at all.

The doctor left the room to prepare a death certificate when, suddenly, a big flash of yellow burst across the grey sky. Carlos's mom said she felt it so strongly, it was as if it had hit the foot of her hospital bed. The crackle of lightning gave way to an ethereal wail. Carlos, as the story goes, had returned from the dead.

These events were little more than a bedtime story for the young boy as he grew into a man. Then, he met Sandra and Cecilio, and started learning the ways of the *yatiri*.

Sandra says Carlos is still in the process of accepting who he is. A *yatiri* can sense the feelings and emotions of others, and that takes time. You have to tune in to the right frequencies and tune out the clutter. Unlike a shaman, a *yatiri* doesn't live apart from society and doesn't need any hallucinogenic substances to reach greater clarity. It's a gift they carry with them always – and use only when asked. And so, eventually, as I learn more about this side of Carlos, I work up the courage to ask for a reading. I want to see what the coca leaves might divulge.

Carlos agrees, but he says we can't do it right away. He tells me to sleep for two nights with a pouch of coca leaves under my head, handing me a pillow case in which to place them. The first night, I get barely any sleep. I skim the surface of it, dreaming wildly and waking often, as you're apt to do at altitude. The second night is no different.

We do the reading after sunset on my penultimate evening in Coyo. Carlos takes me to a table in the garden. It's got a red *manta* draped over top. It's lit only by the flame of a solitary candle. I hand him the pillow case of coca, which I've cradled these past days. He opens it up, pours the leaves into his hands, and asks me to blow on them. Then, he empties the ovular, emerald-green herbs onto the table. He studies the ways in which they've landed. How many lie face up? How many are face down? How and where have they gathered?

Carlos is silent for well over a minute, chewing on a wad of coca leaves that puff his cheeks out to such a degree that he resembles a chipmunk with an acorn. I break the hush to ask him about this trip in the Atacama, about my crippling doubts about whether the experiences I've had and realizations I've come to will add up to anything. He tells me to think of my journey in Chile as some inner animal that needs time to grow into its form. I should nurture the animal and shape it and make sure it has a solid foundation, he explains. Then, with great prudence, I can release this metaphorical creature from my mind and let it steer me onward, either down familiar roads, or in the direction of paths unknown.

I ask him what to make of this. A twist of fate brought me to a country that I couldn't have pinpointed on a map until I met a stranger in New Zealand a decade ago. How do you find meaning in that? Is Chile the known road or the path unknown? He says I've traveled a lot over the years, but that my life got split in two when I arrived in this country. I've spent seven years going down the same path, and if I stay another seven years, I'll keep heading down it.

Change has been a constant in my life, he continues, so what a change it might be if I enjoyed a bit of stability. What's the harm in spending time appreciating what you have around you and not looking for the next thing? There may not be major milestones or grand surprises in the years ahead, but there will be a rhythm to my life if I choose this path. I might, in staying, he says, find a better sense of belonging.

What I don't say out loud to Carlos is that there was a moment, not so long ago, when I started thinking about Felipe in the past; it happened when he was present right in front of me. I began wondering what it would feel like if this story ended. If we ended. He was thinking it too. Neither of us had the guts to say it out loud yet. But we both knew, deep down, that our decade-long romance had turned cold.

Before I set off on this trip, it was as if we were helplessly morphing from lovers into friends. And as will happen when you let any friend overstay their welcome, the little annoyances begin to pile up into a mountain of anger. And that anger turns into a resentment. And the resentment starts to overpower the love.

It's still there, the love; I know that now. But for a while, I just didn't have the drive or empathy or willingness to see it. Eventually, the resentment just fizzled into sadness, and the only thing I could do to make myself feel better was dream about freedom: the thrill and the fear of it. I thirsted for the high of being completely out of my element again. Someone new to blow my mind, to divert me to that strange nook of my brain that scares me and electrifies my nerves.

It's easier that way. It's harder to stay and fix what's gone wrong.

This journey is part of that process. I thank Carlos for everything. I thank Sandra. I thank the coca leaves. And 36 hours later, I'm on the road again.

The owner of the Qori Inti restaurant in the oasis of Pica was adamant: I must visit the Salar de Huasco salt flat. And if I was going (which I wasn't) here was a crazy idea: What if she, Ruth Moscoso, came along, too? Now that she was coming, maybe she should invite her 21-year-old daughter, she said, planting ideas as fast as she maneuvered them into plans. I should probably sleep at the small guesthouse behind her restaurant. And we should leave at seven a.m. Or, better still, six a.m. She would wake me first thing in the morning, she concluded, because we were going to the altiplano.

This wasn't the reason I came to Pica.

The tiny town had appeared on the horizon earlier that day, like a magical forest, an ovular patch of green in the sea of shifting sands. Everyone in Chile knows the place, even though it's home to just 6,000 people. Its highly acidic marble-sized limes, called *limónes de Pica,* are the key ingredient in all the pisco sours from Arica to Punta Arenas. The orchards radiate the tropical hues of mangos, guavas, papayas and passion fruit, too, while street vendors line the roads selling the kinds of juices travelers crave – but rarely find – in a desert.

These fruits were not the reason I came to Pica, either.

I had, in truth, come to meet with Ruth. But our initial plan was much simpler: to try her cooking. A local entrepreneur, Ruth has pioneered new methods of preparing ancestral Andean cuisines (which predate European contact) at Qori Inti, which she told me means "radiant sun" in her native Aymara language. Out front of the unassuming venue are four parabolic solar cookers she aims at the sun to heat traditional dishes made with quinoa and native potatoes.

"In our culture, we have a strong environmental awareness," she'd explained when we first met at the restaurant. "So we said, let's do something that takes into consideration our traditions and our customs of caring for Mother Earth, but also our tradition of being thrifty and optimizing what we already have here, which is sun and heat.

"So it's really a convergence of tradition and innovation," she added, clearly proud of her achievements.

The vast majority of Ruth's ingredients come from her local Aymara network, while her energy source comes from Inti (the sun god). She's spent years melding the two to create solar-cooked versions of foods like *chuño* (a starchy freeze-dried potato used in various dishes), *sopa milenaria* (an umami-rich soup whose broth is made from llama bones) and *kalapurka* (a chili-spiced stew).

"I wanted to include these typical plates that we do in the altiplano, which are dishes most people have never tried," she continued over dinner that night, showing me a new kind of solar oven she's using to cook food inside a glass evacuated tube. With the help of a regional grant for small businesses, she's just purchased six of these cookers, which will enable her to add new dishes to her menu, including a solar version of *huatia andina*, a meat and potato feast typically cooked under hot stones in an earthen hole.

After a gut-warming dinner of *kalapurka* with tender llama meat, Ruth began scheming. Within minutes, she'd convinced me to take her and her daughter up to the altiplano. Now, not enough sleeping hours later, at five a.m., she's in the kitchen preparing Andean tortillas (a thick naan-like flatbread) to bring with us on our trip.

While she cooks, she hands me three bulging bags filled with things she says we'll need on the way. I load them into the trunk of my car for what will turn out to be a 15-hour journey through both the contours of the high Andes and Ruth's wandering mind.

^ ~ ^

We begin long before sunrise, headed east from Pica. Ruth puts on some fairytale-like *zampoña* panpipe music to set the mood, singing along. Her daughter, Mayra, is asleep in the back, covered in a cobalt-blue poncho. Mayra is studying to be a psychologist at a local university, but she looks more childlike than I'd imagined. Maybe it's the small line of drool seeping out of her mouth, which blings with shimmering braces.

We rustle her awake about an hour into the trip. The first sun-rays have made a jagged silhouette out of the Andes, and Ruth wants to give an offering of coca leaves at a roadside *apacheta*, a large pyramid of rocks where travelers can communicate with the *apus*, or mountain gods. "It's a place where we ask for safe passage and good energy for the trip," she explains, adding: "This way we won't have a flat tire or fall into a ditch."

Ruth is quick to joke, a grin snaking across her broad face every time she does. But she's just as quick to swing toward sorrow. It can be unnerving. One minute we're discussing the death of her great-grandfather, who she says was hunted and killed by white men jealous of his superior mining skills – and the next she's poking fun at the Changos, an Indigenous group that's recently applied for official recognition. "I always thought they'd disappeared," she laughs, "but I guess, now, they're reappearing again."

The other thing I learn about Ruth is that a second of silence in her world is a second wasted. She wants to know everything about me, and tell me everything about herself in return. As we zigzag around cavernous potholes, she dives into her childhood. Ruth was one of seven children. But, with her boundless energy, she was such a handful in an already large family that her mother gave her to her aunt, who raised her like her own.

Ruth wasn't given much in life, but she says she's always had an entrepreneurial spirit. It began when she observed an untapped market for Aymara products in the lowland cities where many now live. So she started selling Aymara-language Christmas cards with Andean patterns. Then, a few years later, she became an Aymara-language teacher in local schools ("the Evangelicals always hate my lesson plans," she jokes). Now, in addition to teaching, she's trying to share Aymara cuisine with non-Aymara Chileans who, by and large, are wholly unacquainted with it.

It's my turn to share now, and Ruth wants to hear about my travels in the world beyond Chile. I tell her and Mayra stories about my wandering 20s, when I vagabonded around Asia, taking odd jobs along the way. I feel a strong sense of comfort in their presence, so I get more personal. I explain that I don't think I knew how to travel the way I do now until I met Felipe in New Zealand. I'd lived in – and moved about – the world beyond America, but with him, travel was on an entirely different scale. To do so meant to leave everything behind. And that was unlike anything I'd ever done.

When we met in Franz Josef, he and Carla were already stashing away colorful kiwi dollars to travel around Asia until their money ran out. Whether our relationship continued or not depended on my participation in that trip. "Four months in Southeast Asia," he said. "Then two months in India and Nepal."

We'd try to do it all on about NZ$4,000. I spent the better part of a year saving up funds just in case we lasted that long.

Then, one November day, we set off for Kuala Lumpur. We befriended the kathoey on Ko Lipe and the NGO workers in Luang Prabang. We got in a fight at a noisy club in Bangkok and made up at the serene Temples of Angkor. We celebrated Christmas at the street stalls in Hanoi and Holi with prismatic powder fights in Goa. We got chased out of the hills in Darjeeling by Gorkha rebels and nearly froze to death in the Annapurna Range of Nepal when our mountain guide abandoned us. We succumbed to food poisoning by the Taj Mahal and shriveled into gaunt waifs just in time to ride camels through the Thar Desert.

We ran so far away from the life I knew that, by the time we arrived at the airport in Delhi six months later, all I knew was that there was no turning back. So we kept running. First to Australia. Then to Chile. For Felipe, it was a homecoming. For me, it was a whole new marathon. That is, until it wasn't. Seven years later, I'm still here. I've stopped running. And I'm not sure who I am when I'm staying still.

I fear I may have lost them chasing memories, but Ruth tells me she feels a kindred spirit with India. She's saving up money in hopes of visiting one day. Mayra, meanwhile, is desperate to go to Korea to see her favorite K-pop bands.

We talk more about the world beyond Chile, about my family near Washington, DC, about how American food is much more than hotdogs and hamburgers. We agree that Santiago really is worthy of its nickname, Santiasco (*asco* means disgust in Spanish), on account of all the smog.

"*Santiago no es Chile*" (Santiago is not Chile), Ruth reminds me. Chileans from elsewhere love to repeat this phrase to anyone from the capital. Yet almost half of the population – 40 percent of all residents – lives in the metropolitan region. No other Chilean city comes even close in size or influence. And nothing happens in the country without people in the capital calling the shots. That's why, in many ways, it often feels like Santiago *is* Chile. Of course, it's not; *Santiago no es Chile*. This trip has made that perfectly clear.

I tell them I'm on a mission to understand Chile better beyond the capital, and part of that mission is understanding its Indigenous inheritance, which is so often hidden in the national narrative. I thank them for sharing and trusting me with their stories.

A cartoonish dust devil whips across the dirt road just as the mountains flatten out into *puna*, emitting a whine of elemental stress. The funnel-shaped twister dances leftward, then right again, raising loose earth before collapsing into oblivion. At around 11,000 feet (3353 m) we pass a small sign for the Salar de Huasco, but Ruth has another idea. "Let's go first to Cancosa," she says, explaining that this is her ancestral homeland.

On the way, we pass several pea-green patches in the moon-grey rubble, which Ruth tells me are quinoa farms. I'd assumed that the current star power of this ancient grain had made Andean farmers rich, or at least slightly richer than they were a decade ago, when quinoa was seen as the protein of the poor.

"Not at all," says Ruth. "It's such a labor-intensive process to do it in the ancestral way that these people can't compete with the new commercial farms."

Communities in the Andean highlands have been hand-harvesting and sun-drying this gluten-free grain (technically an edible seed) for at least 5,000 years. But it's now mass-produced (and often mechanically harvested) in 75 countries as disparate as Denmark, Kenya and India.

When Ruth first saw quinoa in a grocery store, she was shocked. Not because its nutty flavor had caught on – that was inevitable – but because it was being marketed as a single product. "For me, there is a different quinoa for soups, for stews, for salads," she explains. "You don't just have one quinoa."

Ruth grabs one of her mysterious bags as we approach Cancosa, and asks me to pull over. We stop at some of the small adobe homes along the road into town. Each time, she yanks out some tropical fruits – mangos, papayas, guavas – and distributes them to friends and family – all of whom live four hours from the nearest market.

"In the old days, the people from the altiplano always traded with the people from the valleys and coast down below," she explains. "They'd walk out of the mountains with *charqui* [jerky], trade it with the Changos for fish, and then walk back up toward the clouds."

Knobby hills with snowy domes curve along the horizon beyond Cancosa, which is well camouflaged in the grey-brown desert. Its mudbrick homes have roofs of *paja brava*, the same reeds alpacas munch on along the periphery. Swaths of dark green saltbushes and pea-green *yareta* cushion plants are the only touches of color.

Cancosa feels both ancient and timeless. It's also largely deserted, with just a few aging herders left. These are the valiant stragglers willing to muster the fortitude for such an extreme environment in the 21st century. A life lived here, on the upper edge of earth, is a brave, bright, miraculous struggle.

Ruth says the town does burst into activity a few times each year for Aymara ceremonies when ex-residents like her ascend from the lowlands. That's why her family maintains a communal home here. Yet the person who keeps the key is nowhere to be found. Ruth, of course, has another plan: we set out a *manta* on a shady patch of dirt next to a hot spring on the edge of Cancosa. It overlooks a trickle of water – the Río Ocacucho – and has a small concrete shelter for bathing.

Mayra makes me a tea infused with *chachacoma negra*, a bitter herb she says will cut the pressure of the altitude. Then, we rip apart our tortillas and eat them with some nutty goat cheese Ruth brought from Pica. As we snack, talk turns to Chile's new constitution. Elisa Loncón, a Mapuche linguist and Indigenous rights activist, has been tasked with leading the Constitutional Convention, which Mayra hopes will give Chile's Indigenous populations more representation and respect.

"I go to school with all of these girls whose last names are Aymara, but they'll never join me at Indigenous marches," she says. "Either they don't know their background, or they're afraid to identify as Indigenous because they think they'll be discriminated against in Chilean society."

With Loncón leading the convention (often wearing traditional Mapuche clothing) – and 16 other Indigenous representatives from the ten officially recognized groups included in the process – Mayra hopes her generation can have more pride in their culture. But she also wants changes within the Aymara community itself.

"I don't love all of the ways Aymara culture treats women," she says. "There are certain musical instruments we have that are only for men – I can't even touch them. And when a woman marries, there is always an issue over whether she will inherit the family's land."

Ruth shakes her head. "There is a spiritual meaning for all of this," she chides.

As a mom, she takes pride in showing her daughter the beauty of her Aymara identity. But she admits that she, too, struggles with it sometimes. Down below, in Pica, Ruth gets discriminated against because her mother's last name is associated with drug trafficking over the Bolivian border. Up here, she's more respected, but because her father wasn't born in Cancosa, the village doesn't give her a voice in local politics (even though she uses her own money to throw community gatherings at her restaurant in Pica).

A herd of vicuñas appears on the horizon, and Ruth swings, as she's apt to do, from grief to delight, joking about how much she wants to shave these protected animals. "When I see vicuñas, all I think about is money with legs," she laughs, noting that the ultra-soft fur is among the most expensive in the world, worth between US$400 and US$600 per kilo (2.2 pounds). In the time of the Inca, vicuña wool was so highly valued that only royalty could wear it, she adds.

After lunch, I take a quick dip in the spring, but it's so scalding hot that, when I emerge, I'm red as a clown's nose. Ruth and Mayra laugh at the sight of me. I chuckle, too. They struggle to regain their composure, so I slip into the shelter and switch back into my winter clothes. We then head together up a hill on the edge of town to visit a small cemetery. On the way, Ruth dives into her complex relationship with Catholicism.

"Spaniards colonized Latin America with Catholicism, right? But I hear they don't even use the churches in Spain anymore," she says. "So if they are now abandoning their churches, should we do the same?"

Her community's version of Catholicism has always been fused so tightly with Aymara traditions that she can't really decipher what's what anymore. So while the graves in this cemetery all have large wooden crosses and wreaths of fake flowers, they also have special alcoves for offerings. These are to appease the spirits that populate the syncretic belief system of the modern Aymara.

Ruth's brother, father, grandmother and aunt (the one who raised her) are all buried here. "If I don't come to see them, they'll know," she says. "They may even curse us with bad weather."

Ruth pulls coca leaves out of her *ch'uspa*, a vibrantly patterned bag with neon pompoms that's used for storing the sacred herb. She then scatters the leaves atop her family's graves, instructing me to crumple them up and do the same. When we arrive at Ruth's aunt, she pours Mayra and me shot glasses of Coca-Cola. "She always had such a sweet tooth," Ruth says, shooting me a sad smile.

We drink the Coca-Cola and pour another shot onto the parched earth as an offering to Pachamama. Then, we split open some fruits from Pica, eating half and leaving the rest on the graves. It's a way, Ruth says, of sharing the moment with her relatives.

Later, Ruth digs a book out of an alcove at the bottom of her father's grave. It's a collection of photos about the old llama herding routes through the altiplano. We flip it open. Inside are a handful of family images. There are shots of her father smiling at a *fiesta del floreo* ceremony for the llamas. There's her stern-looking grandfather, who's driving alpacas down a stone-paved stretch of the Qhapaq Ñan, the ancient Incan trail network. She reads a bit of the text. It's as if she wants to show me the written proof that their way of life still mattered enough for someone to immortalize it in a book.

This cemetery keeps filling up with the llama and alpaca herders featured on these pages. Ruth says she isn't sure what will happen to Cancosa when more of them perish. She brings her daughter here to pass down the traditions she experienced as a kid. But if no one is living here when her daughter has a daughter, then what will be left to pass along? After all, what becomes of a town when its cemetery is its main attraction? What happens when it's nothing more than a vessel for memories?

^ ~ ^

Ruth bids me farewell with a surprise breakfast. On a table in her restaurant, she's placed *api*, a delicious purple corn drink served hot and spiced with cloves and cinnamon sticks. Next to it are some addictive sopaipillas de quinoa, deep-fried pastries made with quinoa flour, which she tells me to eat with the light and salty queso fresco.

We chat briefly about an earthquake that rocked me awake in the middle of the night. I recall its low grumble; I simulate the suppressed trembles. The quake, registering 6.2 on the Moment Magnitude Scale, sent me racing out of my room in my undies. Ruth looks surprised; she didn't even feel it. I'm shocked...but then I'm not. *Of course she didn't.* Chileans are hard-wired to ignore casual tremors, and Ruth lives in her own world. It's been a joy to live in that world with her for a few days.

I promise after breakfast that I'll send her some animal photos I took at the Salar de Huasco, our original destination, which we turned into a pit stop on a much deeper journey together. She wants to use the photos in her Aymara language lessons in the local school. In return, she promises to send me some of her recipes.

I leave with the sense that Ruth doesn't often feel seen in Chilean society, but that having a foreigner care about her story meant something. She tells me as much.

I sometimes think being gay is a superpower that helps me

connect with people who feel invisible. I know what it's like to be othered, to become invisible, and so I know, too, what it's like to be seen. Of course, I can't begin to understand what it's like to be an Indigenous woman in a society like Chile's, which falsely claims to be monoethnic, but I can listen and learn.

On this trip, I'm learning the power of listening. It can be a much more valuable than speaking. More gratifying, too, especially when it comes to the voices of those in Chile who, for so long, have gone unheard.

As I drive away, Ruth is busy preparing her solar ovens for a group of 25 tourists from Santiago. It's her way of opening their eyes to the culture of the land's original inhabitants. She'll place dishes her guests have never heard of in pots, aim the parabolic cookers at the sun and wait for them to heat up, wearing more traditional Aymara clothes than she ever would in daily life. All the while, she'll chat with anyone who'll listen. She'll share her stories and make her voice heard.

^~^

The fruit orchards of Pica give way to a spindly forest of *tamarugos* as I descend from the Andean foothills into the pampa. An hour later, I arrive in the village of La Tirana. It's Sunday, and there is a line out front of the church 50 people deep. I instinctively join the queue, inching ever closer to this colonnaded landmark on the central plaza. Thirty minutes pass before I've reached the interior dome, which has been painted like an indigo sky speckled gold with stars.

This church is the setting of a massive religious celebration each July in honor of the Virgin of Carmel. The festival, which blends Aymara traditions with Catholic rites, lures a quarter million pilgrims to La Tirana, which normally has just 800

people. Videos displayed in a small museum in the church base-
ment show streets packed with costumed dance troupes – men
in devil masks, women in billowing hoop dresses – stomping
away to snare drums and whistles. These parades, I learn, are the
preamble to a procession of the Virgin and a mammoth open-air
mass attended by thousands.

Panpipe music blasts from loudspeakers as I exit to the plaza,
where vendors sell a fermented pineapple drink called *chicha de
piña*. Nearby, stores hawk devotional paraphernalia: fake flowers,
wood-carved saints, devil masks straight out of an Andean
nightmare, with protruding eyes and menacing grins. I follow
the pilgrims to a small lunch place for oven-baked empanadas.
Then, I wander through the nearby desert, which is riddled in
geoglyphs. Ruth said I could travel back in time here to better
appreciate the pre-Columbian Atacama.

Chile, she'd told me up in Cancosa, rarely recognizes the legacy of her Indigenous ancestors, preferring instead to champion
the stories of "heroic" colonizers. "But if you don't know our history," she mused, "then how can you understand our present?"
And so, I take her words to heart, setting off in search of the
messages they left behind.

8 IT'S BLOOMING BONES

(THE ANCIENT ATACAMA)

My boots kick up small white fragments that tumble like confetti down a peanut-colored hill. At first, as I walk a sandy path near Caleta Camarones, these little pearls are all I see. Then, continuing south, I come across full arm bones and leg bones. There are skulls stuffed with silt, as well as fibers nearby that once held together entire skeletons. I knew ancient remains like these were often found at this remote cove; what I hadn't realized was how easy they are to find.

I've traveled to Caleta Camarones to hear a story about bones – about what can and can't be explained by them, and the tales we choose for them to tell. It begins more than 7,000 years ago in this valley of bushy green scrub where the Río Camarones trickles out to sea. This is the place where humans did something with bones that no one else in known history had ever done before.

The story goes something like this: ancient settlers were in the midst of pushing into the most remote and inhospitable parts of South America, the final frontier of human migration, when tragedy struck at Caleta Camarones. Archeologists believe there was an epidemic of stillborn babies. Mothers, it seems, were unwittingly poisoning themselves simply by drinking the local river water.

Studies show that the Río Camarones has the highest natural arsenic level in the Americas. It's 100 times higher than modern safety levels. This may have led to a ceremonial treatment of the dead that resulted in the oldest purposefully created mummies on earth, made 2,000 years before those in ancient Egypt. What's more remarkable still is that these people, the Chinchorro, weren't some advanced civilization, but rather preceramic hunter-gatherers who roamed the coastlines of northern Chile and southern Peru from about 7000 to 1500 BCE.

Ironically, increased humidity in the desert is giving us greater access to one of the Atacama's wildest chapters. "Every time it rains, the desert blooms with bones," Jannina Campos, a young and eager archeologist charged with monitoring this area, explains. "They used to say it only happens once every 100 years, but because of climate change, it's happening more often and getting stronger each time."

The Atacama is in the midst of shedding its buried history, as we can plainly see before us. We pass filaments twisted into braids, a pelvic bone caught between rocks, even a body-shaped mound emerging from some ancient tomb. We spot towering shell middens to our right and an entire burial layer to our left that's been exposed on the hill's edge. The secrets of the past lie bare. Because, here, they were never truly lost; they've simply been waiting, in situ, for the right inquisitive minds to bring them back to life.

Instead of taking these remains out of the earth every time it drizzles, Jannina says she simply registers the bones. She notes their coordinates and buries them back in the same soil that's preserved them for thousands of years. "All of this cultural material is better kept in its natural state where there's an equilibrium," she explains. "The moment you take it out of the ground it begins to deteriorate."

The Chinchorro would make incisions in a body, remove its main organs, dry its cavities and mold it using sticks, reeds and clay. After it regained volume, they stitched it back together – or patched it – with human or animal skin. On the head, they would often place a wig – a short wig in the early period, around 5000 BCE, and a longer one in the later period, around 2000 BCE. In some cases, they painted the body black, using manganese oxide; in others, red, using iron oxide. There were at least four different types of artificial mummies, with the most intricate being the "black mummies" (5000–3000 BCE) and "red mummies" (2500–1500 BCE).

The mummies at Caleta Camarones are the oldest and most primitive. They're protected from grave robbers only by the isolation of this unfrequented cove. Government-sponsored education programs have helped empower members of the small fishing community here to care for the unmarked graves and understand their historic value. As evidence, Jannina points to modern rock art on a barren hill above town, where a sign made of gathered stones welcomes visitors to the cradle of the Chinchorro culture.

The sun finally emerges following a long morning of clouds, so I part ways with Jannina to search for shade and grab some lunch. In town, which is little more than two dirt lanes lined in basic homes, almost all of which have Chilean flags waving in the eternal sea breeze, I find myself at a creaky roadside stand. I chat with a weathered chef as he tosses a scallop and cheese empanada into a bubbling fryer. When I ask him about the arsenic in the adjacent river, he just laughs. People have been living here for so many generations, he explains, that they don't even think about it anymore.

I, however, don't dare ask for a glass of water...

Munching on my gooey, greasy lunch, I learn that the fisherfolk who live here have a unique adaptation in their genes allowing them to metabolize the arsenic without any major health issues (scientists have even proven this by testing their levels against those of other coastal communities). The Chinchorro may have lost their babies here, but 7,000 years later, the modern-day residents of Caleta Camarones are doing just fine.

After lunch, I follow a string of newly built Chinchorro statues out of town. The first, *El Cantar del Viento* (The Song of the Wind) is a pair of stylized 16-foot (5 m) mummies with flutelike holes that transform strong gusts into breathy, ethereal melodies. Other statues lie further along the street as it winds up the sharp-hewn river valley. They depict young boys and girls – perhaps fetuses? – wrapped in fibers and wearing haunting masks.

There are seven monumental statues in total lining the roads between Caleta Camarones and the regional capital of Arica, two hours to the north. The local government commissioned them to tame the distance between these two major Chinchorro sites. The hope is that they might lure tourists here by helping them visualize the great unseen, offering a tangible reminder of the past as well as a glimpse of what the future may hold if the Chinchorro finally attain the global recognition they deserve.

^ ~ ^

I spend the following morning at Playa Chinchorro, a wide beach of brown sugar sands that curves along the edge of Arica, the capital of Chile's northernmost region. The ocean here is surprisingly calm and the water is at-long-last warm (or at least more welcoming than it's been all trip). Meanwhile, the cuisine at seafront restaurants is more Peruvian than Chilean, even though the border is still 12 miles (19 km) away.

Dozens of palm trees line the beach, nearly tricking me into thinking I'm somewhere greener. Yet, while I've now crossed into the tropics, Arica is anything but tropical. In fact, it's the driest city on earth, once enduring 173 months without a single drop of rain; by comparison, the driest city in the US – Yuma, Arizona – receives close to three inches (7.6 cm) every year.

It was here, in 1917, that German archeologist Max Uhle came across a peculiar collection of human remains. Walking down the interior edge of this beach, as I'm doing just over a century later, he stumbled upon bodies poking out of the sands. It was clear, even then, that they were unique. They'd been manipulated with sticks and reeds. Some had natty wigs of human hair; others evocative masks. "Many corpses, especially of children, show post-mortal injuries that are truly curious, such as the replacement of the head by another false one, breaking of the head with adequate mending, [and] straw arms or legs replacing the genuine ones," wrote Uhle.

These early South Americans were excavated and later documented in scientific papers, where they collectively assumed the name of the beach on which they'd been found. Then, like the country from which they came, they were largely forgotten.

Intensive studies wouldn't take place for another 50 years. Another half a century would pass before UNESCO named the Settlement and Artificial Mummification of the Chinchorro Culture to its World Heritage list. This helps explain why, despite the Chinchorro mummies' importance in human history, most people have never heard of them.

I have, of course. Chileans love to brag that their country is home to the oldest mummies in the world. You find them as prize exhibits in Santiago museums. I've even visited Arica before to do a story about them. That's why, upon returning, I call up an old source, Bernardo Arriaza, a physical anthropologist who's been at the forefront of Chinchorro research.

We meet at his lab at the Universidad de Tarapacá, where I find him arched over a microscope in the most professorly of outfits: burgundy pants, white-collared shirt and blue sweater vest – all topped with a fedora. Naturally, he's examining 3,000-year-old lice.

Many of the samples, he says, excited, were found on the elaborate turbans of camelid hair worn by the Chinchorro in their later years. Others were found in human hair, which he also studies to look for things like what people ate (mostly seafood) or how much arsenic they had in their bodies (a lot!).

"You open the door to their secrets doing this micro work," he explains while showing me the lab and its recently acquired machines, which have techie acronyms like SEM and EDX. "Because this is an extremely dry environment, we can have a marvelous preservation of what their daily life looked like. We can reconstruct their diet, the resources they used, the manufacturing of artifacts…and what you find is a coastal population that, very early on, adapted and survived and flourished in the Atacama Desert."

Bernardo shows me cuts made on bones during the mummification process, when the Chinchorro had to take the body apart to transform it into something else entirely. He thinks those early communities in Caleta Camarones, spurred by grief and pain, stumbled upon something they came to regard as beautiful. They found that they could extend the life of those no longer living, and in doing so, keep them around in the community. The mummies became almost like ancestral monuments denoting territory and symbolizing cultural identity. So they manipulated more bodies, painting them in new colors and adding fresh elements as the idea spread.

"What we can see clearly is a specialization where very early humans became masters of the dead," Bernardo says. To make the mummies, the Chinchorro had to search for pigments, grind them up and process them, build brushes, and use complex artistry to manipulate the body. It was a lot of brainpower for such early humans, and showed a real knack for aesthetics – particularly in Arica, where they perfected their craft.

Some mummies were bandaged up to resemble how the person looked in life. In other cases, any resemblance of their former appearance was erased by coating a layer of clay over the entire body to protect it from rotting. Whatever the method, they were generally interred in the sandy coastal desert in shallow communal graves.

Over the years, as Arica expanded from a provincial backwater to a city of 230,000 people, it became clear that much of it had been built atop a necropolis. Nowhere was that more apparent than beneath the *morro*, a 425-foot (130 m) promontory that rises over the south end of the city. Bernardo takes me to its northern slopes to visit Colón 10, a building slated to become a hotel until construction halted indefinitely with the discovery of a giant Chinchorro cemetery in 2004. Now, it's owned by the university and operated as a site museum where you can walk atop glass panes looking at 48 mummies, which lie in situ below. They're gathered in different positions, often enveloped in funerary bundles and bandaged in bird skins. Some were naturally mummified into bare elegant bones. One exposed skull has a mark Bernardo says may be evidence of human conflict. On another, I see teeth that were mangled working reeds into ropes.

Across the street, he shows me a plot of empty desert with some derelict water tanks. They look to me like industrial trash, but inside them, he sees potential for a future interpretation center that might include dioramas and interactive mummy replicas. It's part of a commitment he made to UNESCO while he was leading the campaign for the Chinchorro sites in Arica and Caleta Camarones to join the World Heritage list. He needed to prove that, at these graveyards, there would be something a visitor could actually put their eyes on.

"When you see the sites, they're underground," he explains. "And when it's underground, people say, 'What is there to see?' If you have a pyramid, it's obvious; it's a megasite. In the case of the Chinchorro, you have cemeteries, you have debris, you have shell remains, you have landscapes."

Most sites we associate with world heritage tend to have grand structures: your Machu Picchus and Angkor Wats, for example. "The hunter-gatherers have been less visible," Bernardo laments. "The sites themselves are less visible. They're not monumental, so I think they're underrepresented."

That's what he's out to change. But to do so, he needs to create (or incentivize) a tourism infrastructure that could lure people to the northernmost extreme of the Atacama, which is no easy task.

Before he could think about that, he and his fellow research-ers had a more pressing issue: they needed to convince the local population that these mummies were worth protecting in the first place. Neighbors who live around Colón 10 have stories about the bones beneath their homes. They used to play with them in the 1950s and 1960s, when the city expanded up the *morro*. They'd dig them out like treasure hunters, decorating the skulls they found and using them as macabre toys. Bernardo says that, following years of community outreach, the very people who once naively robbed graves have recently transformed into the mummies' biggest defenders.

"We've been working with the community to integrate them into the process so they know more about the Chinchorro," he explains. "Now, people say, 'These are my ancestors.' They feel a connection and a pride associated with the Chinchorro that didn't exist before."

There are Chinchorro-themed restaurants and hotels. Creatives, including artists (Paola Pimentel), novelists (Patricio Barrios) and musicians (Benjamín Aguirre), draw inspiration from the mummies in their works. "This was born in academia, but over time, people have started to take the Chinchorro out of science and attach themselves to these first inhabitants of the Atacama Desert," says Bernardo. "The community feels empowered; they feel like this is part of their identity."

^ ~ ^

The last time I thought this much about bones, I was in the Australian Outback. It was 2014, and I'd traveled to the deceptively named Willandra Lakes Region (whose lakes haven't held water for thousands of years) to cover a story about Mungo Man. This 42,000-year-old skeleton pushed Australia's known human history back by an astounding 20,000 years, while his ritualistic burial proved that a sophisticated culture had emerged on the far side of the Indian Ocean from Africa much earlier than anyone imagined.

Felipe and I were living in Sydney at the time. We had a small basement-level apartment that, in my memories of it, was forever plagued by giant hand-sized spiders. It was in a part of town that Aussies told us was extremely dangerous: Redfern. It felt, to us, as safe as any other inner-city neighborhood we'd ever known. Over time, we figured out that "dangerous" was code for "Aboriginal." We loved our neighborhood, loved what it taught us about Australia.

I wanted to know more about the continent's Indigenous history to understand modern Redfern, and I kept finding myself drawn to the ochre-red heart of the arid Outback. It may be the first desert I ever fell in love with. Sydney was famously gorgeous, but it never really got under my skin. The Outback blew my mind. *All that space. So much silence to fill.* Like the Atacama, it wasn't the empty place it was purported to be. It was full of life, brimming with untold stories.

None fascinated me more than Mungo Man. In him, I found big questions about what bones can tell us, who gets to share their stories, and where such important remains should ultimately lie. Mungo Man, discovered in 1974, had become a potent symbol of the era's Indigenous rights movement as proof of what Aboriginal Elders had stated for decades: that their ancestors were around for far longer than European academics claimed (or, as they put it, since the continent was sung into existence during the "Dreamtime"). Yet, despite calls from Aboriginal leaders for him to be returned to his final resting place in the eroded red-rubble hills of Lake Mungo, he had been locked away at the Australian National University, in Australia's sterile capital, Canberra, for 40 years.

Here were these bones that forever changed Australian history. And here was this group asking for them back. The debate: Who owns the past? It was this ultimate clash between modern science and ancient spirituality that wouldn't get resolved until three years later, in 2017, when officials placed Mungo Man in a casket and sent him off on a funeral procession from Canberra to Lake Mungo (he was ultimately reburied in 2022).

I remember visiting Lake Mungo with a Paakantji Aboriginal guide and being struck by how brilliantly uncomfortable it was, full of prickly silver-blue saltbush and swarms of antagonistic flies. You had to really want to be there – and I was surprised by how much I did. So I sought out other corners of the Outback, from the massive sandstone monolith of Uluru to the opal mining village of Coober Pedy, where residents live in underground dugouts to survive the scorching heat (and become a bit batty because of it).

Felipe and I were fascinated by Australia – mostly by how untamed it still was. We thought it might be the place for us. It would be like New Zealand, but bigger. Yet, as the months passed, he got increasingly unhappy with the kinds of menial jobs he had to take to make a living there. It was unfair, I know. And the unhappiness was contagious. Soon, I was gloomy, too, despite working in my given profession.

We never seemed to make any Australian friends; everyone in our circles was from somewhere else: the Czech Republic, Ireland, Malaysia, Colombia, Argentina, France, even Bhutan. Our visas ran out after a year, and so we packed up and set off for a second go at vagabonding around Asia. Then when Asia ran its course – or rather, the money did – we set our sights on Chile, where Felipe could build a career of his own. When, for me, Chile felt like it might be running its course too, I found another desert to pine for, a fresh reason to keep myself around.

^˜^

Museo Arqueológico San Miguel de Azapa is the underfunded university-run archeology museum where Chinchorro mummies end up once they've left their earthen tombs. It sits on the land of an old olive factory about ten miles (16 km) east of Arica, in the Azapa Valley, a serene and fertile river dale lined with olive groves. Though the collection here spans 10,000 years of human history in the northern Atacama, the Chinchorro exhibit is the clear star. It holds remains mostly dug up in the 1970s and 1980s, when there was a flurry of archeological activity at excavation sites beneath the *morro*.

The main Chinchorro hall, located about 15 feet (4.5 m) underground, was designed to replicate a tomb. Upon entering, I spot primitive harpoons, netted fishing bags and other artifacts of the Chinchorro's lives. Yet the real reason you come here is to learn about their ceremonial deaths.

The first mummies I see are so small and stylized they look like gothic rag dolls. Other, larger ones appear before me like

Halloween scarecrows, their torsos bursting with sticks and reeds and their faces hidden behind haunting masks. The largest collection is on the far side of a glass wall, where more than a dozen mummies lie in white display cases atop metal structures that resemble modern coffins. I count five perfect rows with three or four coffins each – a proper mummy morgue.

There are about 300 mummies in the collection here, but 90 percent of them are off view (saved, one might argue, from the eternal curse of being wondered and marveled at). Mariela Santos, who's in charge of conservation and museums at the Universidad de Tarapacá, gives me a peek behind the curtain to see what lies on the backside of the sprawling facility. We walk over to an unassuming screen door and step inside storage rooms where mummies and their assorted artifacts are stacked high on shelves, sorted on trays and classified with unique ID codes.

"The Chinchorro seemed to be a society that was so simple, but it appears that they were not so simple after all," says Mariela as she pulls out one tray, then another. The mummies I see are even more striking than those displayed within the museum, with masks so intricate and intact they look like chilling works of modern art.

Some seem to have an expression of surprise; others joy or even anguish. On many of the mummies, you can clearly see the patchwork of skin, mud and fibers used to reassemble their bodies into forms that look, at once, both familiar and misshapen. I can't help but admire the Chinchorro; they were uniquely adept at stripping everything down to its core in order to build back a more perfect life.

The storage facility we're in has no air conditioning and limited humidity controls. That wasn't really an issue until the weather in the world's driest city began to change. "Arica, up to this moment, has been a place that's nearly absent of rain," says Mariela, noting that this helped preserve these archeological remains for thousands of years. "But, independent of the desert we live in, we are on the coast, where there is high humidity. We're also having longer El Niño currents and hotter days, which creates problems of evaporation of ocean water. All of this jeopardizes the objects' integrity."

Earth's changing climate means that the mummies are now endangered whether they're in a museum or not. There's no room for any more of them here, so the consensus among researchers is that what remains in the ground should simply stay there. When you take a mummy out of the earth, "there is a violent change in temperature, humidity and luminosity," says Mariela as she puts remains back on a shelf. "Then, begins the process of deterioration."

Preservation strategies typically involve separating the organic from the inorganic. Yet that's difficult in the case of the Chinchorro mummies, Mariela explains, because they mixed materials like clay, reeds and skins. It becomes even trickier when you have greater climate variations and are storing remains in an unstable environment.

Scientists at Harvard University found that climate change has actually triggered microorganisms to attack the mummies' collagen, causing skin to melt into a kind of dark ooze. The research spawned a torrent of salacious headlines: *World's oldest mummies are melting into black slime* (The *Mirror*). *Scientists strive to save melting mummies* (CBS News). *Chinchorro Chilean mummies reduced to slime* (Earth.com).

Mariela admits that "because we don't have an adequate building, they've suffered." But things may be about to change. The government is investing 20 billion pesos (about US$24.7 million) in a new museum set to open on an adjacent plot of land in the coming years. The massive project, fueled by a long-overdue pride in Chile's Indigenous heritage, spans 53,820 square feet (5000 m²) and will allow the mummies to be stored at optimal humidity levels. "Now," Mariela notes, "we'll be able to showcase about 40 percent of the collection instead of the 10 percent currently on view."

The Chinchorro loved life so much they prolonged it. The hope is that, with a new museum, the scientists protecting the world's oldest mummies can extend their lives even longer still.

^~^

Today is my final day exploring the Atacama coast, marveling at the ways in which land here morphs from desert to beach – all with no features to indicate where one ends and the other begins. During this long and winding journey to Arica, beaches like those in Bahía Inglesa and Pan de Azúcar have been places of catharsis. They're visceral, these shorelines. They may have repelled me in Punta de Choros, back at the beginning, when I was still mad at the world for everything going up in flames. But ever since, they've charmed me. They've calmed me. They've become my frenzied blues after blurry days of browns.

When the Atacama starts to feel empty, the Pacific reminds me how full of life it really is. I can understand why the Chinchorro settled here. Even more so when I walk down the coast to one of their favorite spots, Cuevas de Anzota, a string of sea-facing caves six miles (10 km) south of Arica where a path carves its way through hefty coastal hills painted in bird poop the color of pearls.

Seabirds are everywhere, circling in the sky by the hundreds. There are migratory gulls just passing through. Terns battling for space on glaringly white rocks. Hideous turkey vultures soaring over a spirited sea. With 20 species, it's a riot of life. For the Chinchorro, I suppose, it was also a feast for the famished, a place where this desert could both sustain and entertain.

Waves pound through blowholes in thunderous roars, exploding skyward on the far end like liquid fireworks. I let them shower me in salty mist, knowing that the wind will immediately cool me down. I then follow the coastal path as it zigzags further into the caves. I enter and explore them until their roofs become too low to continue. In one cavern, I have a momentary flashback of Jorge and *los 33*, which makes me reconsider crawling too far underground.

Back in the open air, I scan the 900-foot-tall (274 m) cliff walls for Chinchorro rock art. I find both zoomorphic and anthropomorphic creatures. Some look like the hefty lava lizards sunbathing on these coastal boulders; others the winged creatures soaring up above.

I'm reminded of the geoglyphs of Cerros Pintados, which I saw on the drive up from Pica. They blanketed nearly two miles of arid hills like a storybook splayed across the horizon. There were llama-like animals racing up one peak and condor-like animals that seemingly flew off another. There were godlike men radiating the power of the sun and warrior-like men instilling fear with raised staffs.

This open-air epic in Pampa del Tamarugal National Reserve is the largest collection of geoglyphs in South America, with more than 60 panels and 450 or so figures – all rendered between 500 CE and 1450 CE. Similar to the famed Nazca Lines of Peru, each was crafted by removing raw materials to form a contrast between the natural and scraped surfaces.

Slightly north of there, near Huara, I also visited the largest prehistoric anthropomorphic figure in the world. The so-called

Atacama Giant lies on the Pacific-facing side of a solitary mound, Cerro Unitas, on the otherwise flat pampa. It's 390 feet (119 m) tall, has a surface area of 32,290 square feet (3000 m²) and is said to represent the Andean god Tunupa, one of the oldest deities in the region, who controls both creative and destructive forces, such as thunder and lightning, fire and volcanoes.

On its right side is what looks to be a staff. On its legs are feather-like ornamentations, indicating a high social status. It's believed that the decorative lines emanating from its headdress may have served as a kind of crop calendar used to calculate the movements of the moon. The "giant" lies alongside 20 other geoglyphs made by a succession of cultures that inhabited this zone between 1000 CE and 1400 CE.

These figures – like those in front of me now – served as guideposts for caravans crossing the desert, conveying messages to neighbors and intruders, wanderers and would-be dwellers. They were the ultimate expression of the ways in which the Atacama's ancient settlers marked this land as their own. Even today, it's as if these long-dead artists are proclaiming: *I was here.*

Despite their age, these symbols still speak to travelers. We may not understand their messages anymore – they may not guide or warn us – but they move us nonetheless. Their message now is one of reminder: Of an inhospitable land that inspired fear and awe. Of the people who conquered that land. And of their improbable legacy, which commands attention across the centuries.

^ ~ ^

I drive north from the caves that afternoon and stop at a place called Maracuyá (Passion Fruit) to treat myself to one last tangerine sunset melting across the Pacific. The restaurant is one of

Arica's finest, but it lurches over the sea so precipitously you feel like passing pelicans might snatch your meal. Mine – Chilean-style parmesan-smothered scallops (*ostiónes a la parmesana*), then Peruvian-style grilled octopus (*pulpo anticuchero*) – reminds me of everything I've come to love about this desert: how it's so barren, yet so rich.

Traveling from Santiago to Arica, crossing this desert from south to north over a distance about the same as San Diego to Seattle, I've found much to see – and learn – along the way. These past weeks alone, I've come to appreciate the desert's Indigenous history, but also its Indigenous future. I've spent time with chefs, scientists and students all pushing Chile to take more pride in its native legacy. All the while, I've all but forgotten about the pandemic, the *estallido social* and the trappings of my life back in Santiago.

So I spend one last night along the coast in Arica, this small frontier city, which feels to me like a big *pueblo*. Then, the next morning, it's off to Aeropuerto Internacional Chacalluta, the airport one mile from the Peruvian border. I'm now at the end of Chile's 2,090-mile (3364 km) stretch of the Pan-American Highway. But I'm not quite at the end of my journey. Not yet. I've still got one final trip to make, and I won't be doing it alone.

Felipe steps out of the airport into the electric Atacama air. Or rather, he limps out. In my absence, he's torn his hamstring. I've eagerly awaited his arrival, wanting to care for him but not wanting to baby him either. It hurts to watch him hobble past the airport's heavy glass doors, but I'm also excited to share this desert with him, to see it fresh again through his eyes.

We embrace in that quick and awkward way you do at a kiss-and-ride. Then, I toss his bag in the trunk and we drive into the dust, headed in the direction of Bolivia.

9 OUT OF BREATH

(END OF THE ROAD)

We could have gone the short way. We might have followed the Bolivian truckers out of Arica on Ruta 11, skirting the colossal potholes en route to staggering scenery along the alpine border. Instead, Felipe and I set off along the winding byways of La Ruta de las Misiones. This sweeping arc of interconnected roads links former Spanish missions – now lonesome Aymara villages – tucked into the stark river valleys of these otherwise infertile Andes.

Some 35 of them – with their matching 17th- and 18th-century adobe churches – line the roads up to (and across) the border. Most predate the arrival of Spaniards, even if their quaint churches speak to the colonization that followed. Each is in a varying state of abandon. Timar, 8,000 feet (2438 m) above sea level, is the first we find with promising signs of life, so we stop for a bit of hydration.

White adobe homes with stone bases, heavy wooden doors and thick grass roofs line its two cobbled streets. At the only shop (really the street-facing part of a house), we find Ana María Tapia, a stout elderly *señora* with a wrinkled moon-shaped face. Two toy-sized dogs are yapping at her geriatric shoes, and she's busy making jams out of quince, guava and the fibrous *alcayota* squash. When we poke our heads inside, however, she appears excited to have visitors. "Come in, my boys," she entreats. "The dogs don't bite."

Ana María has the frozen grin of a woman conversant with the punctuated boredom of life in the Atacama. Her home is more than 100 years old and looks it. The mud-brick walls have been packed with a century's worth of artifacts: paintings of stern-looking Aymara ancestors, framed work certificates, black-and-white birth photos, a panpipe, the collegiate accomplishments of her three kids, a sun-bleached homage to Jesus (or is it some workaday hippie?). Soon after entering, we find ourselves in the kitchen, sipping tangy homemade *tumbo* juice made from a kind of banana passion fruit and learning all about Timar. It's the place Ana María was born in 1941, and where she plans to die.

Turns out, the not-quite-retired retiree knows more about this place than just about anyone else. "I'm in charge of protecting the heritage here," she proclaims, proudly. "And I'm the only one with the keys to the church."

Ana María gets up from the table and shuffles off into another room, dogs in tow, returning a minute later with some weighty, ancient-looking keys. We then follow her two blocks away to the Iglesia de San Juan Bautista de Timar, a storybook church flanked by two girthy palms.

As we walk – at the glacial pace of an 80-year-old woman – she tells Felipe and I more about the town. There are 42 families. Yet only 20 actually reside in Timar. Most are farmers, and today they're at a fair down in Arica. "When I was a child, it would take 32 hours to travel to Arica by mule to sell our products," she recalls, eyebrow raised. "There was a *tambo* [shelter] in the middle where we'd sleep along the way."

Now, it takes just over two hours by car or bus. But it remains a desolate route. The whole way up to Timar is all crumpled earth and lunar nothingness, as if Pachamama decided to squish an otherwise flat plain into an accordion. It calls to mind the American badlands of the Dakotas – if you completely stripped them of life.

In Timar, thanks to a small stream, there are terraced fields of avocados and citrics. Tropical fruits and vegetables common in the cloud forests of Bolivia flourish here too. "We eat well here," the octogenarian says. "Down in Arica, they just eat bread: bread with cheese, bread with sausage. Here, we have pure water. We eat fresh fruits and vegetables, and we live until our 90s, even our hundreds."

Ana María twists a key into the lock and pushes open the creaky wooden church doors. Inside is a surprisingly ornate altarpiece filled with fussily costumed statues. There are bountiful bouquets of fake flowers, and they look so conspicuously similar to the ones on the old woman's shirt that it's clear she's in charge of the decorating.

"I have to clean the church each week," she says, pointing to a pew caked in a thin layer of dust. "Look, I haven't been here in a few days, and it's already getting dirty. It comes in through the cracks with the wind. Or it blows in when cars come by. That's why you need someone to care for the place."

This church, like all the others here, speaks to the gradual coexistence of two cultures that, for centuries, haggled over traditions. Which would change, and which would endure? It's the Indigenous mixed with the European, which created a new kind of institution just as familiar to one as it was exotic to the other.

Many of the 35 churches do not have an Ana María, and they need more than a simple clean. That's why a foundation, Fundación Altiplano, has been restoring them, little by little, year by year, for two decades, part of a plan to try and revive these towns through cultural tourism.

At the next village, Tignamar, we stop at the Iglesia de la Virgen Asunta, an adobe church with rounded white walls, turquoise doors and a bushy brown roof of grass. It sits in a shady nook of non-native eucalyptus trees near a stark river canyon, offering the perfect pretext for a lunch of *pan con palta* (the original avo-cado toast).

At the village of Lupica, we come across more terraced hills and ancient aqueducts, which have made a swath of the desert fertile. The scrubland above is the domain of hardy goat farmers, who sell their cheese from homes below. Belén, nearby, was the first Spanish colonial town in this patch of cordillera. Located at an altitude of 10,630 feet (3240 m), its streets spill down the Andes toward the namesake church, a maroon version of the ones seen earlier. All homes here have a similar palette: ochres and khakis, grass-greens and olive-greens. Most have stone bases, adobe walls and grass roofs. They are, defiantly, stuck in time.

We dip into a sharp valley that afternoon to reach Socoroma, a hidden village encased in terraced agricultural fields. Unlike elsewhere, here the fields are in full use, overflowing with oreg-ano, corn and prickly pears. The streets knotting together the town below are tight and cobbled, with the same adobe homes meshing one into the other. Besides the squat church, and its grass-roofed bell tower, Socoroma can't look all that different than it did half a millennium ago, when the Great Inca Trail, known as the Qhapaq Ñan, passed right through town.

Each of these altiplanic villages appears, from afar, as a patch of green on the brown horizon. When you enter, the silence they imbue is unnerving and overwhelming – at least, for city folk like us. I tell Felipe how they remind me of the nitrate towns, like Humberstone, rich with history, yet weighed down by ghosts. There are, however, enough Ana Marías around to remind me how alive they still are.

We're now almost 1,400 miles (2253 km) north of Santiago – just about as far as you can drive away from the capital and still be in Chile. Few Chileans have been here, and even fewer think about places like this when they make decisions for the country. It's the Atacama's marginalized extreme; its continued existence is one of absolute torpor.

We climb that evening above 11,000 feet (3353 m) to the "big city," Putre, a provincial capital of just 1,500 people. Its Aymara residents wear traditional clothing: men in ponchos and knitted *chullo* caps; women in bowler hats, patterned shawls and pleated *pollera* skirts, which balloon like hoop dresses from their waists. These fashions speak, once again, to the ways in which imposed European ideas got rebranded in the Andes.

Putre, unlike the smaller villages, has shops, restaurants and lodgings. It is, in other words, a place on the map. It will be *our* place over the coming days, serving as a base camp as we explore the altiplanic parks along the Bolivian border. It is also, fittingly, my final stop in the Atacama. Putre is, in other words, the real end of the road.

^ ~ ^

It was on a Pilates machine that Felipe tore his hamstring ten days ago. He was stressed at work and anger-stretching during a lunch break and pushed himself too far. We didn't think it was *that* serious at first, but then a doctor did some exams and told him that, if he ever wanted to do sports again, the tendons would need to be reattached to the pelvic bone. There was talk of some titanium screws, which sounded awful. I never thought of Pilates as dangerous. Until this happened, I didn't even know what Pilates was other than a thing Felipe did when he couldn't make it to yoga. Now, I know. Now, it terrifies me.

It took a while to nail down a date for the surgery, which won't happen for another week. So Felipe decided to continue with the trip up to Putre, more or less as planned. It has and hasn't been easy. Dressing for the desert, for one, is complicated. With diurnal temperature swings of 40 degrees Fahrenheit (20°C), you have to remove layers as a day progresses, then put them on again when nightfall approaches. Outdoorspeople call it "the onion principle," and it's even trickier when you're hobbling on one good leg. But we get by. *He* gets by.

Our drives kick up dust that signals our arrival everywhere we go. Not that anyone is around to see it. We're among the only people dumb enough to divert from the main trucking route, Ruta 11, into the bumpy hinterlands upland of Putre, where we can ponder the natural world without anyone else pondering it with us.

Hikes are off the table, given the state of Felipe's leg, but there is a remote hot spring in Las Vicuñas National Reserve that's said to have some healing properties. We've no idea what they are, but it sounds therapeutic. So we make it our first destination.

What's not terribly therapeutic is the road out to the park, which is unpaved, unkept and uncaring to the indisposed. It may be the cruelest I've driven all trip, riddled with potholes when it's not rippled into an unending rumble strip. We nevertheless spend much of the morning rattling atop it, headed southeast along the rumpled planes of the interior altiplano. All the while, we search for the reserve's namesake vicuñas, which, as it turns out, are not so hard to find.

I tell Felipe about my newfound love of vicuñas, whose puckered faces, elongated necks and elegant gaits make them the daintiest of all camelids. They roam the *puna* in packs, sharing the land with *ñandu*, or South American ostriches, who, we both agree, possess none of a vicuña's grace. The animals all gather together by small creeks of snowmelt that cut through the yellow-green porcupine grasses bending in the breeze.

Up above, the tops of Andean peaks roll gently on either side of us. The sky, meanwhile, is a deep, vivid blue. It's epically sunny: not cheery but austere. Felipe calls it "a melancholic landscape," and so we listen to melancholic music: Morrissey, Sigur Rós, Sinéad O'Connor.

Morrissey intones "Everyday Is Like Sunday" as Felipe tells me about his stresses at work. The museum has been reprogramming exhibitions delayed by the pandemic. It's been taxing. Even when he's away, in the middle of this desert, he can hardly go 90 minutes without answering text messages and putting out fires. He's also busy revamping the museum store, rebranding the website, even launching a concert series.

Somehow, as we emerge from those darker times, his job becomes even more stressful. It's hard for me to relate when my career is, conversely, waning. This occasionally causes friction between us. I know it's my fault; I need to give him the space to shine even if I can't right now.

It's good that I've sought refuge in the Atacama, alone. I've busied myself with self-imposed chores, spending my free time training my body to become as comfortable as is humanly possible in such an uncomfortable place. Even here, on earth's infuriating edge, I find that my body has, more or less, reached an accord with the altitude. I take it as a sign that the Atacama has finally welcomed me as one of its own.

Felipe is not so lucky. He's got the frog eyes, the foghorn nose and the spiderweb skin. His nerves are twitchy and his breath asthmatic. And then there's his left leg, which seems barely attached to his fragile body, awaiting surgery. I shouldn't have asked him to come here, I know, but I didn't want to end this journey without him.

Sinéad O'Connor belts "Drink Before the War" as we roll into

Guallatire, another half-dead town centered around an adobe church. The only signs of life are fibrous bundles of llama wool hanging out to dry. Their former owners amble through a valley below. We get out for a short, slow walk to see them, before rumbling onward, headed south into the rose-white Salar de Surire.

This remote salt flat is so brilliantly blinding that I can barely keep my eyes open. Perhaps that's why I lose all sense of time and direction, driving aimlessly adrift. It feels like an empty eternity of bleached nothingness – though it may only be a half hour – before we eventually stumble upon a mine of borax (used in cosmetics and cleaning supplies), where Felipe asks some frazzled workmen to point us toward the lagoon.

Finally, it appears: a big blob of steamy teal on the hazy white horizon. Minutes later, we strip down and wade in around the edge, assessing the temperature before venturing deeper. The water is not quite boiling, but it's hotter than hot, turning my skin the color of cooked lobster. I tell Felipe about Ruth and Mayra, and how they laughed at the sight of me like this. I also recall that first altiplanic lagoon near the world's highest volcano, Ojos del Salado, where I bathed, at last, after dusty days lost in flamingo dreams.

There's a solitary flamingo in this lagoon, too, but it pays us no mind, circling around in search of algae. Llamas graze in the spiky grasses beyond. We're the only humans for miles, save the distant borax boys.

It's too windy to commit halfway, so we trudge deeper into the scalding pool. All day, Felipe has been oscillating between excitement, terrible altitude sickness, and worry over his job and hamstring. Here, he lets it all go, sinking into the sweltering abyss.

He tells me again the same thing he said back in the Elqui

Valley: that he gets why I love Chile's less-loved half. I tell him
that I'm glad he finally does.

"It's easy to like it in a place like this," I add. But, much like our
life together, the Atacama isn't always so enchanting, or so easily
understood.

What I've learned, if anything, is that to appreciate Chile's
north is to be okay with complicated dualities. It's to accept that
its staggering beauty is only accessible to those who endure the
blustery chaos.

The Atacama is preposterously poor land that has the ability to
make people preposterously rich. It's a place where history fuses
so tightly with mythology that you don't know where one ends
and the other begins. It's an incubator of social change that's
used as a dustbin for dissidents. It's populated by down-and-out
strugglers, but also society's big winners. It's an endless stream of
Andean dawns and Pacific dusks.

"I'm sad to be ending this journey," I say as we dry off behind a
small rock shelter. "But I'm also ready."

"Oh yeah?" he asks.

When we last swam together in this desert, back in the Elqui
Valley, I didn't know what form this trip would take. It was pure
escapism. It was about getting out of Santiago and clearing my
head. Then, I set some goals for myself. I dove into politics, history, science, geography and identity – things that I used to be so
mystified by, that confused me in casual conversation, that lost
me in the nightly news. Now, I feel closer to understanding.

"Yeah," I respond, a bit late, unable to vocalize how I feel just
yet.

I've grown tired of hearing myself think all the time. Mentally,
it's kind of like I've pitched myself into the void. Now it's time to
crawl back out. For all its dreamlike qualities, this desert grinds

at you. Or it makes you grind away at yourself until you don't have much more to give.

A forest calms me; a desert sets me on fire.

I came for that. And I got what I wanted.

"Yeah," I repeat. "I'm ready. I'm ready to go home."

^~^

This forgotten border region has got me thinking a lot about "the Chilean dream" that lured so many migrants south – instead of north – in search of opportunity. I wonder if it's over, or if it ever really existed in the first place.

I thought that the social uprising, if not the pandemic, might put an end to it. I suppose it did for some. Many of the nearly 200,000 Haitians who flocked here in the aftermath of the 2010 earthquake have begun a perilous trip north to the US through the Darién Gap – that roadless (and lawless) stretch of jungle that connects the North and South American continents – after finding themselves with no work (and no safety net) in Chile.

Less reported in the global media are the equally harrowing journeys still made in reverse through the remote border regions of the Atacama.

Half a million Venezuelans have poured into Chile in recent years amid the socioeconomic and political crisis that began during the presidency of Hugo Chávez and worsened under Nicolás Maduro. The more desperate among them arrive via this desert – not far from where I'm at now, in Putre. They're aided, at times, by human smugglers, who charge up to US$500 to navigate the frigid evenings, waterless wastelands and blinding sand curtains that blow in along the way. Pandemic-induced border closures and airport screenings have only heightened the trend, making the Atacama a key gauntlet one must pass for a chance at some elusive "Chilean Dream."

For Venezuelans, this is the last hurdle in a long journey hopping borders from Colombia to Ecuador and on to Peru or Bolivia. Many lose their way after hiking for days on the remote edges of an invisible border to avoid Chilean guards. Dramatic rescue operations are frequent. Deaths are, thankfully, less so (the Atacama has surprising pockets of cell signal).

The migrants – who also come from neighboring Peru and Bolivia, as well as Colombia – have completely overwhelmed the small Aymara villages they arrive in, which lack shelters or even basic facilities to receive them. Border towns like Colchane, just south of the Salar de Surire salt flat that Felipe and I visited, are now flashpoints in the conflict, breathlessly reported about on the local news, sparking protests and anti-immigration rhetoric in the coastal cities below.

These towns, way up here on the uncomfortably high border, are just way stations. Some migrants will settle in the Atacama's growing cities; most journeys end down in Santiago, on the fringes of town you only see from highways.

I remember walking with Felipe near our apartment in the early days of the pandemic and passing the embassies of various South American neighbors. Migrants had camped out front, forming tent cities. They begged for flights home. Now, many want to come back. Yet this post-uprising, pandemic-recovering nation – still struggling through its own identity crisis – is less inclined to receive them.

Chile was, for much of its recent history, defined by emigration – or rather, exilation. Increasingly, it's become a nation of immigrants, myself among them (though the reasons for my move are vastly different than those of regional migrants).

Remarkably, the foreign-born now make up a larger percentage of the population here than in any other country in South America. This sudden shift hasn't been easy. Immigrants of all stripes are accused of taking jobs from locals, even if some of those very jobs (picking grapes, cleaning homes, watering parks) are no longer desirable to a majority of Chileans.

I often think about the benefits these changes have wrought, which I've witnessed first-hand over the years, traveling back and forth to immigration offices, waiting in longer lines each time. There's greater diversity, a more youthful population and an international feel that Santiago once lacked. There's also better customer service at stores and restaurants, nicer barbershops, an emergent coffee culture, *arepas* (corn cakes).

We foreigners – no matter the circumstances that proceeded our arrival – all bring something different to Chile. But this country changes us, too.

^ ~ ^

This trip has made me realize that I'm becoming more Chilean – or at least less American – in subtle ways that creep up on me. Late one night, after Felipe falls asleep, I sit outside under the altiplanic moonlight and make a list:

I can no longer tolerate spicy food.
I put avocado on everything.
I linger at a table long after a meal.
I drink tea in the afternoon.
I use an electric kettle to make it.
I shop at different places for bread, vegetables and provisions.
I purse my lips to point at things.
I eat seasonally.

I only buy what I really need.
I accept that the customer isn't always right.
I wake late.
I go to bed late.
I roll with the punches.
I check in with my family more.
I block out Sundays for Felipe's family.
I dress in darker colors.
I work longer hours and get less done.
I say yes to plans even when yes means no.
I show up for plans late and expect that others are expecting this.
I expect to be confronted with the unexpected.
I speak intentionally (instead of inevitably).
I prepare for the inevitability of bureaucracy.
I learn when to throw up my hands.
I worry less about rules.
I worry more about countries other than my own.
I worry more in general.

My English is all out of whack, too. I find myself using phrases like "I'm fully booked" (to say "I'm full") or "copy paste" (to say "you're copying me"). Felipe said them so many times, and I found them so cute, that I didn't have the heart to tell him they were wrong (or at least not quite correct). So I simply adopted them as part of my vocabulary.

It's been a long time since I've had a group of friends fluent in the ways that words from back home slip in and out of the vernacular. Plus, I've spent so many of my adult years abroad that I fear I'm losing my grip on everyday life in the States. I challenged Felipe the other day when he made a grand assumption about the pulse of America. His response: *What do you know?*

You haven't lived there in ages. Things change all the time. You're a sudaca (pejorative for South American) *now.*

Perhaps he's right. Or maybe I'm a bit like the strawberries that Felipe sold to make a living back in Australia.

In the 1760s, a 17-year-old amateur botanist working in the gardens of Versailles for King Louis XV got his hands on a rare Chilean strawberry, which had been brought back to Europe in 1714 by the French spy Amédée-François Frézier. The king loved it so much that he ordered a painting of it for the royal library. He then commanded the teenager, Antoine Nicolas Duchesne, to collect all known strawberry species for the gardens. Duchesne later found that the Chilean strawberry readily hybridized with another horticultural curiosity: the Virginia strawberry. So he crossed the North American and South American fruits. What he created was the garden variety we all know today.

I guess, in a sense, I'm becoming that strawberry.

^~^

The adobe town of Parinacota, near the entrance to Lauca National Park, seems both impeccably conserved and entirely abandoned. Like many of its sister villages in La Ruta de las Misiones, it's got its name spelled out in rocks on a hill above town. It's as if these places – closer to outer space than just about any other settlements on earth – need to proclaim to the world they actually exist. Residents themselves need a sign just to continue believing it.

Putre is low enough (and wet enough) to have a few trees. Up here, above 14,000 feet (4267 m), there are none. It's a reminder of how altitude strips everything to the elemental. Thankfully, we've come prepared this time, with bottles of hot water steeped in coca leaves. The bitter tea seems to help with the altitude's all-out assault on Felipe's body. I guess it helps me, too. Perhaps I'm not as comfortable as I want to be up here. Maybe I've only deceived myself thinking I ever was.

In truth, my skin is the texture of jerky. I can't even feel my lips, which seem like hard foreign objects plastered onto my face. My eyes, meanwhile, look bulgier now than during my worst hangovers. I should have known: the Atacama always wins.

From Parinacota, we dip down toward the Lagunas de Cotacotani, a collection of pond-sized pools bisected by small lava islands. The water here is connected underground to an upland lake, Lago Chungará, which is even higher than the legendary Titicaca over on Bolivia's border with Peru.

Cotacotani's lagoons have salt-white edges that fade to daisy-yellow. Intrigued, I drive down to see them. As we navigate a steep hairpin turn, the car jolts and then slides into a sand trap. It all happens before I even realize the danger. The wheel spins, but the vehicle stays still. We try everything – digging the sand out, building it back up – but nothing works. We try pushing it, but the car won't budge.

We're not mad at each other; we're angry about the situation. But we can't help it; we explode.

"How could you drive right into the sand?" Felipe asks. "Didn't you see it?"

I glare back at him.

"Why did we even come down here in the first place?" he continues, furious.

"Why didn't you stop me?" I counter.

"Would you have even listened if I tried?" he replies, knowing I probably wouldn't have.

These past days have been building to this moment. I had envisioned the end of this journey as romantic. It isn't. It's messy.

Like our lives. Like our relationship. We've bickered over his intrusive work calls and the uncertain future of the place we live. We've clashed over our dearth of physical romance. We've shared vastly different opinions about who should lead Chile out of its crisis, and also what to do about our unfinished apartment, which, amid rising interest rates, now feels like a trap we can't crawl out of.

Despite it all, I think these quarrels are a sign we'll be okay. We don't have to untangle the mess of our knotted lives; we just need to find the best way to navigate it together. Talking – even fighting, every now and then – is part of the process.

I always told myself this trip was about understanding Chile better. What I meant, in a way, was that I wanted to understand *Felipe* better. And maybe if I could do that, I could save this relationship from getting as irreconcilably stuck as our car is right now. If I could find peace in living here, in his home, which never truly felt like mine (or at least not mine without him), then maybe we could find some new kind of joy in the stillness and monotony that comes with an aging relationship.

We're not really mad anymore, but we let the squabble run its course, sitting in this desert like unhappy kids in a giant sandbox, passing blame back and forth, arguing about a situation beyond our control. We're quarreling about the ways we are as humans that may have led to this predicament (me headstrong, he distrait). We're fighting with sand, struggling against the condition of it, hand-shoveling piles in all directions in search of a solution.

The car won't budge. So we just sit there for a while, not enjoying a pretty view. Felipe pretends to be busy on his phone, though I know he's secretly snapping photos. I slowly turn my back to both him and the lagoons and, instead of savoring the scenery, build a village of tiny sandcastles. Then, I exorcise the tension of the moment by smashing them all to smithereens.

Eventually, we get back to work and carve enough sand to slide the car downhill. We get far enough away from the sand trap to rev the engine. I grind the accelerator, and race so fast over it that the wheels have no time for sticking. Felipe hobbles up the hill, and we speed back to Putre just in time to sulk in the cabin over an epic sunset.

^ ~ ^

The Chilean flamingos comb the water face down, ass up, like floating fluff balls, doing what flamingos do best: graceful eating. No matter how often I watch them do this, I can't seem to reconcile how creatures so flamboyant and regal can thrive in a place so austere.

Felipe and I have traveled – mostly in a skyward direction – toward Lago Chungará to have a go at an afternoon walk. Now, we find ourselves venturing slowly along its crinkled edge, strolling at a pace he can manage, watching all the while as pink puffs glide across its surface. The wetland is soft and pastel, but the dusty spread all around it is, like much of the *puna*, spiky and built to harm. I tell Felipe that's one of the reasons I love this place so much. It doesn't tolerate casual intruders lured to its riches; it demands, instead, time, patience and respect.

At nearly 15,000 feet (or exactly 4517 m), Chungará is one our planet's loftiest lakes. It's certainly the highest place I've been all trip. I suppose I'm as close to Mars here as I'll ever get on Earth. Yet in contrast to so many other spots I've seen in the Atacama – from its desiccated core to its moon valleys, salt mountains and crusty white *salares* – this really does feel of this planet.

Just beyond the piercing blue waters are twin volcanoes:

Parinacota and Pomerape. One lies in Chile; the other Bolivia. Both are well over 20,000 feet (6100 m). They're conical and robust, riddled with ancient lava flows. These commanding massifs are potent visions of duality for the Aymara. They're also the protagonists of a kind of Andean *Romeo and Juliet* about two forbidden lovers from vastly different lands frozen here in stubborn defiance of a society who wished them apart.

Felipe and I huddle together for warmth on the shoreline, humbled beneath goliaths. We pass bitter coca tea back and forth, sipping at it when we're not breathing in and out in long and raspy breaths. They come not instinctively but rather as a result of deliberate force, with each extended exhalation like a hot cloudburst in the thin Andean air.

We butted heads yesterday, but it was the good kind of head-butting, the type that always seems to cut through months of tension and reset us for the year to come – the type every healthy couple needs once in a while. Now we wallow in the catharsis, resting together on the shores of Chungará in sun-glazed peace.

The landscape here is as soft as it is harsh – the kind of beauty that doesn't scream but whispers. There are the cotton clouds, which blow in and out of volcanic mounds, momentarily obscuring frosted peaks. There is the *paja brava*, which sprawls across the skyscraping plain like hundreds of spiky beige porcupines marching against the breeze. There's the grumbling wind and the celestial glow.

Chungará lends itself well to meditation. We inhale in long and raspy breaths. We breathe out in hot cloudbursts, which float away in the thin Andean air. Coca tea warms and soothes.

We sit, as settled couples do, in quiet, not needing to fill spaces with words, sliding in and out of an altiplanic trance. Suddenly, a wayward vicuña disturbs the peace. Or rather, it disturbs the flamingos. One, two, three, four soar over the lake, low and heavy, pushing hard against punitive winds, battling the electric sky, gunning for Bolivia. Five, six, seven, eight join the afternoon flight. The startled vicuña dashes in the opposite direction with one, two, three, four furry friends in tow.

Suddenly, Felipe and I are alone.

The once-aggressive sun softens in the afternoon sky, melting toward the distant Pacific. Temperatures plunge and winds rise and, for a while, we just sit there, bracing our bodies against the incessant breeze, tense and guarded. Then, without conspiring, we give in. We loosen our shoulders and let it jostle us around, watching as our sinewy silhouettes swell in the lowering light, wiggling out across the roof of the world.

ANIMITAS

THE ALTIPLANO

MY SHADOW COMPANION

CHINCHORRO MUMMIES

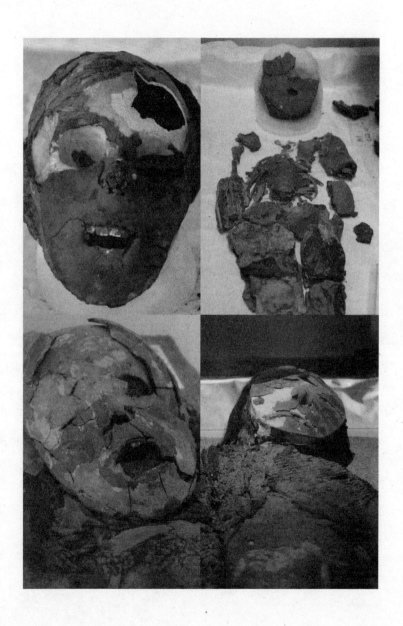

EPILOGUE

I was strolling the National Mall back in Washington, DC, a few months after the Atacama, hopping from museum to museum, soaking up all those imposing Smithsonians, when I came upon the Hirshhorn and, inside it, an exhibit from artist Laurie Anderson. I gravitated to the darkest room and, inside that, a story about stories. It was about the ways we recall them, and how we deceive ourselves along the way.

The piece hit on something I felt deeply in those months following my journey through Chile's northerly extremes. I was trying to tame the contours of this book, untangling the fantasy of adventure from the verity on the ground. How does one tell one's own story about stories? I wasn't sure.

The creepiest thing about stories, Anderson said in her piece, is that you try to get to the point you're making, usually about yourself or something you learned, but in the end, you get further away from it. You find yourself burrowing into moments until you dig so deep you no longer have a view from the ground. "You get your story and you hold onto it, and every time you tell it you forget it more," she explains.

In many ways, I left the desert unsure of what I'd learned, still piecing together the manner in which it had broadened my perspectives. Every time I thought back on it – on the people I assembled and places I absorbed – I seemed to forget it even more. It wasn't until many months later, back in Santiago, that I finally had the distance to appreciate the ways it'd informed me. It crept up, at first, as a feeling: I knew I was no longer marking time in my partner's country. Maybe, just maybe, I was doing the work to stick around.

The truth is that whatever I thought I learned out there, those months in the desert were just the start of a longer education. Chile was already barreling ahead at flash speed, changing again, moving toward an uncertain future. I, too, hurried as fast as I could away from the past, even as I tried desperately not to forget it.

Felipe and I moved into our new apartment in February 2022, two and a half years after we signed the paperwork next to a hole in the ground, and a year behind schedule. I was now officially a homeowner. In Chile. The roots wound deeper. I stuck around in Santiago, building a nest. I cultivated a stronger sense of community, slashed my growing travel schedule and acquiesced to more frequent visits with Felipe's family, my family, which grew increasingly important to him as we emerged from the pandemic.

Around that same time, Chile's youngest-ever president, 36-year-old Gabriel Boric, rode the zeitgeist of the social uprising into office, promising a sweeping overhaul of the status quo. Boric rose to fame in the student protests of 2011 demanding a new framework for public education. Now, he was running the country with a history-making cabinet that included more women than men and Chile's first two openly gay ministers. That March, Chile became one of the last major countries in South America to approve same-sex marriage. Change wasn't just in the air; it was exploding across it.

Santiago still had the scars of a city emerging from three years of protests and economic turmoil. But it had the youthful optimism of transformation, too. I got excited, at long last, to be here. Felipe and I reactivated our lives, hiking up dusty hills, dancing in dingy bars and attending the usual art openings. We joked about – though never truly considered – getting gay married.

Boric's main task that first year was to see the new constitution to the finish line. It was the rallying cry that galvanized him to office; the rest of his term depended on it. Yet all the excitement of his being the new face of the Latin American left – as *Time* magazine put it in an August cover story – seemed to fade by September, when the plebiscite came around. With crime and inflation on the rise, the political tides had suddenly shifted yet again.

Some 78 percent of Chileans voted for a new constitution in 2020, but just 38 percent voted to ratify the draft charter they were ultimately offered two years later. I, newly granted voting rights as one of Chile's more permanent permanent residents, was among the minority. Felipe was too. Our new neighborhood, Ñuñoa, was one of just eight districts in the entire country to vote *apruebo* (approve) this time around.

We watched the results come in that night with Felipe's family, sitting in front of a TV at his brother's apartment. It's about a dozen blocks from ours in Ñuñoa, just past his parents' place. (All of us are in the same barrio now, a grand expression of Chilean familism.) We cooked a big *asado* (barbecue) and blended our pre-meal pisco sours, storing champagne in the fridge for an evening hurrah. In the end, the bubbles never popped. A gut-twisting shock sulked across the room, over-souring the sours. So we quietly excused ourselves to brood alone. We skipped the after parties, having nothing to celebrate, and were instead bedridden with despondency by 11 p.m.

The new charter was not perfect; none of us thought that. With 388 articles, it would have been one of the most verbose in the world. Somehow, even with all those words, it was vague on details; perhaps even a bit woo-wooey at times. There were revelations of problematic behavior by some of the people involved in composing it, including a prominent leftist who rose from street protestor to a leader in the Constitutional Convention channeling sympathy for a cancer diagnosis he never actually had.

Even with all that baggage, it would have been revolutionary.

Chile's failed charter could have enshrined gender parity in politics, vastly expanded LGBTQ+ rights, made the government responsible for mitigating climate change and recognized Chile as a plurinational state, giving Indigenous groups more autonomy over their lives and lands. The changes it proposed were so sweeping, so progressive, that the majority of the nation just couldn't get on board.

The one thing meant to bring about a change to Chilean society – to make it more fair, equal and representative of all – failed spectacularly. Yet that didn't alter the fact that citizens had voted for a new constitution. So, in 2023, the nation felt obliged to try again.

This time around, in a vote for a more streamlined Constitutional Council, the ultra-conservative Republican Party soared to a supermajority thanks to the vitriolic leadership of José Antonio Kast (the son of a Nazi and brother of a Chicago Boy), who modeled himself after Brazil's Jair Bolsonaro, seeding fears over crime, immigration and cultural change. Remarkably, it was now a group of far-right representatives that was rewriting a constitution instilled under a far-right dictatorship – a constitution they'd already voted not to change in the first place. It felt like a cruel farce, especially landing as it did in 2023, the 50th anniversary of the coup.

How far the pendulum had swung in the aftermath of the *estallido social*. All that hope. All that disappointment. It was hard to reconcile how the clamor for change, which triggered this process, could lead us right back to here. But it did, and here we are: the nation chugs on.

I could have remained despondent, but I didn't. I was ready to end this chapter of my life – the Chile chapter – when I set off into the Atacama. But the journey gave me the space to find the reasons to stay. It made me more capable of jumping the hurdles of life in South America. More capable, too, of savoring its mercurial ways. So here I am, chugging on too.

The Atacama, meanwhile, is everywhere these days. It's in your phones, your laptops and your cars. It's on the cover of newspapers and the tops of money-makers' minds. Everyone is buzzing about its "white gold," which is the key to unlocking the great energy transition from fossil fuels to renewables. Lithium, they say, is Chile's ticket to a bright future, and the Atacama is, more than ever, its roaring economic engine.

Boric whipped up plans in 2023 for the country to overtake Australia as the world's biggest lithium producer. He also wants the state to be present throughout the entire production cycle via a National Lithium Company. The foreign financial media labeled it a "nationalization," but the plan only calls for over 50 percent of the shares in joint ventures to be under state control. Even if Boric gets his way, I can't help but wonder how much of this imminent bonanza will ever benefit everyday Chileans. What will be gained in the process, and what will be lost along the way?

For me, the Atacama will never be a series of treasure holes planted with the flags of global superpowers. When I think of it now, I see instead the muscly volcanoes, irritable geysers and blinding salt flats. I picture the enigmatic cliffs scraped with stories and the soaring dunes taming violent seas. Every memory is blanketed in that holy mind-bending sunshine, which softens into evenings so rapturous you can read the shadows of the Milky Way. No matter what happens, you can't take that away.

Some nights in Santiago – when wafting reggaeton rattles my walls, when the neighborhood dogs howl across apartment blocks, when the fire trucks wail and warble – I close my eyes and channel the hush of the desert. I listen for the whoosh of air through *puna* grass, the crackle of crumpled earth under my boots. I remember the smell of solitude. I race through dream-time dust clouds toward the end of paved roads, pining for the lonely backlands beyond.

ACKNOWLEDGEMENTS

Writing a book, as it turns out, is nothing like writing a story for a newspaper or magazine; it's an entirely different beast, demanding bewildering amounts of time and energy and anguish. Thankfully, I did not get to where I am now on my own.

I owe a huge debt of gratitude, first and foremost, to the people of the Atacama who took the time to chat with a nosy stranger (despite his funky Spanish). You shared your toughest struggles, wildest dreams and ageless wisdom with me. Through you, I learned how to see this unknowable desert in a way that would've been impossible on my own. Some of you do not appear on the pages of this book, but all graciously offered stories and trusted me to tell them well.

Thanks to Vanessa Petersen, Annie Merkley and Zelda Zinn for reading early versions of my manuscript when you had no professional obligation to do so. Your support, encouragement and feedback were invaluable at a time when I was terrified at the prospect of releasing this work into the world. I'm also appreciative of the time I spent back in the Atacama at the arts residency La Wayaka Current, which gave me the space to retool this project and find new inspiration for what would become chapter 6.

Thank you to my friends in Santiago who appear on the pages of chapter 1, which should be viewed as a memory of a very specific moment in time. I did not yet know this book would exist, so our discussions in the months and years that followed (as well as our shared photographs) allowed me to rewind and to recreate those pivotal events, which set me off on this journey.

Mars on Earth might have never existed if it weren't for my agent, Max Sinsheimer, who was the first person to truly believe in the story I wanted to tell. Thank you for guiding me through an unfamiliar process, and for fighting to make this book the best it could be at every step along the way. Thanks ongoing, also, to Don Gorman and all the folks at Rocky Mountain Books for shepherding this book to the finish line, and to my astute and supportive editor, Peter Norman, for his key role in that process.

To my parents, thank you for opening my eyes at an early age to the joy of travel. You encouraged all of your children to think critically about the world beyond – to appreciate cultures, landscapes and ways of being different from our own – and we are all better off for it. Finally, I owe an immeasurable thank you to my partner, Felipe. You not only allowed me to share intimate details of our personal journey together; you also accompanied me on the winding road of turning this book into a reality. *Un beso, y te quiero mucho.*

We would like to take this opportunity to acknowledge the Traditional Territories upon which we live and work. In Calgary, Alberta, we acknowledge the Niitsítapi (Blackfoot) and the people of the Treaty 7 region in Southern Alberta, which includes the Siksika, the Piikuni, the Kainai, the Tsuut'ina, and the Stoney Nakoda First Nations, including Chiniki, Bearpaw, and Wesley First Nations. The City of Calgary is also home to Métis Nation of Alberta, Region III. In Victoria, British Columbia, we acknowledge the Traditional Territories of the Lkwungen (Esquimalt and Songhees), Malahat, Pacheedaht, Scia'new, T'Sou-ke, and W̱SÁNEĆ (Pauquachin, Tsartlip, Tsawout, Tseycum) peoples.

SELECT BIBLIOGRAPHY

PROLOGUE

Achenbach, Joel. "Strange DNA Found in the Desert Offers Lessons in the Hunt for Mars Life." *Washington Post*, February 23, 2023. https://www.washingtonpost.com/science/2023/02/21/mars-life-atacama-microbiome.

Dunbar, Brian. "NASA – Mars-Like Atacama Desert Could Explain Viking 'No Life' Results," n.d. https://www.nasa.gov/audience/for-students/postsecondary/features/N_Mars_Like_Desert_prt.htm.

Bull, Alan T., Juan A. Asenjo, Michael Goodfellow, and Benito Gómez-Silva. "The Atacama Desert: Technical Resources and the Growing Importance of Novel Microbial Diversity." *Annual Review of Microbiology* 70, no. 1 (September 8, 2016): 215–34. https://doi.org/10.1146/annurev-micro-102215-095236.

Kargel, Jeffrey S. *Mars: A Warmer, Wetter Planet*. London: Springer, 2004. https://link.springer.com/book/9781852335687.

NASA. "Mars Rover Tests Driving, Drilling and Detecting Life in the Desert," n.d. https://www.nasa.gov/feature/ames/mars-rover-tests-driving-drilling-and-detecting-life-in-chile-s-high-desert.

Navarro-González, Rafael, Fred A. Rainey, Paola Molina, Danielle R. Bagaley, Becky J. Hollen, Jose M. de la Rosa, Alanna M. Small, et al. "Mars-Like Soils in the Atacama Desert, Chile, and the Dry Limit of Microbial Life." *Science* 302, no. 5647 (November 7, 2003): 1018–21. https://doi.org/10.1126/science.1089143.

Schulze-Makuch, Dirk, Dirk Wagner, Samuel P. Kounaves, Kai Mangelsdorf, Kevin G. Devine, Jean-Pierre de Vera, Philippe Schmitt-Kopplin, et al. "Transitory Microbial Habitat in the Hyperarid Atacama Desert." *Proceedings of the National Academy of Sciences of the United States of America* 115, no. 11 (February 26, 2018): 2670–75. https://doi.org/10.1073/pnas.1714341115.

Sun, Tao, Huiming Bao, Martin Reich, and S.R. Hemming. "More than Ten Million Years of Hyper-Aridity Recorded in the Atacama Gravels." *Geochimica Et Cosmochimica Acta* 227 (April 1, 2018): 123–32. https://doi.org/10.1016/j.gca.2018.02.021.

CHAPTER 1

Armus, Teo. "A Californian Economist Loves Neoliberalism. When Chileans Started Protesting It, He Opened Fire on Them." *Washington Post*, November 11, 2019. https://www.washingtonpost.com/nation/2019/11/11/john-cobin-chile-shooting-protesters-video.

Cocker, Isabel. "Chile's University Tuition Fees amongst World's Highest." *Santiago Times*. September 15, 2017. https://santiagotimes.cl/2017/09/15/chiles-university-tuition-fees-amongst-worlds-highest.

Délano, Manuel, and Hugo Traslaviña. *La Herencia de los Chicago Boys.* Santiago: Ornitorrinco, 1989. https://www.memoriachilena.gob.cl/602/w3-article-98015.html.

Faiola, Anthony, and Rachelle Krygier. "How to Make Sense of the Many Protests Raging across South America." *Washington Post*, November 21, 2019. https://www.washingtonpost.com/world/the_americas/a-government-chased-from-its-capital-a-president-forced-into-exile-a-storm-of-protest-rages-in-south-america/2019/11/14/897f85ba-0651-11ea-9118-25d6bd37dfb1_story.html.

Fundación Sol. "Los Verdaderos Sueldos de Chile (ESI 2018)," August 17, 2023. https://fundacionsol.cl/blog/estudios-2/post/los-verdaderos-sueldos-de-chile-esi-2018-6140.

Herrera, Tania. "Radiografía de un saqueo: ¿Dónde va a parar la mercadería?" *The Clinic* (Santiago), November 23, 2019. https://www.theclinic.cl/2019/11/23/radiografia-de-un-saqueo-donde-va-a-parar-la-mercaderia.

Metro de Santiago. "Annual Report," 2018. https://www.metro.cl/documentos/annual_report_2018.pdf.

Museo de la Memoria y los Derechos Humanos. "Recursos e Investigación," n.d. https://mmdh.cl/recursos-e-investigacion.

OHCHR. "UN Human Rights Office Report on Chile Crisis Describes Multiple Police Violations and Calls for Reforms," December 13, 2019. https://www.ohchr.org/en/press-releases/2019/12/un-human-rights-office-report-chile-crisis-describes-multiple-police.

Reid, Michael. *Forgotten Continent: A History of the New Latin America*. New Haven, CT: Yale University Press, 2017.

Ríos, Marcela. "UN Sustainable Development Cooperation Framework and National Poverty Eradication: The Case of Chile," May 22, 2001. https://www.un.org/development/desa/dspd/wp-content/uploads/sites/22/2021/05/Rios_Presentation_PDF_UNCT_Chile_Poverty1.pdf.

Roddick, Jacqueline, and Philip J. O'Brien. *Chile, The Pinochet Decade: The Rise and Fall of the Chicago Boys*. London: Latin America Bureau, 1983.

UNDP. "Desiguales. Orígenes, cambios y desafíos de la brecha social en Chile," 2018. https://www.undp.org/es/chile/publications/desiguales-or%C3%ADgenes-cambios-y-desaf%C3%ADos-de-la-brecha-social-en-chile.

WID – World Inequality Database. "Chile – WID – World Inequality Database," December 5, 2021. https://wid.world/country/chile/.

CHAPTER 2

Bertero, Mauricio. "¿Cómo y cuándo surge la fama mística del valle del Elqui?" *Comunicacionygestion* (blog), June 13, 2023. https://www.comunicacionygestion.cl/post/como-y-cuando-surge-la-fama-mistica-del-valle-del-elqui.

Castro, Fresia. *Surameris and the Chest of Secrets*. Bloomington, IN: Palibrio, 2012.

Chaud, Pedro Bahamondes. "Un Rasputín a la chilena: Las extravagantes andanzas del Cristo de Elqui." *The Clinic* (Santiago), May 7, 2021. https://www.theclinic.cl/2021/05/07/un-rasputin-a-la-chilena-las-extravagantes-andanzas-del-cristo-de-elqui/.

García-Gorena, Velma, ed. *Gabriela Mistral's Letters to Doris Dana*. Albuquerque: University of New Mexico Press, 2018.

Mistral, Gabriela. *Selected Poems of Gabriela Mistral.* Translated by Ursula K. Le Guin. Albuquerque: University of New Mexico Press, 2011.

Parra, Nicanor. *La vuelta del Cristo de Elqui.* Santiago: Ediciones UDP, 2007.

Rivera Letelier, Hernán. *El arte de la resurrección.* Madrid: Alfaguara, 2010.

Urbatorivm. "Casuística fundacional del misticismo en el Valle de Equi (parte iv): auge y ocaso del 'monasterio' de la Hermana Cecilia," n.d. https://urbatorivm1.rssing.com/chan-6153000/article267.html.

CHAPTER 3

BirdLife International. "*Spheniscus humboldti.*" IUCN Red List of Threatened Species, August 21, 2020. https://www.iucnredlist.org/species/22697817/182714418.

Darwin, Charles. *The Voyage of the Beagle: Journal of Researches into the Natural History and Geology of the Countries Visited During the Voyage of H.M.S. Beagle Round the World.* New York: Modern Library, 2001.

Francaviglia, Richard. *Imagining the Atacama Desert: A Five-Hundred-Year Journey of Discovery.* Salt Lake City: University of Utah Press, 2018.

Medina, Ignacio Cerda, and Fernando Mercader Arriagada. "Expresiones del Desierto Florido," 2021. https://www.cultura.gob.cl/wp-content/uploads/2021/04/expresiones-del-desierto-florido.pdf.

Memoria Chilena: Portal. "Animitas," n.d. https://www.memoriachilena.gob.cl/602/w3-article-100572.html.

Memoria Chilena: Portal. "Ferrocarril Caldera-Copiapó," n.d. https://www.memoriachilena.gob.cl/602/w3-article-3401.html.

Universidad de Atacama UDA English Center. "La Copiapó Locomotive," n.d. http://www.uec.uda.cl/index.php?option=com_content&view=article&id=513&Itemid=477.

Zepeda González, Carlos. "La historia no contada ¿Esconde Bahía Inglesa un tesoro pirata?" *Atacama Viva Magazine*, 2018. https://www.letrabrava.cl/reportaje-la-historia-no-contada-esconde-ba-hia-inglesa-un-tesoro-pirata/.

CHAPTER 4

Ahmad, Samar. "The Lithium Triangle: Where Chile, Argentina, and Bolivia Meet." *Harvard International Review*, January 18, 2020. https://hir.harvard.edu/lithium-triangle/.

Cordero, Raul R., Sarah Feron, Alessandro Damiani, Edgardo Sepúlveda, Jose Jorquera, Alberto Redondas, Gunther Seckmeyer, Jorge Carrasco, Penny M. Rowe, and Zutao Ouyang. "Surface Solar Extremes in the Most Irradiated Region on Earth, Altiplano." *Bulletin of the American Meteorological Society* 104, no. 6 (June 1, 2023): E1206–21. https://doi.org/10.1175/bams-d-22-0215.1.

Ellerbeck, Stefan. "Lithium: Here's Why Latin America Is Key to the Global Energy Transition." *World Economic Forum*, January 10, 2023. https://www.weforum.org/agenda/2023/01/lithium-latin-america-energy-transition.

Gajardo, Gonzalo, and Stella Redón. "Andean Hypersaline Lakes in the Atacama Desert, Northern Chile: Between Lithium Exploitation and Unique Biodiversity Conservation." *Conservation Science and Practice* 1, no. 9 (August 2, 2019). https://doi.org/10.1111/csp2.94.

Gutiérrez, Jorge S., Johnnie N. Moore, John Donnelly, Cristina Dorador, Juan G. Navedo, and Nathan R. Senner. "Climate Change and Lithium Mining Influence Flamingo Abundance in the Lithium Triangle." *Proceedings of the Royal Society B: Biological Sciences* 289, no. 1970 (March 9, 2022). https://doi.org/10.1098/rspb.2021.2388.

Kuchs, O.M. "Monografía del Ferrocarril de Potrerillos," n.d. https://revistas.uchile.cl/index.php/AICH/article/view/34146/36082.

NASA. "Scientists Offer Sharper Insight into Pluto's Bladed

Terrain," August 6, 2017. https://www.nasa.gov/feature/
scientists-offer-sharper-insight-into-pluto-s-bladed-terrain.

Vergara, Angela. *Copper Workers, International Business, and Domestic Politics in Cold War Chile*. University Park: Penn State University Press, 2012.

CHAPTER 5

Advis, Luis. *Cantata de Santa María de Iquique*. Quilapayún. DICAP, 1970, vinyl.

Alberdi, Maite, dir. *La Once*. Micromundo Producciones, 2014. 1 hr., 10 min. https://www.netflix.com/title/80097217.

Bernetti, Martin. "Chile's Desert Dumping Ground for Fast Fashion Leftovers." AFP. August 11, 2021. https://www.aljazeera.com/gallery/2021/11/8/chiles-desert-dumping-ground-for-fast-fashion-leftovers.

Contardo, Óscar. *Raro, una historia gay de Chile*. Barcelona: Planeta, 2011.

Dorfman, Ariel. *Desert Memories: Journeys Through the Chilean North*. Washington, DC: National Geographic, 2004.

Franklin, Jonathan. *33 Men: Inside the Miraculous Survival and Dramatic Rescue of the Chilean Miners*. New York: Berkley, 2011.

Fredes, Cristóbal. "El significado de la once." *La Tercera* (Santiago). November 14, 2014. https://www.latercera.com/noticia/el-significado-de-la-once/.

Gross, Daniel A. "Caliche: The Conflict Mineral That Fuelled the First World War." *Guardian*, June 2, 2014. https://www.theguardian.com/science/the-h-word/2014/jun/02/caliche-great-war-first-world-war-conflict-mineral.

Ojeda, Cristian Ascencio. "Underwater Deforestation Is Mobilizing Fishermen and Scientists," n.d. *Historias Sin Fronteras*. https://www.connectas.org/especiales/bosques-marinos-chile-peru/chile-en.html.

Rivera Letelier, Hernán. *Santa María de las flores negras*. Barcelona: Seix Barral, 2002.

Salazar, Diego, Donald Jackson, Jean Louis Guendon, Hernán Salinas, Diego Morata, Valentina Figueroa, Germán Manríquez, and Victoria Castro. "Early Evidence (ca. 12,000 BP) for Iron Oxide Mining on the Pacific Coast of South America." *Current Anthropology* 52, no. 3 (June 1, 2011): 463–75. https://doi.org/10.1086/659426.

Tobar, Héctor. *Deep Down Dark: The Untold Stories of 33 Men Buried in a Chilean Mine, and the Miracle That Set Them Free*. New York: Farrar, Straus & Giroux, 2014.

Vergara, Eva. "Mass Grave Fills Another Page in Grim History of Chilean Desert Village." *Los Angeles Times*, August 12, 1990. https://www.latimes.com/archives/la-xpm-1990-08-12-mn-949-story.html.

CHAPTER 6

Barrera, David. "Adiós al último yatiri de San Pedro de Atacama." *Chululo* (San Pedro de Atacama), September 29, 2016. https://www.chululo.cl/pages/opinion2.php?id=30092016_060531.

Capriles, José M., Calogero M. Santoro, Richard J. George, Eliana Flores Bedregal, Douglas J. Kennett, Logan Kistler, and Francisco Rothhammer. "Pre-Columbian Transregional Captive Rearing of Amazonian Parrots in the Atacama Desert." *Proceedings of the National Academy of Sciences of the United States of America* 118, no. 15 (March 29, 2021). https://doi.org/10.1073/pnas.2020020118.

Chile Precolombino. "Llama Caravans in the Desert," n.d. http://chileprecolombino.cl/en/arte/piezas-selectas/el-trafico-con-recuas-de-llamas/.

Guevara, Ernesto "Che." *The Motorcycle Diaries: Notes on a Latin American Journey*. Translated by Ann Wright. London; New York: Verso, 1996.

Markel, Howard. *An Anatomy of Addiction: Sigmund Freud, William Halsted, and the Miracle Drug Cocaine*. New York: Pantheon, 2011.

CHAPTER 7

Ahmed, Osman. "Inside the Business of Vicuña, the Wool Worth More Than Gold." *The Business of Fashion*, April 14, 2017. https://www.businessoffashion.com/articles/sustainability/inside-the-business-of-vicuna-the-wool-worth-more-than-gold/.

Bazile, Didier, Sven-Erik Jacobsen, and Alexis Verniau. "The Global Expansion of Quinoa: Trends and Limits." *Frontiers in Plant Science* 7 (May 9, 2016). https://doi.org/10.3389/fpls.2016.00622.

Censo 2017. "Efectivamente Censados: Resultados Definitivos Censo 2017," n.d. http://www.censo2017.cl/wp-content/uploads/2017/12/Presentacion_Resultados_Definitivos_Censo2017.pdf.

CHAPTER 8

Apata, Mario, Bernardo Arriaza, Elena Llop, and Mauricio Moraga. "Human adaptation to arsenic in Andean populations of the Atacama Desert." *American Journal of Physical Anthropology* 163, no. 1 (2017): 192–199. https://doi.org/10.1002/ajpa.23193.

Arriaza, Bernardo. *Beyond Death: The Chinchorro Mummies of Ancient Chile.* Washington, DC: Smithsonian Institution, 1995.

Arriaza, Bernardo. *Cultura Chinchorro*. Santiago: Editorial Universitaria De Chile, 2016.

Cole, Hamish. "Mungo Man, Mungo Lady Buried Despite Traditional Owners' Legal Challenge." ABC News (Australia). May 25, 2022. https://www.abc.net.au/news/2022-05-25/nsw-regs-mungo-burial-despite-legal-challenge/101098908.

Daley, Paul. "Finding Mungo Man: The Moment Australia's Story Suddenly Changed." *Guardian*, November 13, 2017. https://www.theguardian.com/australia-news/2017/nov/14/finding-mungo-man-the-moment-australias-story-suddenly-changed.

Karoff, Paul. "Saving Chilean Mummies from Climate Change," Harvard John A. Paulson School of Engineering and Applied Sciences. March 9, 2015. https://seas.harvard.edu/news/2015/03/saving-chilean-mummies-climate-change.

Uhle, Max. "Los Aborígenes de Arica y el hombre americano." *Revista*

Chungara, vol. 3 (1974): 13–21. http://www.chungara.cl/Vols/1974/ Vol3/Los_aborigenes_de_Arica_y_el_hombre_americano.pdf.

CHAPTER 9

Allen, Mike. "The 18th-Century Spy Who Gave Us Big Strawberries." *Atlas Obscura*, November 16, 2017. https://www.atlasobscura.com/ articles/big-strawberries-spy-chile-france.

Doña-Reveco, Cristián. "Chile's Welcoming Approach to Immigrants Cools as Numbers Rise." Migrationpolicy. org, May 18, 2022. https://www.migrationpolicy.org/article/ chile-immigrants-rising-numbers.

Droppelmann, Veronica, and Martín Lecanda. "Ruta de las Misiones-Saraña: recorriendo las joyas patrimoniales de la Región de Arica y Parinacota." *Ladera Sur* (Santiago). January 21, 2020. https:// laderasur.com/destino/ruta-de-las-misiones-sarana-recorriendo-las-joyas-patrimoniales-de-la-region-de-arica-y-parinacota/.

Torres, Cristián. "Una crisis humanitaria desborda a pequeños pueblos del norte de Chile por la masiva llegada de migrantes venezolanos." *Infobae* (Miami), February 3, 2021. https://www. infobae.com/america/america-latina/2021/02/03/crisis-humani-taria-en-pequenos-pueblos-del-norte-de-chile-desbordados-por-la-masiva-llegada-de-migrantes-venezolanos/.

EPILOGUE

Convención Constitucional de Chile. "Propuesta de Constitución Política de la República de Chile," 2022. https://www.chileconven-cion.cl/wp-content/uploads/2022/07/Texto-Definitivo-CPR-2022-Tapas.pdf.

Nugent, Ciara. "Chile's Millennial President Is a New Kind of Leftist Leader." *Time*. August 31, 2022.

ABOUT THE AUTHOR

Mark Johanson is a seasoned freelance journalist who lived on four continents before settling in Santiago, Chile, in 2014. His stories about travel, food, culture, and the environment have appeared in distinguished publications including *Travel + Leisure, National Geographic, Conde Nast Traveler,* AFAR, *Newsweek, Financial Times, Food & Wine, Dwell, Men's Journal, Backpacker, The Economist, The Guardian, The Sunday Times, Bloomberg, World Wildlife Magazine,* BBC, CNN, *Vox, Narratively,* and others. He has co-authored a dozen Lonely Planet travel guidebooks to destinations across the Americas and Southeast Asia, including Bolivia, Cambodia, the Caribbean, Chile, Indonesia, Laos, Peru, and the United States. He has similarly co-authored several coffee table books for the iconic travel brand. Learn more at www.markjohanson.com.

INDEX